Answer Key for
120 Bible Stories "For Reflection" Questions

3558 S. Jefferson Ave., St. Louis, MO 63118-3968
1-800-325-3040 • www.cph.org

Prepared by Emily Barz and Alicia Wosepka

Edited by Rodney L. Rathmann

This publication may be available in Braille, in large print, or on cassette tape for the visually impaired. Please allow 8 to 12 weeks for delivery. Write to Lutheran Braille Workers, P.O. Box 5000, Yucaipa, CA 92399; call toll-free 1-800-925-6092; or visit the Web site: www.LBWinc.org.

Manufactured in the United States of America

4 5 6 7 8 9 10 31 30 29 28 27 26 25

Contents

The Old Testament

The Beginning (Creation to the Flood)

The Patriarchs (2091–1859 BC)

Moses and the Return to Canaan (1526–1406 BC)

Judges Rule God's People (1217–1060 BC)

Great Prophets and Kings (1049–587 BC)

God's People in Exile (722–533 BC)

God's People Return to Judah (538–430 BC)

The New Testament

Jesus' Childhood (4 BC–AD 11)

Jesus' Public Ministry (AD 29–32)

Jesus' Passion, Death, and Resurrection (AD 33)

The Holy Spirit Leads God's Church (AD 33–95)

The Old Testament

The Beginning (Creation to the Flood)

1. God Creates the World (Genesis 1–2)

For Reflection

1. Identify three ways you use God's good creation. ◆ **Answers will vary. We preserve, conserve, and rightly manage all of God's creation as one way of living for Him who died for us and rose again.**

2. What does it mean that Adam and Eve were made in God's image? ◆ **God created Adam and Eve holy, without sin.**

3. What special work do you do that is like the work God gave to Adam and Eve? ◆ **Specific examples will vary. We show the power and presence of Jesus in our life by doing our work faithfully and competently, joyfully serving God Himself (Ephesians 6:6–7).**

2. The Fall into Sin (Genesis 2–3)

For Reflection

1. What things tempt you to sin? What consequences do you experience? ◆ **Responses will vary. Many are the ways the devil tempts us to abandon Jesus for the desires and seduction our sinful world readily provides. Jesus faced and overcame temptation in our place and on our behalf.**

2. Because of sin, Adam, Eve, and all people experience pain and death. But God made a promise that He would save us. What does it mean that Eve's Offspring (Jesus) would bruise the serpent's head? ◆ **Jesus crushed Satan's head by defeating Him through His death on Calvary's cross for the sins of all people. The resurrection was the completion of the victory.**

3. Jesus was tempted also (see page 164 of *120 Bible Stories*). How did Jesus defeat Satan? How will reading and learning God's Word help when you are tempted? ◆ **Jesus defeated Satan when He resisted temptation in our place. Jesus' defeat of the power of the devil means our freedom from the condemnation of sin. Now, through God's Word, God's Spirit strengthens us to resist temptation and encourages us for the new life God has given us to live for Him.**

3. The Children of Adam and Eve (Genesis 4)

For Reflection

1. God warns Cain to think before he acts because sin is "crouching at the door" (Genesis 4:7). How does God help you to think before you act? ◆ **Through God's Word, the Holy Spirit moves us to think and act according to God's will.**

2. How did God show grace (undeserved love) to Cain? How have you been marked by God with His grace? ◆ **God protected Cain by placing a mark on him so that he would not be killed. God protected us by sending Jesus to be our Savior. By faith, we are marked for salvation in Him (see also Galatians 6:17).**

3. When Seth's son Enosh was alive, people began to call upon the name of the Lord. When today do you call upon God? How do you know God is listening? ◆ **People today call upon God when they praise Him and pray to Him either alone or in the company of others. God promises to hear us; He says so in His Word.**

4. Noah and the Flood (Genesis 6–9)

For Reflection

1. Why did God choose Noah to keep people and animals alive during the flood? ◆ **God is gracious; He saved Noah because Noah trusted and believed in Him. He kept people and animals safe on the ark so they might populate the world after the flood.**

2. Draw a rainbow. On it, list the promises (covenants) God made in this story. How did God keep these promises? List other promises that God made and kept. ◆ **The rainbow reminds us that God keeps His promises; among these are His promise never again to cover the world in a flood and His promise that the seasons by which we measure time would not be disrupted. God keeps every promise. God's promise to Adam and Eve and to their descendants to send a Savior from sin was kept in Jesus.**

3. God grieves (suffers extreme sorrow) when He sees the people He created sin. What do you learn about God from this? ◆ **God is just; He punishes sin.**

4. How does Noah's ark symbolize the Church? ◆ **Just as God saved Noah and his family in the ark, God saves His people through the Means of Grace, which He has given to His Church.**

The Patriarchs (c. 2091–1859 BC)

5. God Calls Abram (Genesis 12–13)

For Reflection

1. How did God protect Abram and Sarai in Egypt, even though Abram tried to take care of things on his own? In the New Testament, who was sent to Egypt for protection? ◆ **First, God protected Abram and Sarai from famine by sending them to Egypt. Then, after Abram reacted in fear and told a lie to protect himself, God afflicted Pharaoh and his house with plagues because of Sarai. Instead of taking Sarai for himself, Pharaoh sent Abram and Sarai away. Much later, God sent Mary and Joseph to Egypt to protect baby Jesus from those who sought to harm Him.**

2. When Lot took the best land, what promise did God make to Abram? ◆ **God promised Abram that He would give all the land of the region to Abram and his descendants. Here, God had promised to make Abram and his descendants into a great nation and that all people would be blessed through him. With these words, God was referring to Jesus, who would be born as a descendant of Abraham. Jesus came to save all people from their sins. He desires that all people be saved.**

3. Name a difficult thing God has asked you to do. How did He help you do it? ◆ **Answers will vary but are likely to reflect God's daily gifts of health and the necessities of life so that we may live and serve both God and others.**

6. Abram Rescues Lot (Genesis 13–14)

For Reflection

1. Talk about a time you chose something that turned out to be bad for you. What did you learn that will help you make better choices in the future? ◆ **Examples and learnings will vary. Because we love and trust in Jesus, we can trust in Him to work all things for our ultimate good.**

2. Although Lot had taken the best land, Abram wasn't angry and rescued his nephew and the other captives. How has God rescued you from your wrong choices? ◆ **Jesus came to save all people from their sins. He also rescues us at times by delivering us from evil as we ask Him to when we pray the Lord's Prayer.**

3. Abram gave Melchizedek a tenth of what he brought back because he was thankful for God's help. What can you offer God to thank Him for rescuing you? ◆ **Each of us can show our love for God in the unselfish way we deal with others. We can tell them of God and His love for us and for all people through Jesus. We can serve and love others. We can offer back to God a portion of His generous gifts to us, just as Melchizedek did.**

7. God's Covenant with Abram (Genesis 15; 17)

For Reflection

1. Why did God give Abram and Sarai new names? When did you receive a new name from God? ◆ **God gave Abram and Sarai new names to designate that they had been set apart to receive special blessings from Him. Somewhat similarly, God set us apart in Baptism when we received the name "Christian" to designate us as followers of Jesus.**

2. God promised Abraham that all nations would be blessed through him. God kept this promise when He sent Jesus. How are all people blessed through Jesus? ◆ **Jesus came to live, die, and rise again to earn forgiveness, new life, and eternal salvation for all people.**

3. List ways you are a blessing to others because you know Jesus is your Savior. ◆ **Because we know and believe in Jesus as our Savior, we want to tell others about Him so they, too, come to believe in Him. We also desire to share His love with others through our words and actions.**

8. Abraham's Visitors (Genesis 18; 21)

For Reflection

1. Who were Abraham's visitors? How did Abraham make them feel welcome? ◆ **Abraham's visitors were the Lord and two angels. Abraham ran to meet them, invited them to his tent, and provided a meal for them.**

2. Why did Sarah think she could not have a baby? Is anything too hard for the Lord? Why or why not? ◆ **Sarah was well past the age for having children. But nothing is impossible for God. He is the creator and controller of all things. Nothing is outside His almighty power and abilities.**

3. The meal that Abraham shared with his visitors reminds us of a special meal we share as God's people when we worship Him. What is this meal called? What gifts does God give in this meal? ◆ **God's people today share the Lord's Supper—the Sacrament of the Altar. In this meal, participants receive the very body and blood of Christ in, with, and under the bread and wine for the forgiveness of sins, strength for living the new life, and the assurance of eternal life in heaven.**

9. Abraham and Isaac (Genesis 22)

For Reflection

1. In this Bible story, Abraham is asked to sacrifice (make an offering of, give up) his son Isaac. What makes it hard to give up something you love? ◆ **You would miss what you love and the joy and pleasure its presence brings you.**

2. Abraham did what God told him to do, even though he must have been sad. How does this show what it means to "fear, love, and trust in God above all things"? ◆ **By demonstrating his willingness to obey, Abraham showed faith and trust in God. He regarded God above all else.**

3. What other story of a father sacrificing a son do you know from the Bible? ◆ **God loved all people so much that He gave up His only-begotten Son so that everyone who believes in Him will have eternal life.**

4. What blessings come to you because of Jesus and His death and resurrection? ◆ **We have forgiveness of sins, new life, and eternal salvation because of Jesus' death and resurrection for us and for all people.**

10. Isaac and Rebekah (Genesis 24)

For Reflection

1. What did the servant do to find the woman Isaac should marry? ◆ **He traveled to the faraway land of Abraham's relatives and asked God to direct him to the woman He had chosen to be the wife for Isaac.**

2. According to the servant, the Lord led him to Rebekah. Do you think that the Lord would lead you to a person you are supposed to marry? Why or why not? ◆ **Answers may vary somewhat, but God promises to hear and answer all prayer offered to Him in faith.**

3. Through the prophet Jeremiah, God tells you that He has a plan for you (see Jeremiah 29:11, the Words to Remember). How does each person in this Bible story show trust in God and His plan? ◆ **Abraham trusts in God to guide and direct his servant, the servant trusts in God to lead him to the wife he has chosen for Isaac, Laban and Bethuel agree to allow Rebekah to go to a far country to be Isaac's wife, Rebekah willingly agrees to leave her family to marry a man she has not met, Isaac marries the wife God has selected for him—and he loves her.**

11. Jacob and Esau (Genesis 25; 27)

For Reflection

1. Esau would inherit a double portion of Isaac's possessions (his birthright). How did Esau's sale of his birthright show that he did not respect Isaac? ◆ **The fact that Esau was willing to sell (or trade) a special blessing from his father, Isaac, for a simple meal shows how little respect he had for his father and the blessings his father wanted to give him.**

2. Rebekah helped Jacob receive a special blessing. Did Rebekah's plans work out? How does this show that our human choices are affected by sin? ◆ **Rebekah's plans led to Jacob receiving Isaac's blessing, but the consequences were devastating and life changing. One sin often leads to another. Jacob tricked his brother out of his blessing. Esau responded with threats of murder against Jacob. Jacob had to leave home and run for his life.**

3. Jacob didn't deserve the inheritance or the blessing, but he received them anyway. In what ways is this like the gift of faith in Jesus that you have received? ◆ **As God's children, through faith in Christ Jesus, we receive forgiveness of sins, new life, and eternal salvation at the hand of our loving and gracious God. We deserve or merit none of these gifts. They come to us solely through God's undeserved grace and favor toward us.**

12. Jacob's Dream (Genesis 27–28)

For Reflection

1. Beginning with Adam, God had spoken words of promise to His special followers (think about Abraham). How is Jacob's dream another example of this blessing? ◆ **Jacob had sinned by willingly taking part in the deception of his father. Still, God loved, cared for, and provided for Jacob. God assured Jacob of His love and care in the dream He allowed Jacob to have.**

2. Why did Jacob want to remember the place of his dream? What special places do we set aside for worshiping God? ◆ **Jacob wanted to remember God's love and care and the fact that God alone provides the way to heaven. Answers to the second question may vary somewhat. Churches are special places set aside for worshiping God. Some families have a family altar where they read and discuss God's Word and pray to God at family devotion time.**

3. In what ways do God's angels serve His people? ◆ **Angels serve God by defending and protecting people.**

13. Jacob's Family (Genesis 29–31)

For Reflection

1. Jacob tricked his father. Laban tricked Jacob. How does God bring good to Jacob despite these sinful human actions? ◆ **In spite of the deception and trickery in Jacob's life, God continued to bless him. Soon, Jacob had a large family and many sheep and cattle.**

2. You may trick yourself into thinking you deserve good things. But why does God give you good things? What is the best thing God has given to you? ◆ **God blesses us, not because we are good and deserve His blessings, but rather because of His love and undeserved grace and goodness. The best of His undeserved gifts to us are the blessings of forgiveness of sins, new life, and eternal salvation Jesus earned for us.**

3. What hard thing did God ask Jacob to do? God promised to be with Jacob. List ways you know that God is with you. ◆ **God told Jacob to move his large family and livestock back to his family in Canaan. The list of ways we know God is with us may vary, but it needs to include God's Word and the Sacraments, through which God strengthens our faith and assures us that in Jesus our sins are forgiven and that we have a new and eternal life in His name.**

14. Esau Forgives Jacob (Genesis 32–33)

For Reflection

1. Why was Jacob afraid to meet Esau? ◆ **When they were younger, Esau expressed that he wanted to kill Jacob.**

2. The man who wrestled with Jacob was God. What did God do for Jacob when morning came? How do you think this helped Jacob to face Esau? ◆ **God blessed Jacob, giving him a new name—Israel. These actions of God would certainly have assured Jacob of God's loving protection and care.**

3. Who else in Jacob's family had a name change? Why does God change a name? ◆ **God changed the names of Jacob's grandparents, Abraham and Sarah. God changes people's names to signify a new direction or purpose He is bringing into their life.**

4. As soon as Jacob bought the land, he built an altar to God. How does this show that God is important to Jacob? How do you show that God is important? ◆ **Jacob built an altar so that he might worship God. We show that God is important to us when we worship and pray to Him, both when we are alone and when we join others in worshiping Him.**

15. Joseph's Dreams (Genesis 37)

For Reflection

1. Describe Joseph's dreams and how others reacted to them. ◆ **Joseph's dreams showed his family members bowing down and paying homage to him. Jacob kept these dreams in mind, but Joseph's brothers resented them.**

2. The evil thoughts of Joseph's brothers led to evil actions. Explain why this happens. Where do evil thoughts come from, according to Matthew 15:19? ◆ **We act according to what we feel and believe. God's Word reminds us that evil actions find their origin in the human heart.**

3. The sons of Israel (Jacob) tricked him into thinking Joseph was dead. Whom did Jacob trick? Recall the story. ◆ **Jacob tricked his father, Isaac, into giving him the birthright he intended to give to Esau.**

4. Reuben interceded for (tried to help) Joseph. Who has interceded for you? How? ◆ **Jesus has interceded and continues to intercede on our behalf before His Father in heaven. He stood in our place when He died for our sins on the cross, and now, because of His sacrifice, He pleads our case of innocence before God the Father.**

16. Joseph in Egypt (Genesis 39–41)

For Reflection

1. How did God help Joseph? How does God help you in difficult situations? ◆ **God worked good in Joseph's life in spite of all the hardships, difficulties, and setbacks he encountered. Similarly, God continues to bless and sustain us in spite of our challenges and difficulties. Jesus continues to forgive our sins and strengthens us with His redeeming love; ultimately, He will save us out of this vale of tears and bring us to Himself in heaven.**

2. Explain the connection between this Bible story and God's promises to Abraham, Isaac, and Jacob that through their offspring all nations would be blessed. ◆ **Bringing Jacob and his family to live in Egypt was part of God's plan to grow this family into a great nation of people, the nation into which the Savior of the world would one day be born.**

3. Because of sin, you experienced a famine (suffering from extreme need) for God and His forgiveness. Compare what Joseph did for the hungry people with what Jesus has done and continues to do for you and for all people. ◆ **As we come to**

recognize our sin and feel the need for help, by the power of the Holy Spirit we turn to God for the forgiveness and new and eternal life Jesus offers to us freely through His life, death, and resurrection.

17. Joseph Forgives His Brothers (Genesis 42–45)

For Reflection

1. Although Joseph could have been angry, how did he show mercy (love) to his brothers? In what ways does God show mercy to you? Why does God show you mercy? ◆ **Joseph told them not to be distressed or angry because they had sold him into slavery, for God had sent him before them into Egypt so their lives might be saved. God showed His mercy to us and all people by sending Jesus to save us from our sins. God shows His mercy to us simply because He loves us, not because we deserve or merit His grace and love.**

2. What was Judah willing to do for Benjamin? How does Judah remind you of Jesus? ◆ **Judah volunteered to serve as a substitute for Benjamin. Jesus became our substitute, living a holy life and dying the death we deserved in order to save us.**

3. Describe a time that God made something good happen to you, even though things started out badly. What is the best "good thing" that God has done for you? With whom can you share this good gift? ◆ **Examples of "good from bad" will vary. The ultimate good thing God did for us was sending Jesus to rescue and save us. Answers to the final question will vary.**

18. Jacob's Blessing (Genesis 45–49)

For Reflection

1. Review what you have learned about Joseph. How did God work in Joseph's life to bring good things? How does God work in your life to bring good things? ◆ **God used Joseph's tragic captivity and slavery in Egypt in order to put Joseph in a position from which he could eventually save His people from starvation. Examples from individual lives will vary.**

2. When Jacob blessed his sons, he said, "The scepter shall not depart from Judah." What is a scepter? Why did Jacob give Judah this blessing? Who would be part of Judah's offspring (see Matthew 1:1–17, especially verses 2–3)? ◆ **A scepter is a type of staff (baton) symbolizing royal authority. Kings would come from the family of Judah. Chief among these would be Jesus of Nazareth, our Savior and the King of kings.**

3. Why did Jacob command his sons to bury him in the land of Canaan? ◆ **Jacob's desire to be buried with his wife, parents, and grandparents draws attention once again to God's promise to give the land of Canaan to Abraham and his family. From this family, and in this land, the Savior of the world would one day be born.**

Moses and the Return to Canaan (1526–1406 BC)

19. The Birth of Moses (Exodus 1–2)

For Reflection

1. Despite all the rough treatment by the Egyptians, God continued to be with the people of Israel. What parts of the Bible story show this to be true? ◆ **Answers may vary somewhat. Possible responses include that the midwives feared God and let the male children live, God allowed Moses to survive when he was a baby, and God allowed for Moses to escape the murderous intent of Pharaoh when he was a grown man.**

2. Moses' mother saved him by putting him in a small boat—a basket covered with pitch so that It would float. How is this like God's plan for Noah? (See page 14 of *120 Bible Stories.*) ◆ **The boat by which baby Moses was saved was very much like a little ark. God rescued Noah and the animals by allowing them to float unharmed in a large ark on the waters of the great flood.**

3. God protected baby Moses so he could grow up and rescue God's people from slavery. What other baby was born to rescue people? How did He rescue you? ◆ **Jesus was born a baby; He came to save all people by living a holy life and dying an atoning death for all people everywhere.**

20. God Calls Moses (Exodus 2–4)

For Reflection

1. Identify examples from this Bible story that show God listens to prayer. ◆ **God heard the prayers of His people as they suffered bondage in Egypt; He provided them deliverance through Moses. God heard the prayers of Moses, and then He talked, reasoned, encouraged, and equipped Moses for the work God had planned for him to do.**

2. How did God call Moses? What words and signs (miracles) did God give to Moses to prove to the people of Israel that God had sent him to save them? ◆ **God called to Moses from out of a bush that was burning, yet was not consumed. God told Moses to tell the people that "I AM" had sent him to them. Signs included a staff turning into a serpent and then back into a staff, and Moses getting leprosy and then being cured.**

3. What special gifts has God given to you? How can you use these gifts to serve others and tell them about God's plan of salvation in Jesus? ◆ **God provides His people today with His Word and the Sacraments of Baptism and the Lord's Supper and with the help, support, and encouragement of our brothers and sisters in the faith. Also, He has given each of us unique talents and abilities to use in the lives He has given us to live for Him. Individual answers will vary.**

21. Moses and the Plagues (Exodus 5–10)

For Reflection

1. How did the signs and wonders God did through Moses and Aaron answer Pharaoh's question, "Who is the LORD?" How would you answer this question? ◆ **Through these signs and supernatural acts, God showed His power and His willingness to use His power to help and save His people. Student answers may vary but may identify the Lord as the triune God—Father, Son, and Holy Spirit—the same God as in the Old Testament who acts mightily to save His people. God rescued all people through Jesus.**

2. What do you think it means that God "hardened" Pharaoh's heart? How does God send His Spirit to soften your heart toward Him? ◆ **God allowed Pharaoh to remain resistant to the Holy Spirit and His power to work repentance, faith, and obedience in human hearts. Through God's Word, the Holy Spirit softens hard human hearts and changes fallen sinners into people of faith.**

3. God sent darkness on the land of Egypt for three days. Of what New Testament event does this remind you? How does God use you to shine His light on others? ◆ **When Jesus was suffering and dying on the cross, the sky became dark for several hours. We shine the light of Jesus to others when we help and serve them, especially when we tell them the Good News of salvation by grace through faith in Jesus.**

22. The Passover (Exodus 11–13)

For Reflection

1. What was the tenth plague that God brought upon the Egyptians? ◆ **On the night before the departure of God's people from Egypt, the angel of death passed over the houses of Egypt, bringing death to those households not protected with the blood of the lamb.**

2. What instructions did God give to the people of Israel to keep them safe during the tenth plague? Why did they call this special meal "the Passover"? ◆ **They were to eat roasted meat with bitter herbs and bread made without yeast; they were to eat it in haste and be ready to leave on a journey. They were to spread the blood of a lamb on the doorposts and lintels of their houses.**

3. The blood of the lamb was a sign that those in the house were protected from death. Earlier, you read that God sent a ram for Abraham to sacrifice instead of his son Isaac. Whose blood has saved you? (Hint: He is called "the Lamb of God"!) ◆ **Jesus shed His blood for the salvation of us and all people.**

23. Crossing the Red Sea (Exodus 14–15)

For Reflection

1. What visual reminder of His presence among them did God give to the Israelites? ◆ **God led His people, providing a pillar of cloud to guide them by day and a pillar of fire to direct them at night.**

2. Compare and contrast the events of the exodus (departure) from Egypt with the way in which Jesus has redeemed (bought back) all people from the power of sin, death, and the devil. ◆ **God led the people out of slavery in Egypt after the Passover; Jesus allowed Himself to be nailed to a Roman cross to rescue all people from the bondage of sin and the power of the devil. This rescue is for every person who ever lived or who ever will live.**

3. Describe a time when you felt like the people of Israel, caught between the Red Sea and the Egyptian army. How does this story give you confidence in God? ◆ **Responses to the first question will vary. God is with us. Our loving Savior has promised never to leave us (Matthew 28:20).**

24. God Provides Manna and Quail (Exodus 16)

For Reflection

1. About what did the people of Israel grumble? Were they angry with Moses and Aaron, or were they angry with God? Explain. ◆ **The people grumbled and complained that they were hungry; they remembered the food they had to eat when they were in Egypt. The people grumbled against Moses and Aaron; but since Moses and Aaron were God's designated leaders, the people were really grumbling and complaining against God.**

2. What two foods did God provide for the people? What special rules were the people supposed to follow? What happened when they didn't obey God? ◆ **God gave the people quail to eat at the evening and breadlike manna to eat in the morning. Each day, they were to gather enough manna for that day. On the sixth day, they were to gather twice as much as any other day so that they would also have enough for the Sabbath day. The people were to eat each day all of the manna they gathered. When they disobeyed, the manna became filled with worms and stank.**

3. In John 6:32, Jesus calls Himself the "true bread from heaven." Because you have been given the gift of faith in Jesus, how does this "fill up" your heart and life? ◆ **In Jesus, we find all we need for our life. In Jesus, we can find fullness of happiness and sustenance.**

25. God Gives the Law (Exodus 19–20)

For Reflection

1. List the ways God showed His presence on the mountain. List the ways God comes to you today. Do you need to be afraid of God's presence? Why or why not? ◆ **God demonstrated His presence with smoke, fire, and the trembling of the mountain. God comes to us today through His Word and Sacraments. We need not be afraid of God. Rather, we can trust in His love for us and in His desire and ability to help, protect, and save us. His sacrifice of Jesus for us demonstrates the extent of His great love.**

2. God describes Himself as "jealous." This means He wants you to love only Him. Who loved God perfectly so that you can enjoy God's steadfast love forever? ◆ **Jesus loved and served God in our place, without sin. His righteousness becomes ours by grace through faith in Him.**

3. Moses was an advocate (someone who pleads for others, like a lawyer) for the people before God. Who is your Advocate before God? ◆ **Jesus is our Advocate. He continues to plead with His heavenly Father on our behalf. We are sinners; but by faith, His righteousness is ours. When God looks at us through Christ Jesus, He sees us only as holy and forgiven, covered by the blood of Jesus.**

26. God's Covenant with the Israelites (Exodus 32–34; 40)

For Reflection

1. While Moses was with God on the mountain, how did the people of Israel sin? What other gods do you sometimes worship? ◆ **The people of Israel had time on their hands as they waited for Moses to come down from the mountain. They made an idol and began to worship it in place of the true and living God. We sometimes worship the gods of popularity, possessions, and activities that take the place of the worship of the one true God.**

2. Moses implored (begged) God to forgive the people. Identify parts of the story that show God forgave the people. Who has made it possible for God to forgive you? ◆ **God provided the people with the tabernacle, ark, and other furnishings, and also with the cloud and fire as visual indications of His presence. Jesus has made it possible for God to forgive us. He paid in full the penalty we deserve because of our sins.**

3. What items in your church show God's presence? Draw a picture or create a word cloud that expresses "the glory of the Lord" and "[God] will walk among you." ◆ **Possible responses include the altar, the baptismal font, the eternal light, images shown on the stained glass windows, and other specific works of art.**

27. The Twelve Spies (Numbers 13–14)

For Reflection

1. What report did the spies bring to the people of Israel? How did Joshua and Caleb show their trust in God? ◆ **The spies reported that the land was bountiful, but then they added that the occupants of the land were formidable and impossible to be defeated by God's people. Joshua and Caleb expressed their trust in the ability of God to give the new land to His people. They also warned others about rebelling against God.**

2. When the people rebelled against (disobeyed) God, what did Moses ask God to do? In what part of the worship service do we say words like Moses said to God? ◆ **Moses asked God to forgive the people for their sin and rebellion against God. We speak similar words during the Confession part of the worship service.**

3. Think of a tough job you are facing (a test or project, a new family member). Ask God to help you trust that He will give you everything you need to do the job. ◆ **Obstacles and individual prayers will vary. Stress God's love and the strength He offers us through Christ Jesus, our Lord.**

28. Water from a Rock and Fiery Serpents (Numbers 20–21)

For Reflection

1. What did God tell Moses and Aaron to do to make water come out of the rock? What little action did Moses add to God's command? ◆ **God told Moses and Aaron to tell the rock to yield its water. Instead of simply speaking to the rock, as God had commanded, Moses struck the rock twice with his staff.**

2. What consequences did Moses and Aaron receive because they did not do exactly what God had said? What does this tell you about how God views sin? ◆ **Because of their disobedience, Moses and Aaron were not permitted to enter the Promised Land. God hates and punishes sin.**

3. How is Jesus like the bronze serpent that Moses put on the pole in the wilderness? How does Jesus' death and resurrection remove the consequences of your sin? ◆ **Like the serpent, Jesus was lifted up between heaven and earth so that all who believe in Him could have eternal life (John 3:14–15). Instead of eternal punishment in hell—the consequence for sin, which Jesus' death and resurrection removed—we have a new and blissful home in heaven awaiting us in the presence of our God and Savior.**

29. The Death of Moses (Deuteronomy 18; 31; 34)

For Reflection

1. What command does Moses give to the people before they enter the Promised Land? Do you think the people will follow Moses' command? Explain. ◆ **Moses told the people to avoid the sinful practices of those living in the land of Canaan and to serve God blamelessly. The people did not obey Moses. Like us, they are sinful by nature, inclined to do evil.**

2. God chose Joshua to lead the people. Who has God chosen to be a leader in your life? Ask God to make the leaders in your life strong and courageous. ◆ **Possible responses include parents and other significant adults, such as pastors and teachers. Pray with the child that he or she will follow leaders who are bold and courageous for Jesus.**

3. Moses said that God promised to send a prophet "like me." Who is this Prophet? What words of God has He shared? How does He lead you to the promised land? ◆ **Jesus is the Moseslike prophet. Jesus is the Word of God—the Word made flesh. Jesus saved us by living a holy life and by dying in our place for our sins. Knowing His forgiving, empowering, eternal love, we follow Him into the promised land of heaven.**

30. Rahab Hides the Spies (Joshua 1–2)

For Reflection

1. The first words that God says to Joshua are a promise. What is the promise? Has God made a similar promise to you? When was this promise made? ◆ **God told Joshua, "Be strong and courageous. . . . The Book of the Law shall not depart from your mouth, but you shall meditate on it day and night." God made a similar promise to each of us when He claimed us as His own in Holy Baptism. As we study God's Word, His Spirit strengthens and encourages us. Therefore, God invites us to make frequent and regular use of His Word, both alone and as we receive it in the Sacraments.**

2. How does Rahab show strength and courage that could come only from God? In exchange for keeping their escape secret, what does Rahab ask the spies to do? ◆ **Rahab defied the king of the ungodly land and hid the spies instead. Later, she helped them to escape. Rahab asks the spies to spare her family when they conquer her people.**

3. Describe a time that God gave you strength and courage to help someone. ◆ **Specific examples will vary. Knowing Jesus' forgiving, empowering, eternal love, we can boldly face all that comes to us in life as we serve God and others.**

31. Israel Enters the Promised Land (Joshua 3–5)

For Reflection

1. When Israel crossed the Jordan, what things did God do that were the same as when the people crossed the Red Sea? What things were different? ◆ **During both events, the people crossed through the middle of the water, miraculously, on dry ground. At the crossing of the Red Sea, Moses held his staff over the water and the waters parted. At the crossing of the Jordan River, the waters parted and returned as the feet of the priests who carried the ark of the covenant entered and left the bank of the river.**

2. What was the purpose of the 12 stones Joshua set up? Who has told you what God has done for you? ◆ **The 12 stones made up a monument that served as a reminder for the people of God's care and deliverance of them. Answers to the second question will vary.**

3. Who was the commander of the Lord's army who talked with Joshua? How do you think this meeting prepared Joshua for the battle ahead? ◆ **Answers may vary somewhat. The commander of the Lord's army may have been none other than the preincarnate Jesus. The visit of the commander of the Lord's army would certainly have reminded Joshua of God's help and presence with him.**

32. The Fall of Jericho (Joshua 6; 24)

For Reflection

1. Recall God's promises to Abraham (see page 22 of *120 Bible Stories*). Beginning with the birth of Isaac, describe in as much detail as you remember how God kept these promises. ◆ **God promised to make Abraham's family into a great nation. This promise's fulfillment can be seen in the large numbers of Israelites entering Canaan to occupy it. God's promise to give the land of Canaan to Abraham and his family is being fulfilled even as they enter Canaan to possess it. God's promise to bless others through Abraham's descendants is being fulfilled in the rescue of Rahab, who becomes an ancestor of Christ, the ultimate blessing to all people.**

2. The walls of Jericho were strong, yet only a shout brought them down. Is there anything God cannot do? Explain. ◆ **There is nothing our almighty God cannot do. He controls all things, including all natural forces.**

3. The names Joshua and Jesus both mean "the Lord saves." How did Joshua and Jesus each save people? Why is it so important to believe that Jesus saves you? ◆ **God brought salvation to His people as they followed His directions under the leadership of Joshua; God saved us through Jesus, who obeyed God sinlessly in our place and took our punishment on Calvary's cross. Jesus' salvation brings us forgiveness of sins, life, and eternal salvation. These are the most important blessings anyone can receive.**

Judges Rule God's People (1217–1060 BC)

33. Deborah the Prophetess (Joshua 2; 4–5)

For Reflection

1. What had the people of Israel done so that God allowed them to be under the control of Jabin, the king of Canaan? ◆ **The people did evil in the sight of the Lord.**

2. Deborah told Barak that even though he would defeat Sisera's army, Sisera would be defeated by a woman. Tell how Jael defeated Sisera. ◆ **Jael drove a tent peg into Sisera's temple as he lay sleeping in her tent.**

3. Moses praised God with a song (see page 56 of *120 Bible Stories*). What words in Moses' song are similar to Deborah and Barak's words? What causes you to sing praises to God? ◆ **Both songs refer to singing to the Lord because of the victory He has provided. Somewhat similarly, we sing praises to God because of the victory over sin, death, and Satan's power that Jesus has won for us.**

34. Gideon Defeats Midian (Judges 6–8)

For Reflection

1. Gideon tells the angel that God had forsaken the people because He wasn't doing any "wonderful deeds." List 10 "little things" that God is always doing for you. ◆ **List items will vary. God gives us all we have and are able to do; He enables us to draw our each and every breath.**

2. Gideon started with at least 32,000 men. Why did God choose only 300 to defeat the Midianites? Read the fifth paragraph of the story (page 80 of *120 Bible Stories*) to help with the answer. ◆ **God knew that unless only a few soldiers were given victory, Israel would boast that they had won the victory by their own might.**

3. Read Psalm 118:8, the Words to Remember. Explain what this verse means for you, now that you have read the Bible story about Gideon. ◆ **God always has our best interests foremost in mind; we do well to trust in Him above all else.**

35. God Makes Samson Strong (Judges 13; 15–16)

For Reflection

1. How do you know that God had a plan for Samson even before he was born? In the first part of the Bible story, what actions show that God was with Samson? ◆ **Before Samson's birth, God said of him, "He shall begin to save Israel from the Philistines." Samson's feats of great strength indicate that God was with him.**

2. How did Samson lose his strength? Think of a time that you have finally given in to temptation. What were the consequences? How did God save you? ◆ **Samson gave in to unbelieving Delilah, who shaved his head. Samson lost his great strength. God saved us by sending Jesus to defeat sin, death, and Satan's power in our place.**

3. Who was the real source of Samson's strength? How does God strengthen your faith in Him? List three ways you can thank God for never leaving you. ◆ **God's Spirit was the source of Samson's strength. God's Spirit brings people to—and sustains us in—the one true faith. Responses will vary to how we can thank God but may include in our words and songs of praise, by loving and serving God, and by loving and serving others as God has commanded.**

36. Ruth (The Book of Ruth)

For Reflection

1. Ruth told Naomi, "Where you go, I will go." Ruth loved Naomi so much that she left her home. Who loved you so much that He left His home to save you? ◆ **Jesus left His home in heaven to live, die, and rise again in our place.**

2. Boaz was Naomi's redeemer (the person who could protect her inheritance). How does Jesus, your Redeemer, protect your inheritance of faith, forgiveness, and life? ◆ **First, Jesus earned these things for us; then, He makes them available to us freely by grace through faith; and finally, He gives us His Holy Spirit to sustain us in faith.**

3. Many years after Ruth lived, Jesus was born to one of her descendants. How does Ruth's Moabite background remind you that Jesus came to redeem all people? ◆ **As true man, Jesus, the world's Savior, was descended not only from Jewish people but from other people groups as well. He came to be the Savior of all (2 Corinthians 5:15).**

37. Hannah and Samuel (1 Samuel 1–2)

For Reflection

1. What did Hannah ask God in prayer? List the women in previous Bible stories who were unable to have a child. How did God keep His promises to these women? ◆ **Hannah prayed that God would give her a son. Included among Old Testament women who were unable to have children are Sarah and Rebekah. God not only gave these women children, but through their children, He also gave them many, many descendants.**

2. How did Hannah show her thankfulness to God for giving her a son? ◆ **Hannah dedicated her son to the Lord and to His lifelong service.**

3. Compare Hannah's song with the song Mary sang when she learned she would be the mother of Jesus (see page 150 of *120 Bible Stories*). List all the words that describe our great God. Use them to make your own song of praise to the God who keeps His promises. ◆ **Both Hannah's song and Mary's song compare their humility with the greatness and power of God and praise Him for the great things He has done. Words listed that describe the greatness of God will vary somewhat, as will individual songs of praise.**

38. God Calls Samuel (1 Samuel 2–4)

For Reflection

1. Eli's sons were supposed to become priests like their father. How did their actions show that would be a problem? Who is doing what Eli's sons should be doing? ◆ **Eli's sons were worthless men; they did not know the Lord and they treated the offering of the Lord with contempt. Samuel served the Lord under Eli.**

2. God called to Samuel and spoke with him. What does God use to call and speak to you? ◆ **God calls and speaks to us through His Word.**

3. Eli and his sons died because God does punish sin. Who took the punishment for your sin? Because of Jesus, what does God give to you instead of death? ◆ **Jesus took the punishment we deserved because of our sin. Jesus took our sin upon Himself, and He gives us His holiness.**

Great Prophets and Kings (1049–587 BC)

39. Saul Becomes King (1 Samuel 8–11)

For Reflection

1. What did the elders of Israel ask for because of the actions of Samuel's sons? Why did God call this request a "rejection"? ◆ **The elders asked for a king. The people had rejected God as their King.**

2. What characteristics did Saul have that made him seem to be a good choice for a king? ◆ **Saul was tall, strong, and handsome.**

3. How did the Lord show He was with the people of Israel, even though they wanted an earthly king? How does the Lord show He is with you, even though you sin? ◆ **God granted their request. God continues to bless, sustain, and offer salvation to us and all people, even though we sin.**

40. Samuel Anoints David (1 Samuel 15–16)

For Reflection

1. What did the Lord tell Saul to do when he fought the Amalekites? How do the results of Saul's actions show that God expects complete obedience? ◆ **Instead of destroying the Amalekites and their possessions, Saul spared King Agag and the best of the sheep and oxen and all that was good. God commands perfect obedience.**

2. Explain what God means when He says He doesn't look at outward appearances but at the heart. Why is this a good thing? ◆ **God loves all people. He desires all people to come to faith in Him and be saved. That faith grows in the heart and is not dependent on outer appearances.**

3. Who creates faith in you? Who renews you from the inside out—your spirit, will, attitude, and desires? ◆ **Working in us through God's Word and the Sacraments, God's Spirit creates faith and changes us from the inside out, making us into new people who desire to live for Him who died for us and rose again.**

41. David Fights Goliath (1 Samuel 17)

For Reflection

1. Sometimes only the strongest man from each side fought to decide a battle. The "champion" who fought was often the king. What was Saul's response to Goliath's challenge? Compare this with the response of David, the Lord's anointed king. ◆ **Saul and all Israel were greatly afraid. David expressed fearless trust in God to provide him with victory over the enemy champion.**

2. How did David show his complete trust in the Lord to give him the victory? ◆ **David said, "You come to me with a sword and with a spear and with a javelin, but I come to you in the name of the LORD of hosts, . . . whom you have defied. This day the LORD will deliver you into my hand."**

3. Who is the Champion sent by God to fight for you against the devil? How do you know that the victory is yours? ◆ **Jesus. He has already won the victory for us over all that would finally destroy us. God's Word proclaims the comforting assurance that nothing can separate us from His love (Romans 8:38–39).**

42. David and Jonathan (1 Samuel 18; 20)

For Reflection

1. How did Jonathan show that he was not jealous that God had chosen David to be the next king of Israel? ◆ **Jonathan loved David as his own soul. He gave David his robe, his armor, and even his sword and his bow and his belt.**

2. List characteristics (loyalty, honesty, sense of humor) that make a good friend. Circle those that David and Jonathan showed toward each other. Place a cross over those that Jesus shows toward you. ◆ **Characteristics of good friends will vary. The best friends believers can find are those who share their faith in Jesus as the Son of God and Savior of the world.**

3. How does God, your heavenly King, show that He is well disposed (acting favorably) toward you? ◆ **He sacrificed His only Son so that we might have forgiveness of sins, new life, and eternal salvation.**

43. God's Covenant with David (2 Samuel 7)

For Reflection

1. What special building project did David want to complete for God? What was God's response to David's plan? ◆ **David wanted to build a house for the Lord. God told David that David's son was to be the one who would build a house for the Lord.**

2. Where did David go to speak with God? How did David show his thankfulness for all that God had done for him? ◆ **David went to the tabernacle (tent church). He thanked and praised God as he recalled God's goodness to His people.**

3. How did God keep His promise to David to "establish" the throne forever? Which of King David's descendants brought blessing to his house forever? ◆ **God established a line of faithful offspring from the line and family of David. Among these was born Jesus, the Savior of the world.**

44. Solomon Becomes King (1 Kings 2–3)

For Reflection

1. What guidance do the adults in your life give to you? What is the most important part of David's advice to Solomon? Why? ◆ **Examples of guidance offered by adults will vary. David's most important advice to Solomon was to keep the charge of the Lord (faithfully rule the people), to walk in the ways of God, and to obey Him.**

2. How does God show He is pleased with Solomon's request for an understanding mind? How does Solomon display the gift of wisdom that God gave to him? ◆ **God answered Solomon's prayer for a wise and discerning heart; He added to Solomon the blessings of riches and honor as well. Solomon ruled the people wisely, as evidenced in his handling of the case of the two women who claimed the same child.**

3. Solomon made offerings to God in thanksgiving. List all the gifts God has given to you (family, friends, talents, Jesus). Thank God specifically for these gifts. ◆ **Expressions of thanks to God will vary.**

45. Solomon Builds the Temple (1 Kings 5–6; 8)

For Reflection

1. Why would making a treaty with a neighboring king show Solomon's wisdom? ◆ **Through the treaty, Solomon received the wood he needed from Lebanon and the King of Tyre received payment in the form of food.**

2. The glory of the Lord filled the temple Solomon had built. How does the glory of the Lord fill your church when you gather with Gods' people to worship Him? ◆ **The glory of God's presence evidences itself in the words that are spoken, read, and sung during worship; His glory is also received in the Sacraments.**

3. Prayers can include adoration, confession, thanksgiving, and supplication (ACTS). With an adult's help, identify what parts of Solomon's prayer fit in each category. Compose your own prayer that follows the ACTS model. ◆ **Solomon's prayer began with adoration, then moved into supplication, and then into confession. His offering of the sacrifice may be seen as an act of thanksgiving.**

46. God Provides for Elijah (1 Kings 16–17)

For Reflection

1. How did God provide for Elijah during the drought and famine? ◆ **God sent ravens to bring food to Elijah in the morning and evening at the brook Cherith; later, God sent the widow of Zarephath to care for Elijah's needs.**

2. Elijah pleaded with God, and God brought the widow's son back to life. Compare this with the story of Jesus bringing Jairus's daughter back to life (see page 184 of *120 Bible Stories*). How do these Bible stories show God's power over death? ◆ **God showed His power over death by returning the widow's son to life. Jesus' victory over death means that God will also one day raise our bodies to life and give us a new and eternal home with Him in glory.**

3. Jesus said, "I am the resurrection and the life" (John 11:25). What proof can you point to so you can say, like the widow, that these words of the Lord are true? ◆ **Jesus raised His body from the dead after having been dead for three days. His victory over death is our victory.**

47. Elijah and the Prophets of Baal (1 Kings 18)

For Reflection

1. Like King Ahab and the Israelites, you sometimes follow false gods. Identify people, things, or ideas in which you are tempted to place your trust rather than in God. ◆ **False gods that people worship today include satanic arts and witchcraft, money and possessions, and friends and influence.**

2. God responded to Elijah's prayer and showed His power. Share a time God answered your prayer. Thank Him for always being awake and ready to help. ◆ **Responses may vary, but may include the idea that we pray for and receive forgiveness of sins because Jesus took our sins to the cross.**

3. Elijah called the people back to faith in God. How do you show people your faith in God and tell them Jesus is the Savior from sin? ◆ **Specific actions and words that witness our faith in Jesus will vary.**

48. God Takes Elijah to Heaven (1 Kings 19; 2 Kings 2)

For Reflection

1. How did Elijah "fight the good fight" of calling the people of Israel back from their sinful actions? How did God protect and comfort Elijah? ◆ **Elijah killed the prophets of Baal and remained faithful to God. God sent an angel to bring Elijah food and water and spoke to him in a whisper.**

2. What did Elisha ask of Elijah? How does God send His Spirit to work in your life? Who has God put in your life to teach you about God like Elijah taught Elisha? ◆ **Elisha asked for a double portion of Elijah's spirit. God's Spirit works to strengthen our faith through God's Word and the Sacraments. Examples of teachers of the faith will vary.**

3. How did Elijah go into heaven? How did Elisha know that God was with him even as He had been with Elijah? How do you know God is always with you? ◆ **A chariot and horses of fire appeared, and Elijah was carried to heaven in a whirlwind. God allowed Elisha to watch Elijah go into heaven, which meant he had received a double portion of his spirit. Immediately afterward, Elisha struck the water with the cloak of Elijah and the waters parted so Elisha could cross through them. We know God is with us because He has promised in His Word to remain with us.**

49. Naaman and Elisha (2 Kings 5)

For Reflection

1. How did God use the servants and messengers in this Bible story? ◆ **The young girl in this story told her mistress about the help available through God's prophet in Samaria. Also, Naaman's servant encouraged Naaman to wash in the Jordan River when he became angry at the request.**

2. Naaman was cured of his deadly disease by washing in the Jordan River. What "washing" saves you from deadly disease of sin? ◆ **We are washed in the blood of Jesus (see Revelation 7:14). God makes us His own in the waters of Holy Baptism.**

3. Naaman tried to pay Elisha with silver, gold, and clothing, but Elisha refused the gifts. Can you pay God for healing you from your sin? Who paid the price? ◆ **We cannot pay or in any way earn or merit God's forgiveness. Jesus paid the price for us through His innocent life, death, and resurrection.**

4. What words did Elisha say as Naaman left? When do you hear these words? ◆ **Elisha said, "Go in peace." We hear these words during the worship service after we have been assured of the forgiveness of sins.**

50. Jonah (The Book of Jonah)

For Reflection

1. From whom was Jonah trying to run away? Was Jonah successful? Explain. ◆ **Jonah tried to run away from God. He did not want to go to Nineveh and preach against their wickedness, as God had commanded him. You cannot run away from God. God knows and can control all things.**

2. How did God show His love and kindness to Jonah despite Jonah's disobedience? How does God show love and kindness toward you even when you sin? ◆ **After the sailors threw Jonah overboard, God rescued him by providing a great fish to swallow him and eventually bring him to land. God shows His love and kindness to us by forgiving us for Jesus' sake.**

3. Compare Jesus' death and resurrection to Jonah's experience with the great fish. ◆ **Jesus came to earth to die for our sins, earning our salvation for us. Just as Jonah was in the belly of the fish for three days and nights, Jesus was in the tomb and rose from the dead on the third day.**

4. Like the people of Nineveh, we deserve death for our sins, but God has turned from punishing us. Why? Thank God for His great mercy. ◆ **God loves and rescues us solely because of His grace and mercy, without any merit or worthiness on our part.**

51. Isaiah Sees the Lord (Isaiah 6–7; 9; 53)

For Reflection

1. Why was Isaiah afraid (full of woe) to be in the Lord's presence? What did the seraphim do? How have your sins been atoned for (paid for) so you can be in God's presence? ◆ **Isaiah's fear grew from the realization that he was in the presence of the holy and omnipotent God. The seraphim covered himself with his wings, proclaiming, "Holy, holy, holy is the LORD of hosts. The whole earth is full of His glory!" Jesus atoned for our sins through His life, death, and resurrection.**

2. Identify how each of Isaiah's prophecies was fulfilled. ◆ **Specific prophecy fulfillment examples will vary but may include the following: Jesus came to be Immanuel—God with us; He is the light of the world; He suffered and died to earn forgiveness, new life, and eternal salvation for us.**

3. With an adult's help, find hymns or songs that use Isaiah's words. Memorize your favorite hymn and sing it to Jesus to thank Him for atoning for your sins. ◆ **Hymn selections will vary. Many hymnals list Scripture references in the credit lines of the hymns.**

52. King Hezekiah Prays (2 Kings 18–19)

For Reflection

1. How did the leaders of the Assyrian army try to plant doubt in the minds of Hezekiah and his people concerning God's ability to protect them? Compare this with how the devil tempted Eve in the Garden of Eden. ◆ **The leaders commented that none of the gods of Assyria's other enemies had been able to deliver them. Like the devil in his conversation with Eve in the garden, they sought to lead God's people first to doubt God and then to turn their backs on Him.**

2. Hezekiah prayed to the Lord for help. What was God's answer? ◆ **God sent the prophet Isaiah to speak words of assurance to Hezekiah. Then He sent His angel to kill 185,000 of Sennacherib's army.**

3. List ways God protects you through the government and its leaders. Ask God to guide the leaders in your church, school, city, state, and country. ◆ **Through the government, God provides us with public services and resources and helps us to enjoy safe and comfortable lives.**

53. King Josiah (2 Kings 22–23)

For Reflection

1. What did the priest find in the temple and give to the king? What did King Josiah realize after the book was read to him? ◆ **Hilkiah the priest found the Book of the Law. King Josiah realized that God's people had not obeyed the words found in the book.**

2. What changes did Josiah make after he heard God's Word? What was the most surprising change he made? ◆ **After Josiah read the Book of the Covenant in the hearing of all the people, he and all the people agreed to keep God's commands. They removed and burned all items associated with idolatry from the temple, and they reinstituted the Passover observance.**

3. Who makes it possible for you to love the Lord with all your heart and soul and might? Through what activities does the Holy Spirit strengthen your faith in Jesus? ◆ **The Holy Spirit works within us the will and desire to love and serve God. The Holy Spirit works faith in us through God's Word and the Sacraments.**

54. God Calls Jeremiah (Jeremiah 1; 23; 31)

For Reflection

1. What did God call Jeremiah to do? Why did Jeremiah think he couldn't do what God wanted? Can God use you to tell others the Good News about Jesus? Explain. ◆ **God appointed Jeremiah to be a prophet to the nations. Jeremiah said, "I do not know how to speak, for I am only a youth." Yes, God uses persons of all ages to tell the Good News about Jesus.**

2. God promised King David that his house would be established forever (see page 100 of *120 Bible Stories*). Through Jeremiah, God promises to "raise up for David a righteous Branch." Who will fulfill both of these promises? ◆ **Jesus came as a descendant of King David to be the Savior of the world and to establish a kingship that will have no end.**

3. Reflect on the Bible stories in this section. How has God shown His everlasting love? ◆ **God continues to bless and sustain His people in spite of their sin. He keeps alive the promise to bless the world with the Messiah who will be born among God's people.**

God's People in Exile (722–533 BC)

55. Israel and Judah in Exile (2 Kings 17; 24–25)

For Reflection

1. Why were the people of Israel and Judah taken from their land? Should they have been surprised that they were carried off into exile? Why or why not? ◆ **They continually sinned against the Lord. The people should have expected the tragedy that befell them because God sent prophet after prophet to warn them.**

2. Who has taken the punishment for your sins so that you will not be exiled from heaven? ◆ **Jesus has earned for us our eternal home in heaven.**

3. King Jehoiachin was "graciously" let out of prison and fed by the king of Babylon. Compare this to the release from the prison of sin that Jesus graciously gives to you. ◆ **Our release from hell and the bondage of sin is eternal; nothing will be able to separate us from the love of God that is ours in Christ Jesus our Lord (Romans 8:38–39).**

56. God's Promises to the Exiles (Ezekiel 8; 36)

For Reflection

1. What reasons did the Lord give to Ezekiel for leaving the temple? What will happen to the people of Israel? How does this show that God takes sin seriously? ◆ **The glory of the Lord left the temple because of the evil (abominations) the people were doing. God promised that the people would be given into the hands of foreigners. God's judgment upon the people shows that God hates and punishes sin.**

2. What does God promise through the prophet Ezekiel in the last two paragraphs? When does God put His Spirit in you? ◆ **God promises to give the people His Spirit and to cleanse them. God enters our hearts in Baptism and washes away our sins.**

3. Review the Bible stories about Abraham and Moses. Because God kept His promises to Abraham and Moses, what do you know about His promises made through Ezekiel? To what special place has God promised to bring you? ◆ **God keeps all of His promises. To us, He keeps His promise to forgive all our sins for Jesus' sake, to remain with us, to strengthen and encourage us through the Means of Grace, and to bring us at last to our eternal home in heaven.**

57. Three Men in the Fiery Furnace (Daniel 3)

For Reflection

1. How did Shadrach, Meshach, and Abednego witness to their faith in the one true God? What did they trust God to do for them? ◆ **These men refused to disobey or disown the one true God. They trusted in God and in His ability to save them.**

2. God kept the three men safe in the furnace. Who was in the furnace with them? ◆ **God provided an angel to protect them in the fiery furnace.**

3. Describe ways you are tempted to deny your faith in Jesus and go along with the crowd. What has God given to you to resist these temptations? How does God strengthen you to be a witness of His love and forgiveness? ◆ **Temptations may include opportunities to follow the crowd in dishonoring or denying Jesus. Jesus rescues us by forgiving our sins and restoring us as His new people. God's Spirit strengthens us to live as His people as He works through God's Word.**

58. Daniel in the Lions' Den (Daniel 6)

For Reflection

1. Why did the satraps and presidents work to find fault with Daniel? How did they decide to get rid of Daniel? ◆ **These leaders were jealous of Daniel and the favored position he enjoyed. They decided to get rid of Daniel by making it illegal for him to pray to God.**

2. God protected Daniel by sending an angel. God has commanded His angels to "guard you in all your ways" (Psalm 91:11). Name times this fact can comfort you. ◆ **The presence of God's angels can comfort us when we face fearful, dangerous situations.**

3. Compare Daniel's stay in the lions' den to Jesus' stay in the tomb. What things are similar? What things are different? What does Jesus' resurrection mean for you? ◆ **Both Daniel and Jesus were placed into a cavelike structure from which they were not expected to return alive. God's power restored both Daniel and Jesus. Daniel was in the lions' den for one night; Jesus was in the tomb for three days. Daniel was not dead when placed into the lions' den; Jesus was dead, but He returned to life from the tomb.**

59. Daniel Sees Heaven (Daniel 7)

For Reflection

1. Who is the "Ancient of Days"? What books will be opened? What information do they contain? (You can find the answer in Revelation 20:12.) ◆ **The Ancient of Days is Jesus Himself. The books that will be opened are books that will contain the sum of everything everyone did while they were alive. The Book of Life contains the names of all who trust in Jesus as Savior.**

2. Who is the one Daniel says is "like a son of man"? (You can find the answer in Matthew 25:31–34.) ◆ **Jesus, the judge of all.**

3. Are you one of the saints who will "possess the kingdom forever"? How do you know? Thank God for making you a member of His kingdom through Jesus. ◆ **All who trust in Jesus for salvation are among the saints. We know this is true because God's Word says it is so. Expressions of thanks will vary.**

God's People Return to Judah (538–430 BC)

60. A New Temple and a New Wall (The Books of Ezra; Nehemiah)

For Reflection

1. Review God's promises made through the prophet Ezekiel (see page 128 of *120 Bible Stories*). How has God kept His promise to rebuild the desolate places? ◆ **God worked through the events of history so that the exiles could return to their homeland to resettle and reestablish it.**

2. For what do you praise God? Create a word cloud of all the good gifts God has given to you that make you rejoice. ◆ **Responses will vary.**

3. The temple and the wall were dedicated (set apart through words or actions) to God. In Baptism, how were you "dedicated" to God? What does this mean to you? ◆ **In Baptism, God claimed each of us to be His very own in Christ Jesus. Responses to the second question will vary.**

61. Esther and the King (Esther 1–2)

For Reflection

1. Why was the king angry with Vashti? ◆ **Vashti refused to obey him and come into his presence.**

2. How did Esther show that she obeyed Mordecai, the "parent" God had given her? How did Esther and Mordecai show that they obeyed the rulers God had placed over them? ◆ **Esther obeyed Mordecai and did not reveal to anyone that she was Jewish. Mordecai told Esther of a plot to lay hands on King Ahasuerus. Esther revealed the plot in the name of Mordecai.**

3. When you obey your parents and other adults in authority, what blessing does God promise? Praise God for the blessing of parents and other leaders. ◆ **God promises to bless those who obey their parents and leaders with "long life."**

62. God Saves His People (Esther 3–8)

For Reflection

1. Through the prophet Jeremiah, God told His people that "I know the plans I have for you . . . to give you a future and a hope" (Jeremiah 29:11). How is Mordecai's comment to Esther in the second paragraph similar to this prophecy? ◆ **Mordecai's words suggest that God's plan for Esther may be about to unfold.**

2. How does God work through Esther to save His people? ◆ **Esther brings before the king the truth about the evil Haman is planning, and the king acts to save God's people.**

3. The devil wants to destroy you through the power of sin. Who overcame the devil? What future and hope are yours because of Jesus' death and resurrection? ◆ **Jesus overcame the devil and earned forgiveness and salvation for us. By faith, we have the hope of the resurrection and an eternal home in heaven awaiting us.**

63. Waiting for God's Messenger (The Book of Malachi)

For Reflection

1. Who is the messenger, the second Elijah, whom the Lord promises to send? (See pages 148, 152, and 162 of *120 Bible Stories* for the answer.) ◆ **John the Baptist.**

2. Who is the "messenger of the covenant" and the "sun of righteousness"? ◆ **Jesus is both the "messenger of the covenant" and the "sun of righteousness."**

3. Malachi was the last prophet to speak to God's people for hundreds of years. How does God speak to you today? What promises has God made to you? How do you know that He will keep His promises? ◆ **God continues to speak to His people today through His Word. He promises to save all who love and trust in Jesus and to remain with us to strengthen and preserve us until He takes us at last to live with Him in heaven. We can trust in God to keep His promises, because God is faithful to His Word.**

The New Testament

Jesus' Childhood (4 BC–AD 11)

64. The Birth of John Foretold (Luke 1)

For Reflection

1. List three special things about Zechariah and Elizabeth's promised son. Read page 144 of *120 Bible Stories* to find an Old Testament connection between this promised child and Elijah. ◆ **Gabriel told them the baby's name was to be John, that many would rejoice at his birth, that he would be great before the Lord, that he must not drink wine or strong drink, that he would be filled with the Holy Spirit, that he would turn many of the children of Israel to the Lord their God, and that he would go before God "in the spirit and power of Elijah, to turn the hearts of the fathers to the children, and the disobedient to the wisdom of the just, to make ready for the Lord a people prepared" (Luke 1:17).**

2. Read about Abraham's visitors (page 24 of *120 Bible Stories*). How did Abraham react to God's promise? How did Sarah and Zechariah react? ◆ **Whereas Abraham believed and trusted in God, both Sarah and Zechariah met the angel's words with disbelief.**

3. Imagine that, like Zechariah, you can't speak. Use hand motions to tell a friend or family member the good news that Jesus is your Savior. ◆ **Gestures will vary.**

65. The Birth of Jesus Foretold (Luke 1; Matthew 1)

For Reflection

1. What was Gabriel's message to Mary? What was Mary's reaction? How was this different than the way Zechariah reacted to the news that he would have a son? ◆ **Gabriel told Mary that she would have a Son and that she was to name her Son Jesus. Jesus would be the long-awaited Messiah. Unlike Zechariah's immediate reaction, Mary responded in faith and gratitude, yielding to God's will and offering up a song of praise.**

2. What name does the angel tell Mary and Joseph to give to the child? What does this name means? (Hint: Read the last sentence of the Bible story on page 150 of *120 Bible Stories*.) ◆ **The angel of the Lord appeared to Joseph and told him to name Mary's baby Jesus (Matthew 1:21), which means "Savior."**

3. The Words to Remember from Isaiah give another name for Jesus: Immanuel. This name means "God with us." How is Jesus "God with us"? ◆ **God came to dwell with us in human form in the person of Jesus (Philippians 2:6–8; see also Isaiah 7:14).**

66. The Birth of John (Luke 1)

For Reflection

1. Why were their relatives and neighbors surprised that Elizabeth and Zechariah wanted to name their son John? Who gave this name to the child? ◆ **No one among their relatives had that name. The angel told Zechariah to name the child John.**

2. When was Zechariah able to speak again? What did he say once he could talk? What specific job did Zechariah say John would have? ◆ **Zechariah regained his ability to speak immediately after he wrote, "His name is John." Zechariah praised God. Zechariah announced that John would be called the prophet of the Most High and that he would go before the Lord to prepare His ways.**

3. How has God "visited and redeemed His people"? What message would John preach before Jesus "to prepare His ways"? ◆ **Jesus, God's Son, bought us back from sin, death, and the devil's power, taking our sins upon Himself on the cross. John would bring the people knowledge of salvation and tell them to repent of their sins.**

67. The Birth of Jesus (Luke 2)

For Reflection

1. The prophet Micah said that the Savior would be born in Bethlehem (see Micah 5:2). How did God make sure that Jesus was born in this little city? ◆ **Mary and Joseph traveled to Bethlehem because of a government requirement as part of a census.**

2. Identify three things in this Bible account that show Jesus did not come to be an earthly king. Why did Jesus leave heaven and come to earth? ◆ **Jesus' crib was a manger; there was no room for His family in the inn. Among the first to see Him were lowly shepherds. Jesus was born in the humblest of circumstances. He came to save all people, including the poor and lowly.**

3. As the shepherds returned to their flock, they told others about Jesus. Where are you going today? List ways you can tell others the good news about your Savior. ◆ **Responses will vary.**

68. The Visit of the Wise Men (Matthew 2)

For Reflection

1. How did Herod know where to send the wise men who had come looking for the new king of the Jews? What other things did the prophets say about Jesus? ◆ **Herod asked the chief priests and scribes, who knew that the Messiah would be born in Bethlehem because they knew the Scriptures. They also knew that the Messiah would come out of Egypt and that His birth would be accompanied by suffering at the loss of children and that Jesus would be called a Nazarene.**

2. God put a star in the heavens to lead the wise men to Jesus. Who or what has God put in your life to lead you to Jesus? ◆ **Answers will vary.**

3. How did God use Joseph to protect Jesus? How does God use your parents to protect you? Make a card to thank your parents for protecting you. ◆ **The Lord appeared to Joseph in a dream, telling him to escape to Egypt with Mary and Jesus. Somewhat similarly, God gives us our parents to provide for us and keep us safe.**

69. The Boy Jesus in the Temple (Luke 2)

For Reflection

1. For what event did Jesus' parents go to Jerusalem every year? What did this special event commemorate? ◆ **Jesus' parents went to Jerusalem each year to celebrate the Feast of the Passover. The Passover commemorated the salvation God provided His people in Egypt when the angel passed over the homes, sparing the lives of the firstborn in houses with a doorframe on which the blood of the lamb had been spread.**

2. Where did Mary and Joseph find Jesus? Why were they astonished? What explanation for His actions did Jesus give? ◆ **Mary and Joseph found Jesus in the temple, sitting among the teachers, listening to them and asking them questions. They were astonished when they saw Him interacting in this way. Jesus explained that He must be in His Father's house.**

3. Where do you find Jesus today? How does Jesus talk with you? Ask Jesus to help you grow "in wisdom and in stature and in favor with God and man." ◆ **Today, Jesus sits in heaven at the right hand of His Father. He speaks to us through God's Word as it is spoken, read, and reflected upon either privately in devotions or in the company of other believers, as at church. God's Word shows us our sinfulness, tells us what God has done for us in Christ Jesus to redeem and save us, and guides us in our daily Christian life.**

Jesus' Public Ministry (AD 29–32)

70. John Baptizes Jesus (Matthew 3; John 1)

For Reflection

1. What was John doing in the wilderness? How was John fulfilling the prophecy Zechariah made when he named his son? (See page 152 of *120 Bible Stories.*) ◆ **John was preaching in the wilderness. In so doing, he was preparing the way for the Lord, as Zechariah had prophesied.**

2. Identify how the three Persons of the Trinity are clearly present at Jesus' Baptism. ◆ **As Jesus, God's Son, was being baptized, God the Father spoke from heaven and the Holy Spirit descended upon Jesus like a dove.**

3. Jesus tells John that this Baptism will "fulfill all righteousness," which means that it is part of God's will. In what other ways will Jesus "fulfill all righteousness"? How does Jesus' righteousness become your righteousness before God? ◆ **Jesus came to "fulfill all righteousness," or do God's will, sinlessly in our place. This includes the death He died in our place. (See John 1:29, the Words to Remember.) Jesus took our sin upon Himself so that we might be given His righteousness.**

71. The Temptation of Jesus (Matthew 4)

For Reflection

1. Satan's temptations of Jesus appear well-chosen: food (Jesus had not eaten for 40 days), trust in God (Would His Father really save Him?), and power or glory (Jesus is the King, but the world doesn't see it). Read and discuss each of Jesus' responses. ◆ **Content of discussions will vary. Point out that Jesus used God's Word each time to fend off the temptations of the devil.**

2. What does the way Jesus resisted Satan's temptations teach you about what you can use to resist the devil? ◆ **Jesus resisted the devil's power through the use of God's Word. God's power also comes to us as the Holy Spirit works through God's Word.**

3. What does Jesus' victory over temptation and Satan mean for you? ◆ **Because Jesus overcame the devil's temptations, we also can face and overcome them by the power His Spirit provides (1 Corinthians 10:13).**

72. Jesus Calls Disciples (John 1; Luke 5)

For Reflection

1. John called Jesus the "Lamb of God." What made a lamb an important symbol to the Jewish people? (Hint: read page 54 of *120 Bible Stories.*) How would Jesus fulfill John's statement? ◆ **At the first Passover, God saved His people by the blood of the lamb spread on the doorframes of their houses. Old Testament priests also regularly offered lambs for the sins of the people. Jesus would fulfill His role as the Lamb of God when He gave Himself as a sacrifice for the sins of the world.**

2. How did Peter and Nathanael become Jesus' followers? Who can you invite to "come and see" Jesus? How can you lead your friends to Jesus? ◆ **Andrew told Peter about Jesus, and Philip told Nathanael. We can talk to our friends about Jesus and what He means to us.**

3. Jesus called Matthew, Peter, and the others to new lives as they followed Him. How does Jesus call you to follow Him? What does this mean for how you live your life? ◆ **Jesus has called us to be His followers. His forgiving love empowers us in the new life He has given us to live for Him.**

73. Jesus Changes Water to Wine (John 2)

For Reflection

1. What did Jesus' ability to change water into wine reveal to His followers about Him? What does it reveal to you? ◆ **Jesus is true God. He has power over nature and all things. Ultimately, He showed His power over sin, death, and the devil.**

2. How did the disciples react to this miracle? ◆ **The disciples put their faith in Jesus.**

3. Do the math. How many gallons of wine did Jesus provide? Name the ways God has multiplied His blessings in your life. ◆ **Jesus provided between 120 and 180 gallons of wine. Examples of blessings multiplied in individual lives will vary.**

74. Jesus Clears the Temple (John 2)

For Reflection

1. What was happening in the temple that upset Jesus? What activities should have been taking place in the temple? (Hint: read page 158 of *120 Bible Stories*.) ◆ **Jesus found people selling animals for sacrifices and changing money in the temple. The temple should be used for things devoted to God and the reading and studying of His Word.**

2. Some people say Christians should not show anger. What things should upset Christians? What responses might be appropriate when you see sinful activities? ◆ **Christians should be upset when God and His Word are disregarded, disobeyed, or misused and ridiculed. God would have His people take a stand against wrong with the goal of leading wrongdoers to repent.**

3. The apostle Paul says your body is God's temple (see 1 Corinthians 3:16). What do you need to ask Jesus to "throw out" of your life to clean up His house? ◆ **Answers will vary.**

75. Jesus Teaches Nicodemus (John 3)

For Reflection

1. Why do you think Nicodemus came to talk with Jesus at night? ◆ **Perhaps Nicodemus was busy during the day; or perhaps he did not want to be seen coming to see Jesus.**

2. What does Jesus mean when He says to Nicodemus that he must be "born of water and the Spirit" to enter God's kingdom? When were you "born of water and the Spirit"? ◆ **To be "born of water and the Spirit" is to be baptized. We were "born of water and the Spirit" when we were baptized.**

3. What does John 3:16 mean to you? Write your thoughts on a sheet of paper and put it in your family Bible. Each year on Good Friday read your comments and add any new thoughts. Rejoice that because of Jesus you have eternal life. ◆ **Thoughts and comments will vary.**

76. Jesus and the Samaritan Woman (John 4)

For Reflection

1. What clues in the first two paragraphs of this Bible story on page 174 of *120 Bible Stories* show that Jesus was truly a man who had needs like any other human being? ◆ **Jesus was both weary and thirsty.**

2. What did Jesus offer to the woman? How does Jesus show the woman that He is the Messiah, the Christ? ◆ **Jesus offered the woman living water, in other words, eternal life. He told the woman information about her life that He knew because He is God.**

3. The woman witnesses to the people in her town and brings them to hear Jesus. Who can you bring to hear about Jesus, the Savior of the world? ◆ **Responses will vary.**

77. Jesus Rejected at Nazareth (Luke 4)

For Reflection

1. Luke records that Jesus went to the synagogue on the Sabbath "as was His custom." What does this mean? ◆**Jesus regularly went to the synagogue to worship God on the Sabbath.**

2. Identify how Jesus fulfilled Isaiah's prophecy that He read in the synagogue. How has Jesus healed your blindness? How has Jesus set you free? ◆**Jesus has brought us to recognize that He is light of the world. Jesus has freed us from the bondage of sin.**

3. Jesus mentions two Gentiles (non-Jewish people) whom God saved through His prophets. Why is it important for Jesus to show that He came to save Gentiles too? ◆**Jesus came to earn forgiveness and salvation for all people. Most of the world's population is not Jewish.**

78. Jesus Heals a Paralyzed Man (Mark 2)

For Reflection

1. How did the four men bring the paralyzed man to Jesus? Who brings you to hear about Jesus? Thank that person. ◆**The man's friends carried him and lowered him to Jesus after removing a portion of the roof over Jesus. Responses to the second question will vary.**

2. Who criticized Jesus when He forgave the sins of the paralyzed man? Why did these people criticize Jesus for forgiving the man's sins? ◆**The scribes criticized Jesus for telling the man his sins were forgiven. Only God can forgive sins; the scribes thought Jesus was blaspheming. By healing the man, Jesus showed Himself in possession of divine power (showed that He is God).**

3. What seen and unseen blessings came to the paralyzed man, the four men, and to all those in the room who heard Jesus and saw this miracle that He did? ◆**The man received forgiveness of sins and physical healing. The friends got the satisfaction of knowing they helped their friend by bringing him to Jesus. The people in the room witnessed an amazing event and glorified God.**

79. The Sermon on the Mount (Matthew 5–7)

For Reflection

1. The first part of Jesus' sermon is called the Beatitudes, or blessings. How are these statements alike? Most people do not consider poverty, meekness, or persecution to be good things. What does Jesus say? ◆**The statements begin with "Blessed are . . ." These blessings happen when people trust in God and live as His faithful people, trusting in Jesus; God brings a new perspective to human lives.**

2. For nearly 2, 000 years Christians have been praying the words of the Lord's Prayer. Who taught this prayer to you? Thank God for this person. ◆**Responses will vary.**

3. What do you think it means that Jesus taught with authority? Why was this true? ◆**Jesus spoke as if His words came from God Himself. In truth, Jesus' words came from God; Jesus is true God.**

80. Jesus Calms a Storm (Mark 4)

For Reflection

1. In this Bible account, how does Jesus show that He is truly man? ◆**Jesus slept.**

2. In this Bible account, how does Jesus show that He is truly God? ◆**Jesus caused the storm to cease.**

3. Discuss a time that you were scared. What did you do? Who did you talk to? How does knowing that Jesus has the power to calm storms help when you are afraid? Write a thank-You to Jesus, who said to the "storm" that made you afraid, "Be calm!" ◆ **Responses will vary.**

81. Jesus Heals Jairus's Daughter (Mark 5)

For Reflection

1. Describe how both Jairus and the woman in the crowd show their faith in Jesus. How do you show your faith in Jesus? ◆ **Both Jairus and the woman came to Jesus trusting in His ability to help them. We show our faith in Him when we trust in His desire and ability to help us as well.**

2. Jesus shows His power over death as He wakes Jairus's daughter. What other event shows Jesus' complete power over death? ◆ **Jesus' resurrection from the dead shows His full and complete power over death.**

3. You and those you love will experience bodily death, but Jesus will bring all believers to be with Himself in heaven. How does this truth comfort you? ◆ **We need not fear to die, knowing that Jesus will walk with us through death; He will take us to live with Him in heaven after we die.**

82. Jesus Feeds Five Thousand (John 6)

For Reflection

1. What did Jesus do before He passed out the bread and fish? How might this act affect your behavior before you begin to eat? ◆ **Jesus gave thanks. In a similar expression of gratitude to God, His followers down through the ages thank God for their food before eating.**

2. When the people had eaten, what did they decide to do to Jesus? Where did Jesus go to escape their plans? ◆ **The people were about to come and take Jesus by force to make Him their king. Jesus withdrew to the mountain by Himself.**

3. The feeding of the 5,000 shows that God meets all your earthly needs. Discuss the "bread and fish blessings" that God has multiplied in your family. ◆ **Discussions will vary.**

83. Jesus Walks on Water (Matthew 14)

For Reflection

1. Jesus often went away by Himself to pray. Create a word cloud of people and situations in your life that you would like to share with God. Use this to guide your prayers each day. ◆ **Content of word clouds will vary.**

2. How does this story show Peter as both a man of faith and a man of doubt? ◆ **Peter desired to walk on water; for a time, he did so successfully. Peter also doubted when he saw the wind, and he began to sink before Jesus saved him.**

3. Describe a time Jesus pulled you out of the "waves" of doubt. How does knowing that Jesus has saved you help when you need to face something difficult in life? ◆ **Jesus reached out His hand and caught Peter; Jesus, through His Word, reaches us and rescues us, strengthening our faith and encouraging us in our daily life of faith.**

84. Jesus Is Anointed (Luke 7)

For Reflection

1. What was the woman's extravagant gift? ◆ **She wet Jesus' feet with her tears, dried them with her hair, and anointed His feet with ointment.**

2. What is Jesus' extravagant gift to the woman? To whom has Jesus also given this gift? How does Jesus give this gift? ◆ **Jesus gave the woman the gift of forgiveness. Jesus also has given this gift to us. Jesus gives forgiveness freely through God's Word and the Sacraments.**

3. What might be your extravagant gift to Jesus in thanksgiving for all His blessings to you, especially the gift of forgiveness? ◆ **Responses will vary.**

85. Peter's Confession and Jesus' Transfiguration (Matthew 16; Mark 9)

For Reflection

1. In the first part of the Bible story, Peter makes a confession, a statement of belief about who Jesus is. What is your confession of who Jesus is? ◆ **Responses may vary but are likely to include the fact that Jesus is our Savior and eternal friend.**

2. When Jesus was transfigured, His appearance changed. Describe Jesus' transfiguration. Tell what you know about Moses and Elijah. ◆ **In the presence of Peter, James, and John, Jesus' face became radiant and His clothes became intensely white. Moses and Elijah appeared in glorious splendor, talking with Jesus. Moses is remembered by the Jewish people as the Law-giver, and Elijah is chief among the Old Testament prophets.**

3. Who spoke from the cloud? At what other event in Jesus' life did people hear this voice and similar words? Why are these words so important? ◆ **God the Father spoke. He spoke similar words when Jesus was baptized. Jesus is the Son of God, the promised Messiah, long awaited by the prophets of old, and my personal Savior, who died for me and rose again.**

86. Jesus Sends the Seventy-Two (Luke 10)

For Reflection

1. What do you think Jesus means when He says the "harvest is plentiful, but the laborers are few"? Who are the laborers in your church? ◆ **Many need to hear the Gospel, but there are few who are equipped to share it. Laborers in the church are likely to include pastors, teachers, evangelists, and others who share the Gospel.**

2. Jesus sent out 72 men to preach and teach and to heal. They knew Jesus was with them because "even the demons are subject to us in Your name." What has Jesus sent you to do? How do you know that Jesus is at work in your life? ◆ **Jesus has sent us to witness to His grace and love by word and action. We know Jesus is at work in our lives because He has promised to be and remain at work in us through the Means of Grace.**

3. Sing a favorite hymn or song as you rejoice that your name is written in heaven. ◆ **Responses will vary.**

87. The Good Samaritan (Luke 10)

For Reflection

1. How do the lawyer's words summarize the Law of God that Jesus obeyed perfectly in your place? What does Jesus' perfect obedience of the Law mean for you? ◆ **Jesus loved God and others completely and without sin. By faith, Jesus' righteous acts are transferred to each believer.**

2. What does Jesus' parable (an earthy story with a heavenly meaning) say about how you are to treat others? Who are your neighbors? Give examples of how you have shown love to your neighbor. ◆ **God gives His people the desire and motivation to serve others as a way of sharing the love of Christ with them. Examples will vary.**

3. How has Jesus shown mercy (undeserved love) to you? ◆ **Jesus has lived, died, and rose again to earn forgiveness, new life, and eternal salvation for us and for all people.**

88. Jesus Heals a Blind Man (John 9)

For Reflection

1. The disciples thought the man was blind because of a specific sin. What does Jesus say? What kind of blindness do you have? How has Jesus removed your blindness? ◆ **Jesus says, "It was not that this man sinned, or his parents, but that the works of God might be displayed in him" (John 9:3). Without Jesus, all people are held in spiritual blindness.**

2. Who in this Bible story was blind to Jesus' real identity? Discuss the importance of good teachers. Who teaches you the truth about Jesus? ◆ **The Pharisees were blind to Jesus. They said He "is not from God, for He does not keep the Sabbath" (Jesus healed on the Sabbath). Responses and comments regarding good teachers will vary.**

3. How is Jesus the "light of the world"? In the Sermon on the Mount, Jesus said, "You are the light of the world" (see page 180 of *120 Bible Stories*). How is this statement true about you? ◆ **As children of God through faith in Christ Jesus, we are lights in the world when we serve God and give Him glory.**

89. The Good Shepherd (John 10; Psalm 23)

For Reflection

1. Who has Jesus put in your life to shepherd you in the faith? When or through what activities do you hear Jesus speaking through these people? ◆ **Responses will vary somewhat. The best teachers of the faith help us to know and understand God's Word.**

2. When did Jesus lay down His life for you? What do you have as a result of Jesus' death and resurrection? Describe this abundant (full to overflowing) life. ◆ **Jesus laid down His life for us and for all people when He died for our sins on the cross. Because of Jesus' work for us, we can live life happy and confident of God's love and forgiveness for us now and into eternity.**

3. We often hear about Jesus our Good Shepherd and read Psalm 23 at funerals. What is your favorite part of this psalm? Rejoice that Jesus cares for you always. ◆ **Responses will vary.**

90. Jesus Raises Lazarus (John 11)

For Reflection

1. How do Mary and Martha show their faith in Jesus? ◆ **They say that if Jesus would have come earlier, He could have kept Lazarus from dying.**

2. John records in this Bible story that Jesus wept. How does this show that Jesus is truly a man? ◆ **Jesus displays human emotions.**

3. Jesus brings Lazarus back to life just as He did Jairus's daughter (see page 184 of *120 Bible Stories*). How do these miracles show that Jesus is "the resurrection and the life"? Describe the comfort and hope these miracles give when death takes someone you love. ◆ **Jesus' power over death is shown when He brings back to life those who have died. Ultimately, He will raise to life all who have died. Then He will give eternal life to all believers.**

91. The Prodigal Son (Luke 15)

For Reflection

1. Describe the actions of the father in this parable. The younger son. The older son. ◆ **The father is loving, forgiving, seeking, and restoring; first he grants his son's wish, and then he willingly welcomes him back. The younger son takes advantage of his father's goodness and squanders his inheritance; but then he comes to his senses and returns home. The older son resents the father's forgiving attitude toward the younger son.**

2. Like the younger son, sin once separated you from your heavenly Father. Why does God the Father welcome you back? Like the older son, jealousy can cause you to be ungrateful. List all the daily blessings God gives to you as His child. ◆ **God the Father welcomes and accepts us for Jesus' sake. Lists of blessings may vary but are likely to include the blessings of forgiveness and salvation.**

3. Discuss the similarity of the Words to Remember (Luke 15:10) and the father's final words in Jesus' parable. Thank God for finding you and for making you His child. ◆ **Comment that the forgiveness we have in Jesus is indeed cause for thankfulness and joy.**

92. Jesus Heals Ten Men (Luke 17)

For Reflection

1. During Jesus' time, lepers lived separately from healthy people. In what ways would this make life difficult for lepers? How might the separation affect families? ◆ **Being cut off from society would have made it difficult for lepers to secure even the necessities of life. Families would have worried about their loved ones who were lepers, even as they sought to provide for them.**

2. What was unusual about the leper who returned to thank Jesus? ◆ **The other nine were hurrying back to show themselves to the priest so that they might reenter society. The one leper responds first by praising God with a loud voice and thanking Jesus for healing him; and that leper was a Samaritan, an enemy of the Jews.**

3. When you receive blessings from God (food, clothing, good health, special gifts), how do you thank Him? One way to remember to thank God is to list blessings. Better yet, stop right away like the Samaritan and say, "Thank You, Lord!" ◆ **We thank God by offering back a portion of His blessings to us, by serving Him in lives of willing obedience, and by giving Him our thanks and praise individually and in the company of others, as we do during corporate worship.**

93. Jesus and the Little Children (Mark 9–10)

For Reflection

1. What were the disciples arguing about while walking with Jesus? What did Jesus say makes a person "first"? ◆ **The disciples argued with one another about who was the greatest. Jesus said, "If anyone would be first, he must be last of all and servant of all" (John 9:35).**

2. Sometimes you may feel unimportant. How does Jesus show that even children have an important place in God's family? ◆ **Jesus said, "Let the children come to Me; do not hinder them, for to such belongs the kingdom of God" (John 10:14).**

3. What was Jesus' reaction when the disciples tried to keep the children away from Him? How does Jesus take you in His arms and bless you? ◆ **Jesus rebuked the disciples for trying to drive the children away. Jesus "takes us in His arms and blesses us" through the Means of Grace, which assure us of His love and forgiveness.**

94. Jesus and Zacchaeus (Luke 19)

For Reflection

1. What does the Bible story tell you about Zacchaeus? ◆ **Zacchaeus was a chief tax collector, short in stature, and wealthy.**

2. How did Zacchaeus show that he had become a follower of Jesus? ◆ **He gave half of his possessions to the poor and promised to repay four times as much as he had cheated anyone.**

3. Recall another time that Jesus talked about finding the lost. (Hint: read page 204 of *120 Bible Stories*.) What does it mean to you that Jesus found you when you were lost and brought you salvation? ◆ **The account of Zacchaeus may remind us of the parable of the prodigal son. Answers will vary.**

Jesus' Passion, Death, and Resurrection (AD 33)

95. The Triumphal Entry (Matthew 21; Mark 11; Luke 19)

For Reflection

1. How did Jesus' entry into Jerusalem fulfill Old Testament prophecy? ◆ **By riding into Jerusalem, Jesus fulfilled the Old Testament prophecy "Rejoice greatly, O daughter of Zion! . . . Behold, your king is coming to you; righteous and having salvation is He, humble and mounted on a donkey, on a colt, the foal of a donkey" (Zechariah 9:9).**

2. How did the people worship Jesus? What actions did they use? What words did they use? Compare these words and actions with the ways in which you worship Jesus today. What is the same? What is different? ◆ **The people spread their cloaks and branches on the road in front of Jesus and shouted, "Hosanna to the Son of David! Blessed is He who comes in the name of the Lord! Hosanna in the highest!" We worship Jesus publicly in worship services and festivals. We worship Jesus privately in our devotions and prayers. In still another sense, we worship Jesus in lives lived to His glory.**

3. Look at the final sentence of the Bible story. Do you think the crowd really knew who Jesus is? How would you explain who Jesus is? ◆ **It sounds as though the crowd recognized Jesus as a prophet, but all in the crowd may not have known Him as the Messiah, the Son of God and Savior of the world.**

96. The Widow's Coins (Mark 12)

For Reflection

1. How much did the widow put into the offering box? ◆ **She "put in everything she had" (Mark 12:44).**

2. How does Jesus measure the value of a gift? ◆ **Jesus does not measure the amount of the gift but, rather, one's intentions in giving and one's trust in God's promises to provide for all needs.**

3. According to the Words to Remember, what prompts you to give thanks to God? ◆ **We give thanks to God because He is good and His love is an everlasting love. Our understanding of God's love is found in the fact that His Son died for our sins.**

4. List ways you use your time, talents, and treasures to thank God. Does this list represent giving "everything" you have or only giving out of your "abundance"? ◆ **Responses will vary.**

97. The Lord's Supper (Luke 22)

For Reflection

1. How did Judas show that he was following Satan and not Jesus? ◆ **Judas turned his back on Jesus and the forgiveness He freely offered and instead took his own life.**

2. Based on Jesus' own words, what does Jesus give to believers in the Lord's Supper? ◆ **Jesus gives us His very body and blood in a mysterious way in the Lord's Supper.**

3. Compare the Passover meal (see page 54 of *120 Bible Stories*) with the new Meal that Jesus gave to His followers. What names do believers call this Meal? How do these names show the importance of this Meal? What does Jesus give through this Meal? ◆ **The Passover meal featured a lamb without defect; Jesus—holy and sinless—was such a "lamb." The Passover remembered the salvation God provided Israel when He freed them from bondage in Egypt; the Lord's Supper offers Christ's very body and blood, together with the bread and wine, for the forgiveness of sins Jesus earned on the cross. The Lord's Supper is also called the Lord's Table, Holy Communion, the Breaking of Bread, and the Eucharist. These names indicate that the Lord's Supper is a unique and special meal. In the Lord's Supper, Jesus gives us His very body and blood together with the bread and wine for the forgiveness of sins, strength for new life, and assurance of eternal salvation.**

98. Jesus in the Garden (Matthew 26; Mark 14; Luke 22)

For Reflection

1. How does Jesus' prayer to His heavenly Father show that He is true man? What details in this Bible story reveal that Jesus is true God? ◆ **As true man, Jesus began to be deeply distressed and troubled, overwhelmed with sorrow to the point of death in anticipation of the agony about to begin. As true God, Jesus was all-knowing. He knew the suffering He was about to endure. He also called God His Father.**

2. What did Jesus ask the disciples to do? Why were they unable to do as He asked? Compare the actions of the disciples with how Jesus prays and prepares Himself for the suffering He will experience. ◆ **Jesus asked His disciples to watch and pray. Although they desired to remain awake to watch and pray, they were physically exhausted and fell asleep. While they slept, Jesus endured severe agony as part of the suffering by which He earned our forgiveness, new life, and eternal salvation.**

3. Why is it important that Jesus was willing to do His Father's will? ◆ **Jesus submitted to His Father's will in order to earn our forgiveness and eternal salvation by suffering and dying in our place (passive obedience).**

99. Peter Denies Jesus (Matthew 26)

For Reflection

1. What kind of witnesses were called during Jesus' trial? What testimony finally caused the high priest to call for Jesus' death? Was this testimony true or false? ◆ **False witnesses were called. Two false witnesses came forward with the charge that they had heard Jesus say, "I am able to destroy the temple of God, and to rebuild it in three days" (Matthew 26:61). Jesus had spoken these words, but the temple He referred to was His body.**

2. Think of a time that, like Peter, you had the opportunity to say, "Yes, I know Jesus," but you didn't. What prevented you from telling the truth? ◆ **Because we are sinners, we often fail to speak up for Jesus and pass up opportunities to be associated as one of His followers.**

3. How do you know that you have been forgiven, no matter how "bad" the sin? Draw a picture that shows the joy you have because Jesus forgives you. ◆ **We know that Jesus has earned forgiveness for all sins, because God's Word assures us of this truth.**

100. Jesus' Trial (Matthew 27; John 18)

For Reflection

1. At Jesus' trials, the judge wants to know the truth. What is the truth about Jesus? ◆ **Jesus is a king—the king of the universe. He is God's Son, true God and true man, the Savior of the world.**

2. Pilate sentenced Jesus to death even though he knew Jesus was innocent. Why did this happen? You deserve death because of the guilt of sin, yet God gives you life. Why does this happen? ◆ **Pilate gave in to the will of the crowd, putting his desire to appease the masses above his desire to see justice done. God gives me eternal life because of Jesus' life, death, and resurrection for me, solely out of grace.**

3. What gift comes to believers who are covered in Jesus' blood? (Read 1 John 1:7 for the answer.) ◆ **Jesus' blood has been shed so that we might have the forgiveness of sin.**

101. The Crucifixion (Matthew 27; Luke 23; John 19)

For Reflection

1. What do you learn about Jesus from the words He spoke while on the cross? ◆ **Jesus' words from the cross show His willingness to pray for others, to save others, and to be forsaken by God Himself for us and our salvation. They also show His concern for His mother.**

2. How did the actions of Pilate and the soldiers fulfill Old Testament prophecies about the death of Jesus? ◆ **Among the Old Testament prophecies about Jesus' death is one that not one of His bones would be broken and that He would be pierced.**

3. Why did Jesus have to die? Why did God the Father forsake Jesus while He was on the cross? Because Jesus suffered and died, what priceless gift do you receive? ◆ **Jesus had to die to take the punishment we deserved. Being forsaken by His heavenly Father was part of the punishment Jesus took in our place. Because of Jesus' innocent suffering and death, we have forgiveness and life eternal.**

4. How do Joseph and Nicodemus show their love for Jesus? ◆ **They go to Pilate, ask for and receive Jesus' body, bind it with linen cloths and spices, and lay it in Joseph's tomb.**

102. The Resurrection (Luke 24; John 20)

For Reflection

1. How did the women respond to the message of the angels? How did the disciples and other followers of Jesus react to the message the women brought? ◆ **They returned from the tomb and told Jesus' disciples the words of the angel. The disciples did not believe the women.**

2. What did Peter see when he looked in the tomb? ◆ **Peter went to the tomb and saw the linen cloths by themselves. He went home marveling at what had happened.**

3. How did Jesus reveal Himself to Mary Magdalene? How do you "see" Jesus today? Whom can you tell, "I have seen the Lord"? ◆ **At first, Mary thought Jesus was the gardener. She recognized Jesus when He spoke her name. We see Jesus through His Word, the Bible. Names of those we can tell will vary.**

103. Jesus Appears on the Emmaus Road (Luke 24)

For Reflection

1. What words show that the two disciples were still confused about what Jesus had come to earth to do? What kind of redeemer did they think Jesus would be? ◆ **They had hoped Jesus was the one who had come to redeem Israel, but concluded that He could not be because He had been put to death. The Emmaus disciples seem to have been expecting a military-leader type of messiah.**

2. Why it is important to study Moses and the Prophets (the Old Testament)? Identify three Old Testament stories that point to Jesus as our Redeemer. ◆ **The Old Testament stories all point to Jesus and the salvation Jesus came to bring. Specific Old Testament examples will vary.**

3. What action revealed Jesus to the disciples? Where does this action take place today? Who "opens" Scripture for you to reveal Jesus, your Redeemer? ◆ **They recognized Jesus when He took the bread and blessed it and broke it and gave it to them. We also "recognize" Jesus when we receive His body and blood together with the forgiveness and strength in the Lord's Supper. All Christian teachers faithful to God's Word open Scriptures and show us Jesus as He is found in them.**

104. Jesus Appears to Thomas (John 20)

For Reflection

1. Three times in this Bible story Jesus says, "Peace be with you." How did Jesus' death and resurrection bring you peace? How can you share this peace with others? ◆ **Jesus' life, death, and resurrection restored peace between God and humanity. We share this peace with others in our words and in our actions.**

2. Why did Thomas want to see and touch the marks in Jesus' hands and side? Who did Jesus say would be blessed? Why? ◆ **Thomas said, in effect, "I'll believe it when I see it!" Jesus said, "Blessed are those who have not seen and yet have believed" (John 20:29).**

3. According to the last paragraph of this Bible story, why did God cause the Bible to be written? What great gift do you receive because you believe these words? ◆ **The Bible was written so that we may believe that Jesus is the Christ, the Son of God, and that by believing we may have life in His name. By faith, we have eternal life in heaven.**

105. Jesus and Peter (John 21)

For Reflection

1. When Jesus called them to follow Him, many of His disciples were fishing. Why do you think the disciples are fishing again in this Bible story? ◆ **They may have returned to fishing either as a form of recreation or as a way to make a living, or both.**

2. Peter had denied knowing Jesus. How does Jesus' conversation with Peter reveal that Peter has been forgiven? What is Jesus asking Peter to do? ◆ **Jesus asked Peter three times if he loved Him. Jesus is asking Peter to care for His people.**

3. List the people that God has placed in your life to feed and care for you, including those who feed you with the Good News about Jesus. Pray for these people. ◆ **Specific list contents will vary.**

106. Jesus Ascends to Heaven (Matthew 28; Acts 1)

For Reflection

1. What gift did Jesus want the disciples to wait in Jerusalem to receive? ◆ **Jesus told them they would receive power from the Holy Spirit.**

2. What command and promise did Jesus give to His disciples and to all believers before He ascended? ◆ **Jesus' command was to go and make disciples of all nations, baptizing them in the name of the Father and of the Son and of the Holy Spirit, teaching them to observe all of His commands. Jesus promised to be with His disciples to the end of the age.**

3. Although Jesus has ascended into heaven, explain how He is still present with you. ◆ **Jesus remains with His people, just as He promised, even though we cannot see Him (Matthew 28:20). He remains with us through His Word.**

4. Why was it important that the man who replaced Judas was a witness to Jesus' ministry, death, and resurrection? ◆ **As an actual witness, Judas's replacement would be well equipped to teach about Jesus' life, death, and resurrection.**

The Holy Spirit Leads God's Church (AD 33–95)

107. Pentecost (Acts 2)

For Reflection

1. In what ways did the Holy Spirit make His presence known at Pentecost? ◆ **The Holy Spirit came with a sound like the blowing of a violent wind, filling the house. Jesus' followers saw what seemed to be tongues of fire that separated and came to rest on each of them. Then the people began to speak in languages they had never learned.**

2. Summarize Peter's sermon. What question did the listeners ask Peter and the apostles? What was Peter's answer? ◆ **Peter preached a powerful sermon, telling those assembled about the life and death of the Son of God. In sorrow over their sins, the people asked, "Brothers, what shall we do?" Peter replied, "Repent and be baptized every one of you in the name of Jesus Christ for the forgiveness of your sins, and you will receive the gift of the Holy Spirit" (Acts 2:37–38). Those who accepted his message were baptized. That day, over three thousand people were added to the Church.**

3. How is the Holy Spirit at work in your life today? How do you know the Holy Spirit is at work in your church? ◆ **God converts people and keeps them alive in faith through the Means of Grace—God's Word and the Sacraments. We know that the Spirit is at work in both our lives and in the life of the Church according to how regularly and faithfully we receive God's Word and the Sacraments.**

108. Peter and John Heal a Lame Man (Acts 3)

For Reflection

1. What gift did Peter and John give to the man who could not walk? How was this gift better than gold or silver? ◆ **They healed the beggar in the name of Jesus Christ of Nazareth. They restored the man's health and ability to enjoy life and to provide for himself.**

2. The crowds believed that Peter and John healed the man. Who does Peter say healed the man? When Peter says the man now has "perfect health," do you think he is talking only about physical health? Explain. ◆ **Jesus' power healed the man. Peter's words indicate that the man also possessed spiritual health. Peter says "The faith that is through Jesus has given the man this perfect health" (Acts 3:16).**

3. Why does Peter show how Jesus fulfilled the Old Testament prophecies? ◆ **Peter wanted the people to recognize Jesus as the long-awaited, promised Messiah.**

109. God's Servant Stephen (Acts 6–7)

For Reflection

1. Who was Stephen? What did he do among the new believers? What special gifts did the Holy Spirit give to Stephen? ◆ **Stephen was one of seven men set apart to serve tables. Stephen was also doing great wonders and signs among the people. In addition, the Holy Spirit also equipped Stephen to be a powerful speaker.**

2. How did Stephen witness to his faith? Describe a time you told someone about Jesus even though it was difficult to do so. How did the Holy Spirit help you? ◆ **Stephen boldly proclaimed Jesus as the Righteous One, the Messiah. Specific examples of witnessing experiences will vary.**

3. What did Stephen pray as he died? Whose example did Stephen follow? ◆ **Stephen prayed for those putting him to death, just as Jesus did. He said, "Lord, do not hold this sin against them" (Acts 7:60).**

110. Philip and the Ethiopian (Acts 8)

For Reflection

1. Who told Philip about the Ethiopian? ◆ **An angel of the Lord directed Philip to go south to the desert road. Here, Philip met the Ethiopian.**

2. Pretend you are Philip. How would you explain the passage from Isaiah that the Ethiopian was reading? Who will help you tell others the Good News about Jesus? ◆ **Jesus was led like a sheep to the slaughter. Like a lamb before the shearer, Jesus also was silent. Jesus suffered humiliation and death so that we might be saved. Answers to the second question will vary.**

3. After his Baptism, the Ethiopian left rejoicing. Why does knowing that Jesus is your Savior make you joyful? How can you share this joy with others? ◆ **Through His life, death, and resurrection, Jesus has solved our biggest problems. He has earned our freedom from sin, death, and Satan's power. We can share our joy with others through our words, our attitudes, and our actions.**

111. The Conversion of Saul (Acts 9)

For Reflection

1. Describe Saul's role at Stephen's death (see page 244 of *120 Bible Stories*) and at the beginning of this Bible story. How did Jesus change Saul? How did Jesus change you? ◆ **Jesus changed Saul from being a persecutor of Christians to a Christian missionary. When we came to faith, God changed us from enemies to God of believers in Him.**

2. How was Saul blind before Jesus spoke to him? You were blind in the same way. What event healed Saul's blindness? What event healed your blindness? ◆ **Saul did not know Jesus as His Savior. Before we came to faith we, too, were blind—spiritually. Saul's regaining of sight coincided with his Baptism. Without faith, we do not know God or desire Him or His salvation. We received spiritual sight when we came to faith; for many, this happens in the waters of Baptism.**

3. Why would Saul's past actions make others afraid to meet him? Who brought Saul to the apostles? List friends and family members whom you can bring to church. ◆ **Some may have thought Saul was only pretending to be a believer so that he might capture more of them. Barnabas brought Saul to the apostles. List names will vary.**

112. Peter and Cornelius (Acts 10)

For Reflection

1. Why is it unusual that Peter would visit Cornelius? ◆ **Peter was a Jew and Cornelius was a Gentile. Jews were not to visit those who were not Jews.**

2. What is the meaning of Peter's vision? How is God making sure that Peter fulfills Jesus' command to "make disciples of all nations"? ◆ **The unclean animals represent foods eaten by the people groups with which Jews had formerly been forbidden to associate. God wanted to underscore for Peter that God's gift of salvation earned by Jesus is for all people, everywhere.**

3. Who commanded Baptism? Who gave the words that are used in Baptism? What gifts do people receive in Baptism? Why is Baptism important to the Church? ◆ **In Jesus' words that instituted the Sacrament of Baptism (Matthew 28:18–20), Jesus commanded Baptism and gave us the words to speak. Through Baptism, God welcomes us into His family and gives us forgiveness of sin, new life, and eternal salvation. Baptism is important to the Church because Baptism is a Means of Grace; through Baptism, we enter the family of God and desire association with a Christian congregation.**

113. Peter's Escape from Prison (Acts 12)

For Reflection

1. When Peter was put in prison, what did the members of the church do? ◆ **While Peter was in prison, the church was earnestly praying to God for him.**

2. How was Peter saved from Herod's plans? ◆ **Peter was freed from prison by an angel of the Lord.**

3. The apostle Paul tells us that we are to "pray without ceasing" (1 Thessalonians 5:17). How does this Bible story show that God hears prayer? For whom can you "pray without ceasing" today? ◆ **God answered the prayers of the congregation prayed on behalf of Peter. Those for whom we might pray may include those who are persecuted and imprisoned because of their faith in Jesus.**

114. Paul's First Missionary Journey (Acts 13–14)

For Reflection

1. How did the Holy Spirit use Saul, now called Paul, to tell others the Good News about Jesus? In what ways was Paul's message similar to Peter's (see page 242 of *120 Bible Stories*)? ◆ **Paul and Barnabas took the Good News to Jewish people who lived far away from the land of Jesus' birth. Eventually, when their message was rejected by the Jewish people, they took the Good News to the Gentiles.**

2. Why did the apostles always begin with the Old Testament promises and prophecies to prove Jesus is the Savior? How does this history prove their case? ◆ **They looked to show Jesus as the Promised One of the Old Testament. Every one of the Old Testament prophecies was fulfilled in Jesus.**

3. List Bible passages you can share when telling others about Jesus. As a family, memorize these passages and practice sharing the Good News of Jesus. ◆ **Verse selections will vary.**

115. Paul and Timothy (Acts 16; the Books of 1 and 2 Timothy)

For Reflection

1. What relationship did Paul and Timothy have? What evidence do you see in Paul's letters that point to this relationship? ◆ **Timothy was Paul's young friend and trusted co-worker; his "true child in the faith" (1 Timothy 1:2).**

2. Who is the first person you remember teaching you about Jesus? Who today teaches you about Jesus and encourages you to "fight the good fight of the faith"? ◆ **Responses will vary.**

3. Draw the "crown of righteousness" that will be given to you on the Last Day. How do you show Jesus that you "have loved His appearing"? ◆ **With our words, actions, and attitudes, we can show what it means to us to know and believe in Jesus as our Savior.**

116. Paul Tells Lydia about Christ (Acts 16)/ Paul Writes to the Philippians (Philippians 1; 4)

For Reflection

1. In this Bible story, how did God tell Paul where he should travel to share the Gospel? How does God help you share the Gospel? ◆ **God sent Paul a vision that appeared to him at night. God guides and equips us through His Word.**

2. How did Lydia show her faith? How did God use Lydia to take care of Paul and his travel companions? ◆ **Lydia invited Paul and his companions to come to her house and stay. In this way, God provided for Paul and his companions through Lydia.**

3. Paul wrote his Letter to the Philippians while he was in prison. What reasons does Paul have to be joyful? What can give you joy when troubles come? ◆ **Paul urges believers to rejoice in the Lord. We, too, can find joy in Jesus and His gifts of forgiveness, new life, and eternal salvation, in spite of our life situation.**

117. Paul and Silas in Prison (Acts 16)

For Reflection

1. Why were Paul and Silas put into prison? ◆ **Paul's act of casting a spirit out of a slave girl, a spirit that enabled her to tell fortunes, angered her owners. The girl's owners had Paul and Silas arrested for causing a disturbance.**

2. How did the Holy Spirit use the actions of Paul and Silas as a witness to the prisoners and to the jailer and his entire household? ◆ **Paul and Silas prayed and sang hymns, even as they were locked up in prison. After an earthquake, they witnessed to the frightened jailer and later baptized the jailer and his entire household.**

3. Review the way you acted in public today. What kind of witness did your words and actions give regarding your faith? Ask the Holy Spirit to guide your words and actions so that they may reflect your faith and trust in Jesus. ◆ **Responses will vary.**

118. Paul's Letters (The Books of Romans; Ephesians; 1 Thessalonians)

For Reflection

1. How does Paul begin each of these letters? Compare it to how you write messages. ◆ **Paul identifies himself as the sender of the letter and tells to whom the letter is being written. We may or may not indicate similar information on our correspondence today.**

2. What similar message does Paul include in these letters? Why is it important that Paul's message is consistent (similar) to the different churches? How is Paul's message consistent with what Jesus taught? ◆ **Paul wrote to encourage believers in the faith and in the blessings Jesus earned for them that are theirs by grace through faith. There is only one message of truth. Jesus is the only Savior of the world. His blessings come to us freely as God's gift; we do not and cannot earn them. Jesus earned forgiveness and salvation for us.**

3. Read 2 Timothy 1:13, the Words to Remember. What does this Bible passage mean? How does it apply to all the letters that Paul wrote to the churches? ◆ **Paul encourages believers to remain true to God and His Word and not to become confused or deceived. Paul desires all followers to remain faithful to God and not to turn their backs on Him.**

119. Paul Sails to Rome (Acts 27–28)

For Reflection

1. List all the ways God protected Paul and his friends on their journey. How does God protect you each day? ◆ **While en route to Rome, the ship on which Paul was traveling experienced a severe storm, with winds of hurricane force. The storm raged for so many days that the passengers gave up all hope of being rescued. After an angel brought Paul an encouraging message, the ship ran aground, and all found safety on an island. Responses will vary somewhat regarding how God keeps us safe each day. He gives us shelter, clothing, and parents and other adults who watch out and care for us.**

2. Why wasn't Paul afraid during the storm? What promises has God made to you that give you hope and peace even when there are problems? ◆ **Paul knew of God's plan for him; Paul trusted in God. Among other assurances God gives are His promise to always remain with us and to never let anything separate us from His love.**

3. How did the storm and what followed allow Paul to speak about God? Review your day. What opportunities did you have to speak about God? ◆ **Paul was able to share the love of Jesus with those living on the island of Malta. Opportunities to speak about God will vary.**

120. John's Vision of Heaven (Revelation 21–22)

For Reflection

1. John the apostle received the vision that he records in the Book of Revelation. What does the vision describe? ◆ **John's vision describes a new heaven and a new earth and the throne of God.**

2. Who is the Lamb? What gifts do we receive from the Lamb according to this Bible story? ◆ **Jesus is the Lamb. In heaven, there will be perfect happiness, with no sadness, death, pain, or night. Jesus Himself will be our light.**

3. When will John's vision be fulfilled? Draw your "vision" of heaven. Pray with the apostle John, "Come, Lord Jesus!" ◆ **John's vision will be fulfilled on the Last Day. Drawings and prayers will vary.**

Answers to *120 Bible Stories Activity Book*

Contents

The Old Testament

The Beginning (Creation to the Flood)

The Patriarchs (2091–1859 BC)

Moses and the Return to Canaan (1526–1406 BC)

Judges Rule God's People (1217–1060 BC)

Great Prophets and Kings (1049–587 BC)

God's People in Exile (722–533 BC)

God's People Return to Judah (538–430 BC)

The New Testament

Jesus' Childhood (4 BC–AD 11)

Jesus' Public Ministry (AD 29–32)

Jesus' Passion, Death, and Resurrection (AD 33)

The Holy Spirit Leads God's Church (AD 33–95)

1

God Creates the World

(Genesis 1–2)

Reviewing God's Word

The first two chapters of Genesis describe the plan God followed for each day of creation. The first three days are sometimes referred to as days of forming, and the next three days are sometimes called days of filling. On the days of forming, God called into being. On the days of filling, God built upon the work of the days of forming.

Draw a line to match each day of forming with its corresponding day of filling:

Day 1: Light and darkness	Day 5: Sea creatures and birds
Day 2: Sky and water	Day 6: Animals and people
Day 3: Dry ground and vegetation	Day 4: Sun, moon, and stars

Thinking about God's Word

1. What is meant by "the beginning"?
   (At the start of creation)

2. Who lived before the beginning?
   (God)

3. Out of what did God make the world?
   (He made it from nothing. He simply spoke and the world came into being!)

4. In John 1:1–3, Jesus, the Son of God, is called "the Word." What connection is there between "the Word" and "God said"?
   (Jesus is God's Word made flesh. Jesus was present at creation, and "all things were made through Him.")

5. What were the chief differences between people and the other moving creatures?
   (People were created in the image of God, and they were given power to rule and care for the rest of the earth.)

6. Who is meant by "Us" and "Our" when God speaks about making people?
   (The three persons of the Trinity—Father, Son, and Holy Spirit)

7. Which words tell that there was not a mistake or a flaw in anything God had made?
   ("It was good"—"very good.")

8. What did God create on the seventh day?
   (On the seventh day, God rested. We might say that on the seventh day God created rest.)

9. All Scripture points to God and His love for us in Christ Jesus. How does God's designation of the seventh day remind us of Jesus? See Matthew 11:28.
   (God designed the seventh day to be a day of rest. Jesus invites us to find our rest in the forgiveness, new life, and salvation He has won for us.)

Applying God's Word

1. In what way does God continue to create the world today?
   (God continues to populate His creation with plants, animals, and people. He preserves all that He has made.)

2. What does God's Word accomplish in our lives today?
   (Through the Word, the Holy Spirit works faith and grants us the blessings of forgiveness, eternal life, and salvation in Jesus Christ. God's Word also comforts, strengthens, instructs, and encourages us.)

3. How do the teachings of evolution compare with those of Genesis 1?
   (God's Word clearly describes a six-day creation with evening and morning each day. It says God created each animal according to its kind. Nowhere does the Bible suggest that animals changed into other kinds of animals over a long period of time, as the teachings of evolution suggest. Evolution holds that the earth came about by random chance and natural processes. The Bible says creation is a result of God's loving design and almighty power.)

2

The Fall into Sin
(Genesis 2–3)

Reviewing God's Word

Underline the word or phrase that answers each question.

1. Whose fault was it that Adam sinned? (Devil's—Adam's—God's—Eve's)
2. Whose fault was it that Eve sinned? (Devil's—Serpent's—God's—Eve's)
3. Who drove Adam and his wife from the garden? (Devil—Cherubim—God—Wild animals)
4. Why did Adam and his wife try to hide from God? (They were naked—They were like God—They had sinned—They didn't know God)
5. How did God punish Adam, his wife, and the serpent? (He cursed them—He killed them—He abandoned them—He hid from them)
6. Who are sinners? (Only heathens—All people Everyone except Christians—Only adults)
7. For whose sake did God curse the ground? (God's sake—The woman's sake—Adam's sake—Satan's sake)

Thinking about God's Word

1. How did God communicate with Adam and Eve? **(He talked with them directly.)**

2. What special command had God given them? **(Not to eat from the tree of the knowledge of good and evil)**

3. How did the first two people become disobedient? **(They listened to the serpent and ate the forbidden fruit.)**

4. Why did Adam and Eve hide from God? **(They had sinned and they knew they were naked.)**

5. How did Adam and Eve try to make excuses for their sin? **(They placed blame beyond themselves. Adam blamed Eve. Eve blamed the serpent.)**

6. Name four evils that have come into the world because of sin. **(Answers will vary.)**

7. What sentence did God pronounce on the woman? **(Pain in childbirth)**

   on the man? **(Difficulty and frustration [the ground became cursed], death)**

Applying God's Word

1. What tactic did the devil successfully use to tempt Adam and Eve to sin? **(The devil, in the form of a serpent, led Adam and Eve to doubt God's words: "Did God actually say . . .")**

   Does the devil ever use this temptation with you? **(Anytime we doubt God's Word and His promises or ignore His Law, we are falling prey to the same temptation that Adam and Eve did.)**

2. Why did Adam and Eve's relationship with God change when they sinned? **(The fall into sin destroyed the image of God in Adam and Eve. Their sin put separation between them as fallen people and their perfect Creator. They were no longer able to please God or to commune closely with Him, as they had done prior to the fall.)**

   How does sin hurt your relationship with God? **(Sin separates us from God too. Without redemption through faith in Christ, we can't please God or have a close relationship with Him.)**

3. How did Jesus, the offspring of Eve, crush the head of the serpent? **(Jesus crushed the head of the serpent when He lived a perfect life and died an atoning death for the sins of all people. Jesus' words from the cross "It is finished" refer to the completion of this work and the final defeat of Satan.)**

   How has Jesus' work changed your relationship with God? **(Through faith in Jesus, our sins are gone, the separation is removed, and we are made righteous or right with God.)**

3

The Children of Adam and Eve (Genesis 4)

Reviewing God's Word

Fill in the blanks, using the words below. Some words may be used more than once or not at all.

1. **Cain** was the first child born to Adam and Eve.
2. Adam and Eve's second child was named **Abel**.
3. Cain was a **farmer**.
4. Abel was a **shepherd**.
5. The offering that **Abel** brought pleased God.
6. **Cain** committed the first murder.
7. God cursed Cain and made him a **wanderer**.
8. Adam and Eve's third son was named **Seth**.

Cain	Enosh	Seth	Adam
slave	farmer	shepherd	wanderer
Abel	Nod	fisherman	hunter

Thinking about God's Word

1. Whom did Eve credit for the birth of her son?
   (God)

2. What is one way Cain and Abel worshiped God?
   (They brought God offerings.)

3. What warning did Cain receive from God?
   (God told Cain, "If you do not do well, sin is crouching at the door. Its desire is for you, but you must rule over it.")

4. What did Cain ask God in order to try to avoid responsibility for Abel's murder?
   (Cain asked God, "Am I my brother's keeper?")

5. What curse did God put on Cain?
   (God said the earth would no longer let Cain farm and grow produce. Cain would have to leave his family and wander the earth.)

6. Was the mark that God set on Cain a blessing or a punishment?
   (A blessing)

   Why?
   (God put a mark on Cain so that no one would kill him.)

7. How did God show mercy to Adam and Eve?
   (He blessed them with a third son, Seth.)

Applying God's Word

1. How does God's warning to Cain apply to all people?
   (All people should heed this same warning. Sin desires to pull us away from our Savior and hold us firmly in its grasp so that we will not go to God to receive the forgiveness He freely offers us in Jesus.)

2. Answer Cain's question correctly and give a reason for your answer: "Am I my brother's keeper?"
   (Yes, as God's children, we are all brothers and sisters, and God would have us love and care for all people.)

3. God had promised that a Savior would come through Adam's descendants. Then one of Adam's sons was killed and the other was exiled. How did God continue His plan for salvation?
   (God gave Adam and Eve another son, Seth, through whose descendants Christ would come.)

   What does this tell us about God?
   (God is more powerful than human actions and sin, and He always keeps His promises.)

4

Noah and the Flood

(Genesis 6–9)

Reviewing God's Word

Answer each question by circling Yes or No.

1. Did God send a flood to destroy the world because the people were wicked?	**(YES)**	NO
2. Did the flood cover only part of the earth?	YES	**(NO)**
3. Were the mountains covered with water?	**(YES)**	NO
4. Did God forget about Noah and his family?	YES	**(NO)**
5. Did the ark come to rest on Ararat?	**(YES)**	NO
6. Were all people and animals (other than those on the ark) destroyed by the flood?	**(YES)**	NO
7. Does God punish wickedness today?	**(YES)**	NO

Thinking about God's Word

1. What did the Lord see that made Him grieve?
   (People were very wicked and thought only about doing evil.)

2. What did the Lord plan to do?
   (He planned to wipe all people and animals from the face of the earth. God cannot tolerate evil, because God is holy.)

3. How was Noah different from the other people?
   (Noah found favor with God; he walked with God.)

4. What did God tell Noah to do?
   (He told Noah to build an ark and take his family and two animals of every kind onto the ark.)

5. How did Noah show that he believed God?
   (Noah showed his faith in God by doing everything God commanded him to do.)

6. Which people were saved by the ark?
   (Noah, his wife, their sons and their wives—eight people in all—were saved.)

7. What did Noah do after leaving the ark?
   (He built an altar to worship God.)

8. What promise from God did the rainbow symbolize?
   (God promised that never again would He curse the ground or destroy all living things, as He had done during the flood.)

Applying God's Word

1. Why did God declare Noah righteous? See Hebrews 11:7.
   (Noah was saved by his faith. Being warned about the coming destruction, Noah built an ark and showed the unrepentant world that God's judgment was real.)

   How are we declared righteous?
   (We, too, are made righteous by faith in God, through the death and resurrection of Jesus.)

2. God could probably say the same thing about our world that He said about Noah's: The wickedness of man is great and all man thinks about is doing evil. What comfort can we find in the account of the flood?
   (First of all, God always preserves faithful people for Himself. Even when the whole world seemed full of sin, God protected the faith of Noah and his family. Second, God has promised never to destroy the world again by flood. Jesus took the punishment for the sins of the world so that all who believe in Him can be forgiven and receive everlasting life in heaven.)

3. The great flood reminds us of the Sacrament of Holy Baptism. See 1 Peter 3:18–22. Explain.
   (God saved faithful Noah and his family through the waters of the flood. In the same way, God saves people today through faith in the triune God by the washing of water and the Word in Holy Baptism.)

5

God Calls Abram

(Genesis 12–13)

Reviewing God's Word

Draw lines to connect each cause to its effect.

Cause:	Effect:
1. God told Abram to go to a land He would show him.	Lot moved to the Jordan valley.
2. God promised Canaan to Abram's descendants.	Abram went to Egypt.
3. There was a famine in Canaan.	God sent a plague on Pharaoh's house.
4. Abram was worried he would be killed.	Abram built an altar to God.
5. Pharaoh took Sarai into his house.	Abram said Sarai was his sister.
6. Abram and Lot's herdsmen fought.	Abram moved to Canaan.

Thinking about God's Word

1. What command came to Abram, whom God later named Abraham, from the Lord?
   ("Go to the land that I will show you.")

2. What threefold promise did God give with His command?
   (God would make Abram into a great nation; God would bless him and make his name great; all people on earth would be blessed through Abram.)

3. Which of these promises meant the same as the promise given to Adam and Eve after the fall?
   (All people on earth would be blessed through Abram. Abram was a descendant of Adam and Eve, and through his descendants would come Jesus. Jesus would defeat Satan and bring blessing to all mankind.)

4. How did Abram worship God in public after he arrived in Canaan?
   (He built an altar.)

5. Why did Abram lie to Pharaoh about Sarai being his wife?
   (He was afraid and thought lying would save his life. He didn't trust God to deliver them.)

6. How did Abram keep peace between himself and his nephew?
   (He graciously allowed Lot to choose his land first so they could part ways and avoid further conflict.)

7. What promise did God make to Abram about his offspring?
   (God promised that they would be as numerous as the dust of the earth and that they would inherit the land of Canaan.)

Applying God's Word

1. In what way have all people on earth been blessed through Abraham?
   (All people have been blessed through Abraham in that God sent His Son into the world to redeem the world. Jesus was a descendant of Abraham.)

2. How did Abram show his faith in God? See Hebrews 11:8.
   (When God told Abram to leave his homeland and travel to a new land, Abram packed up and went—without even knowing where he was going.)

   How do we show our faith in God?
   (By faith, the Holy Spirit gives us the strength to obey God's commands. Our faith is made visible to those around us when God does good works through us.)

3. Abram took things into his own hands while in Egypt, rather than trusting God for protection. When do you have the most trouble trusting God? What application for your own life can you find in the fact that God delivered Abram and Sarai?
   (Answers will vary, but we can be reassured that no matter how much we struggle to trust God, He always delivers His people.)

6

Abram Rescues Lot

(Genesis 13–14)

Reviewing God's Word

Fill in the blanks, using the words below.

1. Abram settled in the land of **Canaan**, while Lot settled among the cities of the valley.
2. The kings of Sodom and **Gomorrah** were on the losing side.
3. The enemy also took **Lot**, who was living in Sodom, and his possessions.
4. Melchizedek, the king of Salem, brought out **bread** and wine.
5. Melchizedek said, "Blessed be Abram by God Most High, **Possessor** of heaven and earth."
6. Abram said to the king of Sodom, "I would not take a **thread** or a sandal strap or anything that is yours."

Possessor	Canaan	bread
Lot	thread	Gomorrah

Thinking about God's Word

1. What happened in the Jordan Valley, where Lot had chosen to live?
(There was a great battle between the kings of the land, and Sodom and Gomorrah lost.)

2. What did the winning kings take as plunder?
(They took all the possessions and food from Sodom and Gomorrah, and they captured Lot and his possessions.)

3. What did Abram do when he heard what had happened?
(He took his men with him and rescued Lot and his household.)

4. Whom did Abram meet after returning from defeating the enemy kings?
(He met Melchizedek, the king of Salem and a priest of God.)

5. What did Abram do when he met this person?
(He gave him a tenth of everything that he had.)

Applying God's Word

1. God used Abram to rescue Lot. How has God used other people to rescue you from bad situations?
(Answers will vary.)

2. Melchizedek brought out bread and wine to celebrate God's deliverance. What church celebration does this remind you of?
(In Communion, we not only have bread and wine to celebrate God's deliverance, but we also have the assurance that Jesus actually comes to us in body and blood to give us forgiveness of sins, life, and salvation.)

3. How is Jesus like Melchizedek?
(Melchizedek was a priest and a king—a rare combination. Jesus is both a priest who offered Himself as a sacrifice for sin and who goes to God on our behalf and also a king who reigns in heaven forever.)

7

God's Covenant with Abram

(Genesis 15; 17)

Reviewing God's Word

God often used names very deliberately because of their specific meaning.

Using your knowledge of these people, match each name to its meaning.

1. Abraham	A person of royalty
2. Sarah	The Lord saves
3. Isaac	Father of a multitude
4. Jesus	He laughs

Thinking about God's Word

1. How did God comfort Abram's fears?
(God reminded Abram that He was his shield and that He would protect and reward him.)

2. How did God answer him when Abram said he was still childless?
(The Lord promised that Abram's own son would be his heir and that his descendants would be as many as the stars in the sky.)

3. Why did it take great faith for Abram to believe this promise?
(He and Sarai were very old and had no children.)

4. What did God do as a sign of His covenant with Abram?
(He changed Abram's name to Abraham and changed Sarai's name to Sarah. By doing this, God claimed them as His own and gave them a constant reminder of His covenant with them.)

5. When did God say Abraham's son would be born?
(He promised that the child would be born at the same time the next year.)

6. What does it mean to believe in God?
(To trust that God and His promises are real and true, even when what God says in His Word doesn't seem possible.)

Applying God's Word

1. Abraham believed the Lord, and He credited it to him as righteousness. How is God's righteousness credited to people today?
(Just as with Abraham, righteousness or good standing before God is credited to those who believe in Jesus as the Son of God and only Savior of the world.)

2. Abraham asked for one child, and God promised that his descendants would be as numerous as the stars. In what ways has God given you even more than you could ask for or think of? See Ephesians 3:20.
(Answers will vary.)

3. In addition to Abraham's actual descendants, who else is included among the children of Abraham? See Galatians 3:29.
(All who believe in Jesus as their Savior are the children of Abraham, whether they are actual physical descendants or Gentile believers. Truly, his descendants are as numerous as the stars in the sky!)

8

Abraham's Visitors (Genesis 18; 21)

Reviewing God's Word

Underline the word or phrase that answers each question.

1. Who were the three men who came to Abraham's tent? (The Lord and two angels—Pharaoh and two servants—the King of Sodom and two officials—Melchizedek and two priests)
2. What did Abraham offer to his guests? (A place to sleep—Money—Water and a meal—A donkey to ride)
3. What did Abraham tell Sarah to do? (Bring water—Bake cakes—Prepare a calf—Clean the tent)
4. How old was Abraham when Isaac was born? (99—90—95—100)
5. How did Sarah say people would respond to the news of Isaac's birth? (They would cry—They would laugh—They would sing for joy—They would be speechless)

Thinking about God's Word

1. In what form did the Lord come to Abraham at the time of this story?
   (Three men came to Abraham; one was the Lord Himself.)
2. What special message did the Lord bring to Abraham?
   (He told Abraham that he and Sarah would have a son.)
3. How did Abraham show hospitality?
   (He invited the men to stop and rest. He provided them with water for washing and a full meal to eat.)
4. How did Sarah hear the Lord's promise, even though it was not spoken directly to her?
   (Sarah was listening at the entrance to the tent.)
5. How would you answer the question "Why did Sarah laugh?"
   (She laughed because she was old and well past childbearing years.)
6. Why did it make sense for the child to be named Isaac (meaning "he laughs")?
   (Both Abraham and Sarah laughed when they heard the news that they would have a son. No one expected this aged couple to have a baby! Isaac was a true gift of joy.)

Applying God's Word

1. What characteristic of God is suggested by the question "Is anything too hard for God?"
   (God is omnipotent [all-powerful]. Nothing is too difficult for Him to accomplish.)
2. Name a promise God has made to us that has not yet been fulfilled. Do you believe it will be fulfilled? Why can we trust God to keep all of His promises?
   (Answers may vary somewhat. Students may mention Jesus' promise to come again. Because God is perfect, He does not lie [Titus 1:2]. He has been faithful in all He has promised to us in the past, and the whole Bible with thousands of fulfilled prophecies testifies to the surety of God's promises.)
3. In this account, God took on human form to visit His people. When else did God take on human form to live among His people? See Galatians 4:4–5.
   (God sent His Son to be born of a woman and to live on earth and die a human death. He became a man in order to save humanity from the curse of the fall.)

9

Abraham and Isaac

(Genesis 22)

Reviewing God's Word

Fill in the blanks, using the words below.

1. God **tested** Abraham.
2. God told Abraham, "Take your only son, Isaac, whom you love, and go to the land of Moriah. Offer him there as a burnt **offering**."
3. Abraham said, "I and the boy will go over there and **worship** and come again to you."
4. "God will **provide** for Himself the lamb for a burnt offering."
5. Then Abraham took the knife to **kill** his son.
6. The Lord said, "Now I know that you **fear** God, seeing you have not withheld your only son from Me."
7. "In your offspring shall all the nations of the earth be **blessed**, because you have obeyed My voice."

kill	provide	tested	worship
offering	fear	blessed	

Thinking about God's Word

1. How did God test Abraham?
(He asked him to sacrifice his son as a burnt offering.)

2. Why must God's command have been a shock to Abraham?
(Isaac was Abraham and Sarah's only son, born to them in old age. God had promised that many nations would come from Isaac's descendants.)

3. Yet, what did Abraham's faith in God move him to do in answer to God's command?
(Abraham's faith moved him to obey.)

4. In which words did the angel of the Lord tell Abraham that he had passed the test?
("Now I know that you fear God, seeing you have not withheld your only son from Me.")

5. What did the angel of the Lord say Abraham's blessing would be?
(He would have as many descendants as the stars in the sky and the grains of sand on the shore, and through them all nations would be blessed.)

6. Name three ways in which Abraham's son and God's Son were the same.
(Answers may vary but could include that they were both sons of God's promise; they both carried wood to the sacrifice; they both went willingly to be sacrificed.)

7. God spared Abraham's son, but what did He do with His own Son?
(He sacrificed Him for the sins of the world.)

Applying God's Word

1. What things do you love most? Would you be willing to sacrifice them or give them up to God? What great sacrifice did God make for us?
(Answers will vary. We often put other things before God because we are sinful people, but God gave up His only Son to save the world from bondage to sin.)

2. What was Abraham's answer to Isaac's question?
(He told Isaac that God would provide a lamb for the sacrifice.)

With what action did God fulfill a short time later what Abraham said and believed?
(God provided a ram and told Abraham to sacrifice it in place of Isaac.)

What Lamb did God Himself provide as an offering about 2,000 years later?
(He provided His only Son, Jesus.)

3. What did Abraham believe God would do to restore Isaac if he would have sacrificed his son? See Hebrews 11:17–19. Of what great event does this belief remind us?
(Abraham believed that God would, if necessary, raise Isaac from the dead. Some 2,000 years later, God did raise Jesus, the true Lamb of God, from the dead so that someday everyone who believes in Christ will be raised.)

10

Isaac and Rebekah
(Genesis 24)

Reviewing God's Word

Draw a line through the sentences that are not true.

1. Abraham sent his servant to get a wife for Isaac.
2. ~~The servant searched the whole city of Nahor for the right woman.~~
3. ~~The servant chose Rebekah because she was the prettiest woman he saw.~~
4. Rebekah's father was Bethuel.
5. Laban welcomed the servant into his home.
6. Laban and Bethuel agreed that Rebekah should go with the servant.
7. ~~Rebekah had fallen in love with Isaac.~~
8. Isaac and Rebekah married, and Isaac loved his wife.

Thinking about God's Word

1. Why did Abraham send his servant back to his homeland?
(He sent the servant to find a wife for his son, Isaac.)

2. What did the servant do when he arrived in Nahor?
(He prayed that God would guide his search and lead him to the right wife for Isaac.)

3. How did the servant know that Rebekah was the chosen woman?
(She offered not only to draw water from the well for the servant but for his camels as well.)

What does this say about Rebekah?
(She was considerate, hospitable, and willing to serve.)

4. What did Laban do when he heard about the servant?
(He was very hospitable. He prepared space for him and his camels and welcomed him into his home.)

5. Why did Laban and Bethuel agree to send Rebekah with the servant?
(They recognized that this was God's will for Rebekah.)

6. How did Rebekah show her faith in God?
(Without even having met Isaac, Rebekah left her family and went with the servant to obey her mother and brother and do the Lord's will.)

Applying God's Word

1. Why was it important for the servant to go to Abraham's homeland to find a wife for Isaac?
(The land where Isaac was living, Canaan, was full of people who worshiped other gods. Abraham wanted his son to have a wife who worshiped the one true God.)

2. What did the servant do before—and after— finding Rebekah?
(The servant prayed that God would guide him to the right woman for Isaac, and he thanked God after he did find Rebekah.)

How can you follow his example?
(We can pray that God would guide all our decisions, and we can also thank Him when He answers our prayers.)

3. Abraham, the servant, Laban, Bethuel, Rebekah, and Isaac all trusted that God had a plan for this marriage. Why was Isaac's marriage to Rebekah so important for God's great plan of salvation?
(God had promised that the Savior would come through Abraham's descendants. Abraham's son, Isaac, and his godly wife, Rebekah, continued the family line that would ultimately lead to Jesus.)

11

Jacob and Esau (Genesis 25; 27)

Reviewing God's Word

Answer each question with either *Esau* or *Jacob*.

1. Who was the older son? **Esau**
2. To whom did Isaac wish to give the blessing? **Esau**
3. Whom did Rebekah want to get the blessing? **Jacob**
4. When Jacob came in to see his father, who did he say he was? **Esau**
5. Whom did Isaac think he heard speaking when Jacob was in the room? **Jacob**
5. Whom did Isaac think Jacob was when he felt Jacob's hands? **Esau**
6. To whom did Isaac give the blessing of the firstborn? **Jacob**

Thinking about God's Word

1. In what way were both Esau and Jacob gifts from God?
(Rebekah was barren. Isaac prayed for children, and God gave him two sons.)

2. How does this remind you of Isaac's birth?
(Isaac's mother, Sarah, was also barren, and God gave her a son.)

3. What did Jacob give Esau in exchange for his birthright?
(Jacob gave his very hungry brother bread and lentil stew.)

4. How did Rebekah try to take things into her own hands?
(She sent Jacob, disguised as Esau, to Isaac to get the blessing.)

5. What lie did Jacob speak to his father?
(He said, "I am Esau.")

6. Why could Jacob fool his father so easily?
(Isaac was old and couldn't see anymore.)

7. Why did Jacob flee to Laban?
(He heard that Esau was planning to kill him when the days of mourning for Isaac were over.)

Applying God's Word

1. How did Jacob break each of the following commandments?

IV. Honor your father and your mother.
(Jacob deceived his father.)

VII. You shall not steal.
(Jacob stole the blessing his father planned to give to Esau.)

2. Of what was Rebekah guilty?
(Rebekah took matters into her own hands rather than trusting in God. [God had promised that Jacob was to receive the greater blessing.] Even though, as we saw in our last story, Rebekah had great faith in God, she was still sinful and failed at times to trust God.)

3. What do Jesus' life, death, and resurrection mean for all repentant sinners?
(Jesus has earned forgiveness for all sins ever committed, including those of Jacob and his family and those we commit today.)

12

Jacob's Dream

(Genesis 27–28)

Reviewing God's Word

Write the name of the speaker next to each quote. Names may be used more than once or not at all.

1. "God Almighty bless you and make you fruitful and multiply you." **Isaac**
2. "The land on which you lie I will give to you and to your offspring." **God**
3. "This is the gate of heaven." **Jacob**
4. "Take as your wife one of the daughters of Laban." **Isaac**
5. "This is none other than the house of God." **Jacob**
6. "Behold, I am with you and will keep you wherever you go." **God**

God	Jacob	Isaac
Rebekah	Esau	Laban

Thinking about God's Word

1. Why did Isaac send Jacob to the house of Laban?
   (Isaac sent Jacob to get a wife.)

2. How did God appear to Jacob?
   (He appeared to him in a dream.)

3. What vision did Jacob see in his dream?
   (He saw a ladder going up to heaven, with angels going up and down the ladder between heaven and earth.)

4. What blessing did God give to Jacob?
   ("The land on which you lie I will give you and to your offspring. Your offspring shall be like the dust of the earth. . . . In you and your offspring shall all the families of the earth be blessed.")

5. What name did Jacob give to the place where he had his dream?
   (Bethel)

6. What vow did Jacob make before he left Bethel?
   ("The LORD shall be my God. And this stone, which I have set up for a pillar, shall be God's house. And of all that You give me I will give a full tenth to You.")

7. Have you ever been blessed by someone? When? Where? How? Why?
   (Answers will vary.)

Applying God's Word

1. Jacob received the blessing God gave to Abraham. What was the most significant part of that blessing?
   (The Savior of the world would be born as a descendant of Abraham, Isaac, and Jacob.)

2. In what ways do God's angels serve His people?
   (Angels protect, serve, aid, and bring messages to the people of God.)

3. How is Bethel like a Christian church?
   (A church is the house of God—the gate of heaven. A church building is set apart for the worship of God. Here, God Himself promises to be present. Jesus promises that wherever two or three are gathered together in His name, He will be among them [Matthew 18:20].)

13

Jacob's Family (Genesis 29–31)

Reviewing God's Word

Fill in the blanks, using the words below. Some words will not be used.

1. Jacob traveled to the land of the people of the **east**.
2. Rachel was Laban's **daughter**.
3. Jacob agreed to work **seven** years for Rachel.
4. Laban gave Jacob **Leah** in marriage instead.
5. Jacob loved **Rachel** more than Leah.
6. God told Jacob to return to **Canaan**.

Dinah	west	daughter	Nod
Leah	seven	Canaan	Rachel
five	sister	North	east

Thinking about God's Word

1. Why was Jacob so excited to meet Rachel?
(She was the daughter of Laban, his relative. He was very happy to find the household of his kinsman.)

2. How many daughters did Laban have?
(He had two daughters: Leah and Rachel.)

3. Why did Jacob agree to work for Laban for seven years?
(He loved Rachel and wanted to marry her.)

4. How did Laban trick Jacob?
(He gave him Leah in marriage instead of Rachel.)

5. How much longer did Jacob work in order to marry Rachel?
(He worked seven more years.)

6. Which words show that God gave Jacob many gifts while he was working for Laban?
("Jacob's family grew and grew. . . . Jacob's flocks and herds grew large.")

7. What did the Lord tell Jacob to do?
(He told him to go back to the land of his father.)

8. Why did Jacob not have to fear the long journey back to Canaan and back to a brother who had threatened to kill him?
(God promised to be with him.)

Applying God's Word

1. Jacob's earlier trickery and Laban's deceit caused conflict within their families, yet God was at work through it all. What conflicts does your family have, and how might God bring good out of these situations?
(Answers will vary.)

2. Jacob was blessed with twelve sons. Twelve is an important number in the Bible to represent the whole people of God. Can you think of another important group of twelve men in the Bible?
(The descendants of Jacob's twelve sons became the twelve tribes of Israel, the whole of God's people in the Old Testament. Similarly, Jesus had twelve disciples, who became leaders of God's people in the New Testament.)

3. Jacob knew it would be hard to move his whole family back to Canaan and face his brother, Esau, but he trusted that God would be with him. What hard things can you get through knowing that God is always with you?
(Answers will vary.)

14

Esau Forgives Jacob
(Genesis 32–33)

Reviewing God's Word

Underline the word or phrase that makes each sentence true.

1. In his message to Esau, Jacob called himself Esau's (slave—master—servant—hired hand).
2. Jacob told God he wasn't worthy of His (wrath—punishment—steadfast love—anger).
3. (God—An angel—Satan—Esau) wrestled with Jacob at night.
4. God changed Jacob's name to (Isaac—Israel—Abraham—Shechem).
5. Esau (hated—punished—exiled—forgave) Jacob.

Thinking about God's Word

1. What did Jacob send his messengers to tell Esau?
   (He sent them to tell Esau that he was returning with wealth from Laban's house and that he wanted to find favor with him.)

2. Why did Jacob think Esau might attack him and his household?
   (After Jacob tricked Isaac and took Esau's birthright, Esau threatened to kill him.)

3. How did Jacob show humility in his prayer for protection?
   (He told God that he was unworthy of His love and faithfulness.)

4. What blessing did God give to Jacob after they wrestled?
   (God gave him the name Israel because he had struggled with God and men and won.)

5. What did Esau do when Jacob came to him and bowed before him?
   (Esau hugged him and kissed him, and they wept together.)

6. What did Jacob do when he was safely in Canaan with his entire household?
   (He built an altar to God.)

Applying God's Word

1. Jacob remembered in his prayer that he was unworthy of God's love and faithfulness, yet he still prayed for deliverance. Why can we pray for God's blessings, even though we don't deserve them?
   (Although we are sinful and unworthy, Jesus' death and resurrection has forgiven our sins and made us right with God. We don't deserve good gifts from God, but He loves us anyway and delights in showing us grace and mercy.)

2. God changed Jacob's name from Jacob (meaning "he cheats") to Israel (meaning "he who wrestles with God and wins"). How was God setting the stage for more change in Jacob's life?
   (Jacob had been a deceiver early in his life, who tricked his aging father and stole the birthright that belonged to his brother. Now, after hard years of labor for Laban and after being tricked himself, he was willing to kneel before his brother and ask for forgiveness. God was preparing him to be the father of His chosen people, the people of Israel.)

3. In the Lord's Prayer, we pray that God would "forgive us our trespasses as we forgive those who trespass against us." What prompts you, like Esau, to show forgiveness to others?
   (God's people forgive from a joyful recognition that God, in His mercy, has graciously forgiven our every sin through Jesus' death and resurrection and empowers us by His Spirit to forgive others.)

15

Joseph's Dreams (Genesis 37)

Reviewing God's Word

Draw lines to match each person to his action(s).

1. Israel/Jacob	Showed favoritism
	Sold Joseph to the Ishmaelites
2. Joseph	Dreamed about sheaves and the sun, moon, and stars
	Remembered Joseph's dreams
3. Reuben	Threw Joseph in a pit
	Tried to rescue Joseph
	Mourned without being comforted
4. The brothers	Dipped Joseph's robe in blood

Thinking about God's Word

1. Why did Joseph's brothers hate him?
   (Their father, Israel, loved him more than the other brothers. And Joseph told them about his dreams that he would rule over them.)

2. How did Jacob show his great love for Joseph?
   (He made him a beautiful robe of many colors.)

3. What did Joseph's dreams mean?
   (Joseph would rule over his family.)

4. Why did Israel send Joseph to find his brothers?
   (The brothers were pasturing their flocks, and Israel wanted Joseph to check on them.)

5. How did the brothers show their hatred for Joseph and their hard-heartedness?
   (They threw him into a pit. Then they sold him into slavery. They hoped they would never see Joseph again.)

6. How did the brothers deceive their father?
   (They took Joseph's robe and dipped it in goat's blood so their father would think Joseph had been killed by a wild animal.)

7. How did the brothers hurt Joseph, Jacob, and most of all, themselves?
   (Joseph became a slave, Jacob went into a prolonged period of mourning, and the brothers had to live with what they had done to their brother.)

Applying God's Word

1. How is Jacob as a father like our Father in heaven? How is he different?
   (Our heavenly Father loves us enough to provide us with the very best, just as Jacob loved Joseph and gave him a beautiful robe. Jacob, however, showed favoritism toward Joseph, which caused great conflict within his family. Our heavenly Father loves us each equally and to the extent that He gave His only Son to pay for our sins.)

2. Jacob gave Joseph a beautiful robe to wear. With what are those who have been baptized into Christ clothed? See Galatians 3:27 and Revelation 7:13–14.
   (By faith, those who were baptized into Christ have put on Christ. We are covered with a white robe of righteousness because our sins have been washed away in the blood of the Lamb, Jesus Christ.)

3. Reuben pleaded with his brothers for Joseph's life, but in the end, he couldn't rescue him. Who pleads with God on our behalf and did rescue us?
   (Jesus pleads with His Father in heaven for us and for all for whom He has died [Romans 8:34]. Jesus did succeed in rescuing us from the death we deserve because of our sin.)

16

Joseph in Egypt

(Genesis 39–41)

Reviewing God's Word

Underline the word or phrase that best completes each sentence.

1. Joseph (exposed—gave in to—fled—enjoyed) the temptations of Potiphar's wife.
2. But Potiphar (jailed—praised—promoted—exiled) Joseph.
3. The cupbearer told Pharaoh about Joseph (immediately—2 weeks later—2 years later—never).
4. Pharaoh was the (king—captain—president—prince) of Egypt.
5. Joseph said that (he—magicians—Jacob—God) would answer Pharaoh.
6. Pharaoh's dreams told about (14—7—10—8) years of famine.
7. The famine was severe all over (Egypt—Canaan—Ur—the earth).

Thinking about God's Word

1. How did Joseph show that he wanted to do the right thing and follow God's commands?
(He refused to lie with Potiphar's wife.)

2. How did God bless Joseph even while he was in prison?
(The keeper of the prison put Joseph in charge of all the other prisoners.)

3. What did Joseph do for the cupbearer and baker while they were in prison?
(He, by God's power, interpreted their dreams for them.)

4. Why did Pharaoh have to find someone in place of his magicians to interpret his dreams?
(They could not interpret them.)

5. How did Pharaoh know that Joseph could interpret dreams?
(The cupbearer told him.)

6. How did Joseph show his humility as he stood before Pharaoh?
(He told Pharaoh that it was God who revealed the meaning of the dreams to him.)

7. What advice did Joseph give Pharaoh together with the interpretation?
(Joseph told Pharaoh to put a wise and discerning man in charge of the land of Egypt to store up grain for the years of famine.)

8. Whom did Pharaoh put in charge?
(Joseph)

Applying God's Word

1. How did God show Joseph His steadfast love even when things weren't going well?
(Things certainly didn't always go well for Joseph. He was enslaved, falsely accused, and imprisoned. But God was with Him at every moment, and God gave Joseph a high position in Potiphar's house, the prison, and eventually in all of Egypt. Through Joseph, God saved and blessed His people.)

2. What words of Joseph show that the power to interpret dreams wasn't his own?
(Joseph said [to the cupbearer and baker], "Do not interpretations belong to God?" And Joseph said [to Pharaoh], "God has revealed what He is about to do.")

3. God was faithful to Joseph and gave him a position of prominence in Egypt, but he was in prison for two years first. What does this say about God's timing?
(It may seem sometimes as though God has forgotten us or is slow to keep His promises. But God delivered Joseph from prison at exactly the right time to save the world from famine. Even when hard times come—and seem to last a long time!—we can be assured that God is with us and will ultimately bring good out of our suffering.)

17

Joseph Forgives His Brothers (Genesis 42–45)

Reviewing God's Word

Circle Yes or No for each statement.

1. Jacob went with Joseph's brothers to Egypt to get grain.	YES	**(NO)**
2. Joseph's brothers recognized him.	YES	**(NO)**
3. Joseph kept Simeon bound in Egypt.	**(YES)**	NO
4. Joseph invited his brothers to eat with him.	**(YES)**	NO
5. Reuben received the most food.	YES	**(NO)**
6. Benjamin stole Joseph's silver cup.	YES	**(NO)**
7. Judah offered to stay as a slave instead of Benjamin.	**(YES)**	NO
8. Joseph punished his brothers for how they mistreated him.	YES	**(NO)**

Thinking about God's Word

1. How can you tell that there was a famine also in Canaan during the lean years?
   (Jacob sent his sons to Egypt to buy grain.)

2. What did Joseph do to his brothers when they came to him?
   (He accused them of being spies and kept Simeon as a prisoner.)

3. Why might the brothers have not recognized Joseph?
   (It had been many years since they had seen him. He was dressed as an Egyptian. They never expected him to be a high-ranking Egyptian official.)

4. How did the brothers react when they reached home and found their money in their sacks?
   (They were afraid.)

5. Whom did Jacob send with the brothers the second time they went to Egypt?
   (He sent the youngest brother, Benjamin.)

6. Why did Joseph put the cup was in Benjamin's sack?
   (Joseph wanted to see whether his brothers had changed.)

7. How did the words of Judah show that his heart was changed?
   (Judah offered to serve as a slave in Benjamin's place.)

8. How can you tell that this is what Joseph had hoped for in testing his brothers?
   (Joseph wept, told them who he was, and explained that he wasn't angry with them, because God had used his slavery in Egypt for good.)

Applying God's Word

1. How could Joseph easily have taken revenge on his brothers for having sold him?
   (Joseph was now a mighty ruler in Egypt. He literally had the lives of his brothers in his hand.)

   Why didn't he?
   (Joseph believed in God and sought to do God's will.)

2. Judah was willing to give himself up for his brother Benjamin. What prominent New Testament figure was born from Judah's descendants (Matthew 1:1–16)? Why is this significant?
   (Jesus was born of the tribe of Judah. Judah gave a small glimpse of the sacrifice Jesus would make. Jesus willingly gave up His life to save all of mankind.)

3. Although we have sinned against God worse than Joseph's brothers sinned against him, why can we come to God without fear?
   (Although we deserve God's wrath and punishment, God shows us mercy. Jesus took the punishment we deserve when He died on the cross. Because of His sacrifice, we are forgiven and enabled to "with confidence draw near to the throne of grace" [Hebrews 4:14–16].)

18

Jacob's Blessing
(Genesis 45–49)

Reviewing God's Word

Write the name of the speaker next to each quote.

1. "Say to your brothers, 'Come to me. I will give you the best of the land of Egypt.'" **Pharaoh**
2. "Now let me die, since I have seen your face and know that you are still alive." **Israel/Jacob**
3. "Joseph is ruler over all Egypt." **The brothers**
4. "The scepter shall not depart from Judah, nor the ruler's staff from between his feet." **Israel/Jacob**
5. "Do not be afraid to go to Egypt. There I will make you into a great nation." **God**
6. "Do not bury me in Egypt, but let me lie with my fathers." **Israel/Jacob**

God	Joseph	The brothers
Israel/Jacob	Pharaoh	Judah

Thinking about God's Word

1. Why did Joseph send wagons to Canaan?
(He wanted to bring his family to Egypt.)

2. What did Pharaoh promise to Joseph's family?
(He promised them the best land of Egypt.)

3. What did Israel do before he went to Egypt?
(He offered sacrifices to God and sought God's will.)

4. How did Jacob and Joseph show how overjoyed they were to be reunited?
(Joseph wept for a long time, and Jacob said that his life was complete and he was ready to die.)

5. Whom did Jacob bless first?
(He blessed Joseph's sons, Ephraim and Manasseh.)

6. What was the special blessing Jacob gave to Judah?
(He told him that the scepter and ruler's staff would never depart from his descendants, and he would rule over all people.)

7. Why does this blessing make sense in light of Judah's descendants?
(Jesus was a descendant of Judah. His reign will never end.)

8. Where did Jacob ask to be buried?
(He wanted to be buried in the land of Canaan, where his parents, grandparents, and wife had been buried.)

Applying God's Word

1. How did Joseph show his love for his family?
(He wept over his brothers and his father. He forgave his brothers, even after they betrayed him. He blessed his whole family with gifts and the best land in Egypt.)

What are some specific ways you can show love to your family?
(Answers will vary.)

2. Read Romans 8:28. What things seemed evil in Joseph's life?
(He was betrayed by his family, enslaved, falsely accused, and imprisoned.)

How did God work for good in all things?
(Through all that happened, God placed Joseph in a position to save Egypt, his family, and the surrounding world.)

3. Although Ephraim and Manasseh were born in Egypt to an Egyptian mother, they were blessed by Jacob and adopted in as full children of Israel. How has God adopted you?
(We're naturally children of sin and enemies of God. In Baptism, God has adopted us into His family and blessed us. Just as Ephraim and Manasseh's descendants lived and served God's purposes, God uses us, as baptized children, to bless the world.)

19

The Birth of Moses (Exodus 1–2)

Reviewing God's Word

Fill in the blanks.

1. The more the people of Israel were **oppressed**, the more they multiplied.
2. The king of Egypt told the midwives, "When you serve as midwife to the Hebrew women, if it is a son, you shall **kill** him."
3. When Moses' mother could hide him no longer, she made a **basket** of bulrushes.
4. Moses' **sister** stood at a distance to know what would be done to him.
5. Pharaoh's daughter took **pity** on baby Moses and said, "This is one of the Hebrews' children."
6. Pharaoh's daughter asked Moses' mother to **nurse** baby Moses for her.
7. When Moses had grown up, he saw an **Egyptian** beating a Hebrew, one of his people.
8. But Moses fled from Pharaoh and stayed in the land of **Midian**.

Thinking about God's Word

1. How did the Lord bless the family of Israel in Egypt?
   (They grew to a large number.)

   Why didn't the new pharaoh like this?
   (He feared their strength and worried that they might become too powerful.)

2. How did Pharaoh try to stop the growth of the Israelites?
   (He made them slaves and told the midwives to kill any sons born to the Hebrews.)

3. How do you explain the fact that "the more they were oppressed, the more they multiplied"?
   (In the midst of their trouble, God still blessed them.)

   Of which blessing of God to Abraham does this remind you? **(God promised that Abraham's descendants would be as numerous as the stars in the sky.)**

4. Think of two good reasons why the Levite woman did not drown her son. **(She followed God; she loved her son.)**

   Why did she not keep him at home longer?
   (She was unable to hide him anymore.)

5. How were the mother and daughter wise in placing Moses in the rushes?
   (The mother saw an opportunity for the baby to be saved. The daughter saw an opportunity for the baby to be returned to his mother.)

   What did God have to do with their wisdom?
   (God is the source of wisdom, and He blessed their wise thinking.)

6. Why did the princess keep the baby she found?
   (He was crying, and she felt sorry for him.)

7. Who gave Moses his name?
   (Pharaoh's daughter)

   Why did she name him Moses?
   (She named him Moses because she drew him out of the water. Moses sounds like the Hebrew word for "draw out.")

8. What evidence does this story provide to indicate that Moses identified himself with the people of God rather than with the Egyptians?
   (Moses defended the rights of the Hebrew who was being beaten by the Egyptian.)

Applying God's Word

1. How does this account show that God is more powerful than human rulers?
   (When Pharaoh tried to enslave and oppress the Israelites, they grew in number. When Pharaoh tried to kill all the Hebrew boys, the midwives refused to follow his orders. When Pharaoh tried to wipe out the Israelites, God used Pharaoh's own daughter to raise a leader for His people. God is greater than any human ruler, and He uses even unbelieving rulers to accomplish His purposes.)

2. Why might it have been hard for Moses to identify with the people of God?
   (Moses had been raised in the palace in wealth and comfort. The Hebrews were oppressed slaves.)

   Is it ever easier for you to identify with other people who seem to have it all rather than with God's people?
   (Answers will vary.)

3. Compare the birth of Jesus and the birth of Moses. **(Both were born to people in bondage; Moses' parents were slaves in Egypt, and Jesus' mother shared humanity's bondage to sin. Both births were accompanied by the slaughter of children. Both stories involve the land of Egypt: Moses was born in Egypt; Jesus and His parents escaped to Egypt. Other comparisons may be offered.)**

20

God Calls Moses
(Exodus 2–4)

Reviewing God's Word

Underline the word or phrase that answers each question.

1. What did the people of Israel do because of their slavery? (Sulked—Cried out for help—Refused to work—Turned their backs on God)
2. What did God tell Moses to do in His presence? (Fall to the ground—Perform ceremonial washing—Take off his sandals—Be silent)
3. What else did Moses do to show that he feared God? (Hid his face—Ran away—Trembled with fear—Refused to speak)
4. What did God promise would be in the Promised Land? (Green pastures—Flowing water—Rich farmland—Milk and honey)
5. What did the people do when Aaron spoke to them? (Wept—Laughed—Believed and worshiped—Rebelled against Egypt)

Thinking about God's Word

1. Why did God appear to Moses?
(He heard the groaning of the Israelites in slavery and remembered His promises to Abraham, Isaac, and Jacob.)

2. How did the Lord appear to Moses?
(The angel of the Lord appeared to Moses in a burning bush—a bush that was on fire but never burned up.)

3. Why did the Lord call the Hebrews "My people"?
(They are His chosen people, the descendants of Abraham, Isaac, and Jacob.)

Why did the Lord want to help His people?
(God had promised to bless them and give them the Promised Land.)

4. What name for Himself did God give Moses to tell to the people?
(I AM)

5. What signs did God give Moses?
(Moses' staff could turn into a snake and then back into a staff. God gave Moses leprosy and then immediately cured him.)

6. What was Moses' excuse for why he couldn't go?
(Moses said he was slow of speech and tongue.)

7. What did God promise in response to Moses' excuse?
(God said, "I will teach you what you shall speak.")

8. How did the Lord patiently answer Moses when he pleaded with Him to send someone else?
(God gave Moses his brother Aaron to speak for him.)

Applying God's Word

1. Why was Moses hesitant to go to Pharaoh to free the Israelites?
(He said, "I am slow of speech and tongue.")

Do you ever feel unqualified to do what God has called you to do?
(Answers will vary.)

What comfort can you find in God's dealings with Moses?
(God promises to be with us, give us the abilities we need, and send other Christians to help us do His will.)

2. God told Moses to tell the people that "I AM" had sent him. Who else used the phrase "I am" to describe Himself? See John 8:58, as well as numerous other passages in John's Gospel.
(Jesus declared Himself to be "I am.")

Why is this important?
(Jesus is true God with the Father. He is one with the God of Abraham, Isaac, and Jacob, who appeared to Moses in the burning bush.)

3. Who are the leaders of God's people today?
(Pastors, teachers, DCEs, deaconesses, and other church workers, including lay leaders, all lead God's people.)

How are they like Moses? **(They, too, have been called by God and equipped by Him for the work they do.)**

21

Moses and the Plagues
(Exodus 5–10)

Reviewing God's Word

God used the plagues to show the Egyptians that He alone was God. Many of the plagues even corresponded to specific Egyptian gods or values that the real God displayed His power over.

Draw lines to match these plagues to the Egyptian god or value they were directed against.

1. Nile turned to blood	Flies and beetles honored in worship
2. Frogs	Herds and flocks symbolized wealth
3. Flies	Hapi (Nile god and giver of life)
4. Death of livestock	Crops meant food and income
5. Boils	Ra (Egyptian sun god)
6. Hail	Pride in personal health and strength
7. Darkness	Heqt (Frog goddess of childbirth)

Thinking about God's Word

1. How did Moses and Aaron let Pharaoh know that they were sent by God?
(They told him, "Thus says the Lord, 'Let My people go.'")

2. How did Pharaoh respond?
(He refused to let the Israelites go and made them work even harder.)

3. How did the magicians do some of the signs Moses did?
(They used secret arts and may have used sorcery or trickery, but they couldn't repeat most of the plagues. Their trickery was no match for God's power!)

4. Why did God say He would harden Pharaoh's heart and bring plagues on Egypt? **(His purpose was to make the Egyptians know that He was God.)**

5. Whom did the later plagues affect?
(Only Egypt was affected. The Israelites and the land where they lived were untouched by the worst of the plagues.)

6. How did Pharaoh respond to the plague of darkness?
(He told Moses to leave and warned him that he never wanted to see his face again.)

Applying God's Word

1. God sent the miraculous plagues to prove to the Egyptians that He was God. How is this like Jesus' miracles? See John 20:30–31.
(Jesus did miracles—and the disciples wrote them down—so that we would know that He is God and would believe in Him.)

2. God struck down all of the Egyptians' sources of life: water from the Nile, food from livestock, and even light from the sun. What was He proving?
(God alone grants life. God gives us all we need to have and sustain life.)

How does God move us to respond to His blessings?
(We respond with joy and thanksgiving to God for all that He has given to us. We can rejoice that God in His mercy graciously blesses us with all we need to live.)

3. In the ninth plague, God sent darkness over all of Egypt. What do darkness and light often represent in the Bible? See John 8:12.
(Darkness represents life without God. Without faith, we are lost and confused in the darkness of our sin. Jesus is the light of the world. Because we have faith in God, we can live in the light of His wisdom and grace.)

22

The Passover
(Exodus 11–13)

Reviewing God's Word

Draw a line through the statements that were NOT part of God's instructions for the Passover.

1. Take a lamb for each household.
2. ~~Each lamb should be two years old.~~
3. ~~The Passover lamb must be a female.~~
4. Kill the lamb at twilight.
5. Spread blood on the doorposts and lintels.
6. Eat the lamb with unleavened bread and bitter herbs.
7. ~~Save some of the meat for the journey.~~
8. ~~Savor every bite of the special meal.~~
9. Eat with your belt fastened and sandals on your feet.

Thinking about God's Word

1. What was the last plague God sent?
(All the firstborn children and cattle of Egypt died.)

2. What would keep death from coming over the firstborn of the children of Israel?
(The lambs' blood on the doorframes of their houses would cause the LORD to pass over their homes.)
LORD

3. What did God want to show by this plague?
(He was showing the difference between the Israelites, who were His children, and the Egyptians, who didn't believe in Him.)

4. How was the final plague a devastating blow to the Egyptians?
(The firstborn sons were to receive their families' inheritances. They symbolized the power and future of Egypt. God had declared once and for all that He was all powerful.)

5. How were the Israelites supposed to celebrate the Passover festival in the future?
(They were to repeat the meal they ate during the first Passover.)

6. Why were the Israelites supposed to celebrate the Passover every year?
(The Passover was a chance to remember how God had delivered the Israelites and to pass on the story to their children.)

7. How did God lead His people out of Egypt?
(He went before them in a pillar of cloud during the day and a pillar of fire at night.)

Applying God's Word

1. Who is our Passover lamb?
(Jesus)

How did He become a Passover lamb for us? See 1 Corinthians 5:7.
(He shed His blood for us on the cross. Just as the lambs' blood on the doorposts saved the Israelites from death, Jesus' blood saves us from death and gives us everlasting life.)

2. What celebratory meal did Jesus institute while He was sharing the Passover with His disciples? See Luke 22:7–20.
(During the Passover meal, Jesus instituted Communion. He is the Lamb of God. The Israelites ate the lamb they had sacrificed and covered their doors with the blood. In Communion, people eat bread and drink wine and receive the body and blood of Chrit in a mysterious way. This fulfillment of the Passover meal is not just a remembrance of things past but a present reality of God's presence in, with, and under the bread and wine.)

3. How did the children of Israel show that they believed the Lord?
(They did what the Lord commanded.)

How do we show that we believe in God? See 1 John 5:3–4.
(Our faith shows itself in our love for others and our obedience to God's commands. God's love is so strong and powerful that it gives us the desire to obey God's commands and the ability to do so. Commandments are no longer a burden but a joyful response of faith!)

23

Crossing the Red Sea (Exodus 14–15)

Reviewing God's Word

Write the name of the speaker next to each quote.

1. "What is this we have done, that we have let Israel go from serving us?" **Pharaoh**
2. "Fear not. Stand firm. See the salvation of the LORD." **Moses**
3. "Stretch out your hand over the sea, that the water may come back." **God**
4. "What have you done to us in bringing us out of Egypt?" **Israelites**
5. "Let us flee from before Israel, for the LORD fights for them." **Egyptians**
6. "I will sing to the LORD, for He has triumphed gloriously." **Moses/Israel**

God	Moses	Egyptians
Israelites	Pharaoh	Moses/Israel

Thinking about God's Word

1. Why did Pharaoh want the Israelites back?
(He realized he was suddenly without a valuable labor force.)

2. What did Moses say to reassure the people when they saw the Egyptians chasing them?
("Fear not. Stand firm. See the salvation of the LORD, which He will work for you today. The LORD will fight for you.")

3. What miracle did God perform through Moses to enable the people to cross the Red Sea?
(The waters divided, and the people went through the sea on dry land.)

4. How did God bring chaos to the Egyptian army?
(He used the pillar of cloud and the pillar of fire, which had guided Israel, to create panic in the Egyptian army.)

5. What do you suppose the Egyptians thought when they rushed into the Red Sea after the children of Israel?
(They thought they could pass through the same way.)

6. How did the Lord finally punish proud Pharaoh and his army in which he trusted?
(The waters covered them, and they drowned.)

7. How did the Israelites thank God for His wonderful deliverance?
(They sang to the Lord.)

Applying God's Word

1. God came to His people Israel in a pillar of cloud and in a pillar of fire. How does God come to His people today? What visible signs of His presence does He give us?
(God comes to His people today through the Means of Grace—the Word and the Sacraments. In Baptism and Holy Communion, God uses water, bread, and wine to give us visible signs of His presence among us.)

2. God rescued His people from captivity in Egypt. From what forms of captivity has God rescued us?
(Jesus said that "everyone who practices sin is a slave to sin" [John 8:34]. Without faith, we are held captive by our sinful nature and the devil's power. Our slavery to sin, death, and the devil leaves us unable to live fully, have a relationship with God, or act in a God-pleasing manner. In Christ Jesus' death and resurrection, God set us free from this bondage. As Jesus said, "If the Son sets you free, you will be free indeed" [John 8:36].)

3. Moses and the Israelites responded to God's deliverance with a song of praise to God. What are some great things God has done in your life that you can praise Him for?
(Answers will vary.)

24

God Provides Manna and Quail

(Exodus 16)

Reviewing God's Word

Draw a line through the sentences that are not true.

1. The Israelites were so hungry that they wished they had died in Egypt.
2. ~~Moses provided food for the people.~~
3. ~~God ignored the people because they were complaining too much.~~
4. God provided manna to show the Israelites that He was the LORD.
5. The Israelites were not supposed to have any manna left over each day.
6. ~~All the people followed God's instructions.~~
7. God gave special instructions for the seventh day.
8. God provided manna for the people every day until they reached the Promised Land.

Thinking about God's Word

1. Why did the Israelites grumble?
(They had no food, and they were afraid they were going to die in the wilderness.)

2. How did the Lord promise to feed them?
(He said He would send meat at night and bread in the morning.)

How did He keep His promise?
(Quail covered the camp that night, and flakes of bread appeared like frost on the ground the next morning.)

3. What instructions did God give the people about the manna?
(They were to collect only enough for one day and eat it before the end of the day.)

4. Why was Moses angry with the Israelites?
(Some of them didn't listen and left some of the manna until morning. In the morning, the manna they had left was filled with worms and stank.)

5. What were God's special instructions about the Sabbath Day?
(The Israelites were not supposed to gather manna on the seventh day because it was a holy day to the Lord. The manna from the sixth day would keep until the seventh.)

Applying God's Word

1. God gave His people Israel special food from heaven. What special meal has God given us?
(Jesus called Himself the bread of life [John 6:35].) In Communion, we receive Jesus' very body and blood, together with bread and wine, for the forgiveness of sins, new life, and salvation.)

2. Why do you think God let the people collect only enough manna for one day? What could we learn from this?
(God was teaching the Israelites to trust Him. He wanted them to believe that every day He would provide for them exactly what they needed. We can also trust God for "daily bread," as we pray in the Lord's Prayer. God will never skip a day or forget to provide for us. We can trust Him to be present each and every day and to provide everything we need for this life.)

3. God commanded the Israelites to rest on the Sabbath and not collect manna that day. How do we honor the Sabbath today?
(We honor the Sabbath by going to church, listening to the Word being preached, reading God's Word, praying, and worshiping God. Jesus is the fulfillment of the Sabbath, and we find our full and complete Sabbath rest in Him.)

25

God Gives the Law

(Exodus 19–20)

Reviewing God's Word

Fill in the blanks.

1. The Lord called to Moses out of the **mountain**.
2. God said, "If you will keep My **covenant**, you shall be My treasured possession."
3. Then the Lord told Moses, "Go to the people and **consecrate** them."
4. All the people in the camp **trembled**.
5. "I am the **LORD** your God, who brought you out of the land of Egypt."
6. "I am a **jealous** God."
7. In six days, the Lord made heaven and earth and rested on the **seventh** day.

Thinking about God's Word

1. What did God promise to the Israelites if they kept his covenant?
   (He would make them His treasured possession, a kingdom of priests, and a holy nation.)

2. With what signs did God show the people that He had something very serious and important to tell them?
   (He came with thunder, lightning, trumpet blasts, a thick cloud, and fire.)

3. Where did God take Moses to have him receive the Law?
   (He went up on the mountain, Mount Sinai.)

4. Of what did God remind the Israelites before He gave the Ten Commandments?
   (He reminded them that He had delivered them from slavery in Egypt.)

5. What is the focus of the first three commandments?
   (They focus on our relationship with God.)

6. What is the focus of the last seven commandments?
   (They focus on our relationship with other people.)

7. Which commandment comes with a promise, and what is that promise?
   (With the Fourth Commandment—honor your father and your mother—God includes this promise: "that your days may be long in the land that the LORD your God is giving you.")

Applying God's Word

1. Are there any of the commandments that you haven't broken? See James 2:10.
   (No, we have broken all of God's Law, every single commandment. Jesus said that being angry at your brother in your heart makes you a murderer [Matthew 5:20–21]. Even sinful thoughts and desires are sin in God's eyes. Every one of us has broken God's commandments and fallen short of His perfect standard.)

2. God told the Israelites that if they kept His covenant they would be His "treasured possession . . . a kingdom of priests and a holy nation." Our sin has broken our relationship with God. But 1 Peter 1:9 says, "You are a chosen race, a royal priesthood, a holy nation, a people for His own possession." How is this possible?
   (We fail to keep God's Law. But God sent His Son, Jesus, to keep the Law perfectly for us. Because Jesus fulfilled the Law and sacrificed Himself to pay the punishment for our sins, we are holy and chosen before God. Jesus followed all the commandments, and Jesus restored our relationship with God. Praise be to God!)

3. Before giving the commandments, God said, "I am the LORD your God, who brought you out of the land of Egypt." How might God address us in light of our salvation in Christ? "I am the Lord your God, who . . ."
   (Answers may vary. One possibility: I am the Lord your God, who brought you out of the land of sin and darkness into the light of salvation.)

26

God's Covenant with the Israelites (Exodus 32–34; 40)

Reviewing God's Word

Draw lines to match each word to its definition.

1. Consume	Beg or plead
2. Implore	Movable tent of worship
3. Relent	Stubborn
4. Stiff-necked	Formal, binding agreement
5. Pardon	Destroy
6. Covenant	Decide not to punish
7. Tabernacle	Forgive or excuse

Thinking about God's Word

1. Why did the children of Israel become impatient with Moses?
   (He was delayed coming down from the mountain. In fact, he was gone for forty days and nights [Exodus 24:18]!)

2. What did the people start to worship instead of God?
   (They had Aaron make a golden calf, and they worshiped and offered sacrifices to it.)

3. What did God say to Moses when He saw the people worshiping an idol?
   ("Your people have turned aside out of the way that I commanded them.")

   What had God always called these people before?
   ("My people")

4. What did God threaten to do?
   (He threatened to consume the people in His anger.)

5. What did God do when Moses begged Him to relent?
   (He showed mercy on Israel.)

6. How did the people reply when God said He wouldn't go with them into the Promised Land?
   (They mourned.)

   How did Moses reply? **(He pleaded with God to show him His ways.)**

7. What part of God was Moses allowed to see?
   (God let Moses see His back, a glimpse of His glory but not the full expression of His majesty.)

8. What did God in His goodness say when He passed by Moses?
   ("The LORD, the LORD, a God merciful and gracious, slow to anger, and abounding in steadfast love and faithfulness.")

9. How was Moses' appearance changed when he came down from the mountain?
   (His face shone with the glory of the Lord.)

10. How did God show that He had forgiven Israel and still claimed them as His people?
    (He filled the tabernacle with His presence in a cloud of glory by day and fire by night.)

Applying God's Word

1. We often imitate the idolatry of our culture like the Israelites imitated the pagan culture around them. What gods do we make for ourselves?
   (Answers will vary. We are committing idolatry when we make people, money, power, recognition, material possessions, popularity, or anything else more important in our lives than God.)

2. Moses served as an intercessor between the people and God, pleading for their forgiveness. Who pleads before God in our defense?
   (Moses was a forerunner of Christ who served God's people faithfully, but he could never make full atonement for sin. Jesus is our perfect intercessor. He took all of our sins upon Himself, and He still speaks to God the Father on our behalf [1 John 2:1].)

3. God told Moses that man could not see Him without dying, and so He appeared to the people in various forms, including His "goodness," a cloud, and fire. What form did God take on when He came to earth to live?
   (God came in human form when Jesus took on flesh to live, die, and rise again. He veiled His glory so that He could interact with mankind.)

   How does God come to us now?
   (God comes to His people today in the Word and in the water, bread, and wine of the Sacraments.)

27

The Twelve Spies (Numbers 13–14)

Reviewing God's Word

Underline the word or phrase that answers each question.

1. After how many days did the explorers return from Canaan? (25—30—40—50)
2. Which words show that the land was a good land? (grasshoppers—milk and honey—strongholds—camps)
3. Where did the people of Israel want to go? (Canaan—Egypt—wilderness—Cush)
4. What did Joshua and Caleb do in response to the people? (tore their clothes—gave in to the people—set out on their own—wept and moaned)
5. Who of the older Israelites would be allowed to enter Canaan? (Moses and Miriam—Joshua and Caleb—Aaron and Judah—Cain and Abel)
6. For how many years would the Israelites be punished for their sin? (25—75—50—40)

Thinking about God's Word

1. Why did God command Moses to send men into the land before the children of Israel went in?
(They went to see what the land and its people were like.)

2. When they returned, what did the explorers report to Moses?
(The land flowed with milk and honey, and there was good fruit in the land.)

Why didn't they think the new land could be taken?
Powerful people lived there, and the cities were strong and fortified. The people were so large that the explorers said they felt like grasshoppers next to them.)

3. How did the Israelites respond?
(They said, "Our wives and our little ones will become a prey. Would it not be better for us to go back to Egypt?")

4. How did they again show their lack of trust in God?
(They were afraid and didn't believe that with God's strength they could overcome the Canaanites.)

5. What did Joshua and Caleb tell the people?
(They assured the people that the Lord was with them, so they had no reason to be afraid. They said that if God was pleased with them He would give them the land He had promised.)

6. After Moses pleaded with God not to disinherit the people, what did God say would be the punishment for their sin?
(God said that the Israelites would have to wander for forty years in the wilderness and that only Caleb, Joshua, and the children would enter the Promised Land.)

Applying God's Word

1. The spies reported all sorts of reasons why they couldn't enter Canaan: the cities were large and fortified, the people were strong, the people were huge. What things in your life do you feel are too big or too difficult for you to handle?
(Answers will vary.)

2. Describe Joshua and Caleb in the face of what many would consider an overwhelming obstacle.
(Joshua and Caleb trusted in God's ability to bring them victory over the mighty inhabitants of the land.)

What confidence can you have in the face of overwhelming obstacles in your life?
(God is powerful and promises to be with us. There is nothing God cannot do, and nothing we face in life is too overwhelming or too difficult for God Himself.)

3. How would the forty years in the wilderness remind the people of their sin? What knowledge of God's grace did the people possess during their forty years of wandering?
(The forty years in the wilderness would remind the people of the forty days the spies spent in the Promised Land and of their failure to trust God. During their sojourn in the wilderness, the people of God could be confident that, together with Joshua and Caleb, the younger generation would enter Canaan.)

28

Water from a Rock and Fiery Serpents (Numbers 20–21)

Reviewing God's Word

Circle Yes or No for each statement.

1. The people of Israel grumbled against Moses, again.	(YES)	NO
2. Moses and Aaron brought their concern before the Lord.	(YES)	NO
3. God told Moses to strike the rock and bring forth water.	YES	(NO)
4. Moses followed God's instructions.	YES	(NO)
5. God gave the people water from the rock.	(YES)	NO
6. Moses and Aaron entered the Promised Land.	YES	(NO)
7. The people of Israel had no food to eat.	YES	(NO)
8. The people complained about the manna God had provided.	(YES)	NO
9. God sent fiery serpents to punish the people.	(YES)	NO
10. The people were saved from death by eating a special herb.	YES	(NO)

Thinking about God's Word

1. How did Moses and Aaron respond to the people's grumbling?
(They fell on their faces before the Lord and brought their need to Him.)

2. What were God's instructions to Moses and Aaron about getting water for the people?
(He told them to tell the rock to give up its water.)

3. What did Moses add to God's command?
(In addition to speaking to the rock, he struck the rock with his staff.)

4. Whom did Moses say would bring water from the rock?
(Moses said, "Shall we bring water for you out of this rock?" Moses and Aaron took credit for providing for the people rather than giving God glory.)

5. Why was God upset with Moses and Aaron?
(Rather than trusting God and believing that His exact instructions would be enough, they added to God's command. They wanted to claim credit for themselves.)

6. How did God punish the people for complaining again about food and water?
(God sent poisonous serpents. When the serpents bit the people, they died.)

7. When Moses prayed for the people, how did God save the people from the serpents?
(God told Moses to make a bronze serpent and put it on a pole. Everyone who looked at the serpent after being bit would live.)

Applying God's Word

1. How do we sometimes act like the Israelites? **(God has graciously provided for us all we need, but still we grumble and complain about what we don't have.)**

2. Who appeared as a serpent in the Garden of Eden in Genesis 3?
(Satan.)

How is he like the serpents in the wilderness?
(The serpents brought poison and death to the people of Israel. Satan brought sin and death to the whole world.)

3. The people of Israel were saved by a bronze snake that looked exactly like the serpents. How does this remind you of Jesus?
(Jesus became a human being and carried all our sins when He was lifted up on the cross. By looking with faith to Jesus' cross and empty tomb, we are saved from the poison of our sins.)

29

The Death of Moses (Deuteronomy 18; 31; 34)

Reviewing God's Word

Underline the word or phrase that makes each sentence true.

1. Moses told the people that the practices of the Canaanite nations were (admirable—strange—abominable—God-pleasing).
2. God said the role of a prophet was to (make decisions—settle disputes—speak God's words—organize sacrifices).
3. (Caleb—Aaron—Joshua—Moses) was chosen by God to lead the children of Israel into Canaan.
4. It was up to (Joshua—God—the male warriors—the Israelites) to defeat the nations of Canaan.
5. God appeared to Moses and Joshua in the form of a(n) (pillar of cloud—angel—blazing fire—whirlwind).
6. (Joshua—The children of Israel—The LORD—Aaron) buried Moses.

Thinking about God's Word

1. What instruction did Moses give the people for their time in Canaan?
(They were not to follow the abominable religious practices of the nations of Canaan.)

2. Whom did Moses promise that God would send?
(Moses said God would send a prophet like him from among the people of Israel to speak God's Word.)

3. What reasons did Moses give Joshua and the people for being "strong and courageous" as they entered the land?
(God had promised them that the land of Canaan would be theirs. He would go before them, and He would defeat the enemy nations.)

4. How did the Lord show that Joshua was the leader He had chosen for His people?
(He appeared in the tent of meeting in a pillar of cloud to bless and encourage Joshua.)

5. What did the Lord show Moses from Mount Nebo before the prophet died?
(He showed him the whole Promised Land.)

6. Why did the Lord not permit His servant Moses to go into the Promised Land? See Numbers 20:7–12.
(Moses disobeyed God by striking a rock rather than speaking to it, as God commanded. He tried to take credit for the miracle rather than giving God glory.)

7. How did Joshua receive the spirit of wisdom?
(Moses commissioned Joshua, and God blessed Joshua with wisdom.)

Applying God's Word

1. Moses warned the people not to follow the ways of the unbelieving Canaanite people. What practices of unbelievers around us might be tempting to follow but displeasing to God?
(Answers will vary.)

2. What reason did Moses and God give for Joshua to be strong and courageous?
(They both told him to be courageous because the LORD would be with him.)

How is this different from what the world says about courage?
(The world says to look inside you to find courage. We often honor courageous people but forget to give glory to God. You don't have to try to summon up courage on your own. We can be courageous because the all-powerful God of the universe is with us and fighting for us!)

3. Moses served as the leader of God's people for over forty years before he died. The Bible even says that no other prophet knew God face-to-face as Moses did. What comfort can we find in the fact that the Israelite nation still prospered after the death of Moses?
(God is the true leader of His Church. The Church is bigger and stronger than any one leader. God uses many faithful individuals to lead His people, but He will always raise up new leaders when they are needed. Our hope is in God—not men.)

30

Rahab Hides the Spies
(Joshua 1–2)

Reviewing God's Word

Write the name of the speaker next to each quote. Names may be used more than once.

1. "This Book of the Law shall not depart from your mouth." **God**
2. "When the LORD gives us the land we will deal kindly and faithfully with you." **The spies**
3. "Bring the men who have come to you. They have come to search out all the land." **The king of Jericho**
4. "The LORD your God, He is God in the heavens above and on the earth beneath." **Rahab**
5. "Do not be frightened. Do not be dismayed." **God**
6. "Truly the LORD has given all the land into our hands." **The spies**
7. "View the land, especially Jericho." **Joshua**
8. "I know that the LORD has given you the land." **Rahab**

Joshua	God
The king of Jericho	The spies
Rahab	

Thinking about God's Word

1. What instructions did God give to Joshua?
   ("This Book of the Law shall not depart from your mouth, but you shall meditate on it day and night. Be careful to do according to all that is written in it. Be strong and courageous. Do not be frightened. Do not be dismayed.")

2. Why did Joshua send out two men?
   (He sent them as spies to examine the land [especially Jericho] so that the Israelites would be prepared to enter.)

3. How did Rahab protect the spies?
   (She hid them on the roof and told the king of Jericho that they had left the city and he should pursue them. Then she helped the men escape through the window with a rope.)

4. How did Rahab show great faith?
   (She believed that the LORD had delivered the people of Israel from Egypt and that He was the God of heaven and earth.)

5. Why were Rahab's actions so amazing?
   (Rahab was a Canaanite, not one of God's chosen people. She believed simply because she heard how the Lord had delivered the Israelites from Egypt. God wants all people to be saved [1 Timothy 2:3–4], and so He worked faith in Rahab's heart and used her to protect the spies and bring victory to the Israelites.)

6. What did Rahab ask for in exchange for protecting the spies?
   (She asked them to spare her and her family when the Israelites captured the city of Jericho.)

7. How did the spies ask Rahab to identify her house?
   (They told her to tie a scarlet cord in her window.)

Applying God's Word

1. How did God equip Joshua to lead Israel?
   (He gave him the Book of the Law and told him to meditate on it and follow its instruction.)

   How does God lead and equip us today?
   (God uses His Word to strengthen, encourage, and instruct us too. God works in us when we read the Bible and let it guide our words and actions so they are pleasing to Him.)

2. How does the color of Rahab's cord remind you of how we have been saved?
   (Rahab tied a red cord to her window so that the lives of her and her family would be spared in the conquest of Jericho. We are saved by the red blood of Jesus Christ, who gave His life to save us from sin, death, and hell.)

3. Rahab believed in the Lord because she heard how He delivered the Israelites from the Egyptians. What does this mean about how we witness about God?
   (To witness is literally to tell what we have seen or experienced. We can witness to others just by telling them what God has done in our lives or the lives of others. It is God who creates faith, but we have the opportunity to plant seeds by sharing stories of God's grace and mercy.)

31

Israel Enters the Promised Land (Joshua 3–5)

Reviewing God's Word

God often used memorial markers or festivals as signs for people to remember His action in their lives and to teach their children about the Lord.

Draw lines to match each memorial with the event it commemorates. (See previous stories for hints.)

Memorial	Event
1. 12 stones at Gilgal	God's promise to never again destroy the world by flood
2. Rainbows	God preserving the firstborn children of Israel
3. Stone pillar at Bethel	Jesus' death for the salvation of all people
4. Passover meal	God's appearance to Jacob in a dream
5. Crosses	The parting of the Jordan River

Thinking about God's Word

1. When the people were ready to cross the Jordan River and enter the Promised Land, who went first?
   (The priests led the people across.)

   What were the priests carrying?
   (They were carrying the ark of the covenant.)

2. What did the ark of the covenant show the Israelites?
   (It showed the people God's presence.)

3. How was it possible for the Israelites to pass through the Jordan River on dry ground?
   (God miraculously caused the waters to part and the ground beneath the river to become dry.)

4. Of what event from earlier in the history of Israel does this crossing remind you?
   (God parted the Red Sea in a similar fashion to allow the people to cross on dry ground.)

5. Why did the time of year make the parting of the Jordan River especially miraculous?
   (It was during the harvest, when the river was always very high and overflowing its banks.)

6. When did the waters of the Jordan flow as before?
   (The water began to flow naturally again when the priests left the river.)

7. What did Joshua do to commemorate the Israelites' entrance into the Promised Land?
   (He had men set up twelve stones—one per tribe—to mark where they had crossed the Jordan River.)

8. Why did the manna stop falling from heaven?
   (The people could now eat the produce of Canaan.)

9. Who appeared to Joshua near Jericho?
   (The commander of the army of the Lord)

Applying God's Word

1. Joshua told the people to consecrate themselves because the Lord would do wonders among them. How are we made holy and set apart for God's use?
   (Through His sacrificial death, Christ took our sin upon Himself and gave us His righteousness. In Baptism, God grants us Jesus' righteousness in this great exchange. We are now new creations, holy and set apart for service in God's kingdom!)

2. What parts of your church, like the stones in this account, help you remember what God has done for you?
   (Answers will vary.)

3. The stones also served to teach the children about God's deliverance. How would you respond if someone asked you, "What does this cross mean?"
   (Jesus died for our sins on the cross, taking the punishment we deserve. He rose from the dead, and we believe that because of Him we, too, will rise from the dead and live with God forever in heaven.)

32

The Fall of Jericho (Joshua 6; 24)

Reviewing God's Word

Fill in the blanks.

1. "On the seventh day you shall march around the city **seven** times."
2. "Shout, for the LORD has **given** you the city."
3. The spies brought out **Rahab** and all who belonged to her.
4. So **the Lord** was with Joshua, and his fame was in all the land.
5. "Fear the LORD. Serve Him in **sincerity** and in faithfulness."
6. "Choose this day whom you will **serve**."
7. "It is the LORD our God who brought us and our fathers up from the land of **Egypt**."

Thinking about God's Word

1. What was the first thing God said to Joshua as the Israelites approached Jericho?
("I have given Jericho into your hand.")

2. How could God say this was already done when the walls hadn't fallen yet?
(God was in control all along. The victory was already won.)

3. How did the children of Israel show their faith in God's plan to take Jericho?
(They did exactly as God commanded.)

4. What happened after the seventh day of marching when the people shouted and blew trumpets?
(The walls fell down, and the people captured the city.)

5. Why did Joshua tell the people to shout? **(They shouted because God had given them the victory.)**

6. Why did God have the people walk in circles around the city instead of using conventional military tactics?
(This plan made it clear to the Israelites and to the people of Jericho that it was God who had won the battle. Just marching and blowing trumpets couldn't knock down a city, but God's power could make even mighty Jericho crumble!)

7. How did the Israelite spies keep their promise to Rahab?
(They brought her and her family safely out of the city, and she lived with the Israelites for many years.)

8. Why did Joshua's fame spread throughout the land?
(It spread because the Lord was with him and gave him victories over the nations of Canaan.)

9. What choice did Joshua ask the people to make, and how did they respond?
(Joshua told the people they needed to choose whom they were going to serve with their lives. The people chose the LORD.)

Applying God's Word

1. God had won the victory for Israel before they even began marching. What victory has Christ already won for us?
(On the cross, Christ defeated sin, death, and the devil forever. [See 1 Corinthians 15:54–57.] Death has been swallowed up in victory, and Satan no longer has power over us. The victory is ours through Christ Jesus alone.)

2. Why was Rahab saved when God destroyed the city of Jericho?
(Rahab was delivered because she had hidden the messengers. She protected these spies because she believed the God of Israel was the true God.)

   How are we delivered from God's punishment for sin?
(The only way we can be saved from punishment and death is through faith in Jesus Christ, who took God's wrath upon Himself in order to deliver us.)

3. Joshua told the people of Israel they needed to choose whom they were going to serve. How does this apply to you as well, and how is this choice connected to the First Commandment?
(We all serve someone in the way that we use our time, talents, and possessions. The First Commandment says we must not have any gods before the LORD. By the power of the Holy Spirit, who has brought us to faith, we joyfully choose to serve the God who has brought us out of sin and darkness into His marvelous light!)

33

Deborah the Prophetess

(Judges 2; 4–5)

Reviewing God's Word

Write the name of the speaker next to each quote. Names may be used more than once or not at all.

1. "Has not the LORD, the God of Israel, commanded you?" **Deborah**
2. "Turn aside to me. Do not be afraid." **Jael**
3. "Hear, O kings. Give ear, O princes. To the LORD I will sing." **Deborah and Barak**
4. "If you [Deborah] will go with me, I will go." **Barak**
5. "Up! For this is the day in which the LORD has given Sisera into your hand." **Deborah**
6. "Please give me a little water to drink." **Sisera**
7. "I will make melody to the LORD, the God of Israel." **Deborah and Barak**

Jael	Joshua
Jabin	Sisera
Deborah	Deborah and Barak
Barak	

Thinking about God's Word

1. Why were the Israelites under the control of Jabin, king of Canaan?
   (The LORD gave them over to him because the people did not know God and didn't follow His commands.)

2. Who was the judge over Israel at this time?
   (Deborah the prophetess)

3. What had God already commanded Barak to do?
   (God had commanded him to take his men and fight Sisera and his troops.)

4. Why hadn't Barak followed God's command yet?
   (He was frightened and wanted Deborah to go with the army.)

5. What did Deborah tell Barak would be his punishment for not trusting God to be with him and deliver him?
   (Barak would not have the honor of killing the opposing commander, Sisera, but a woman would defeat Sisera instead.)

6. How did Israel win the battle?
   (The Israelites won because the LORD Himself defeated Sisera and his men.)

7. What did Sisera do to try to escape being killed?
   (He fled and hid in the tent of Jael.)

8. How did God bring to pass what Deborah had predicted?
   (While Sisera was sleeping in Jael's tent, Jael took a tent peg and drove it into Sisera's head. When Barak pursued Sisera, he found that the commander was already dead and had been killed by a woman, as Deborah had predicted.)

9. What did Deborah and Barak do after the victory?
   (They sang praise to God.)

Applying God's Word

1. The text says that the people of Israel didn't know the Lord and did what was evil in His sight. How are these two things related?
   (The Bible says that we cannot please God without faith [Hebrews 11:6]. We are by nature sinful, and so without knowing God, we naturally do evil. But, by God's grace, we have been given faith and the knowledge of God. This knowledge empowers us to do what is right in God's eyes!)

2. Barak was frightened and doubtful about God's promise to defeat Sisera. When have you felt a similar fear? What comfort can you find in this account?
   (Specific examples will vary. We, too, are often scared to do the things God asks of us. But we can be sure that the LORD goes with us and that God will give us the strength to do what He has asked of us. Every battle and every victory belong to God alone.)

3. How are the songs of praise we sing to God like the song of Barak and Deborah?
   (We, too, worship God with songs and hymns that remind us of what God has done for us and praise God for all His wondrous deeds.)

34

Gideon Defeats Midian (Judges 6–8)

Reviewing God's Word

Underline the word or phrase that answers each question.

1. Into whose hands did the Lord give Israel? (Philistia—Egypt—Ammon—Midian)
2. Who came to Gideon? (Deborah—The elders of Israel—The angel of the Lord—The king)
3. About what did Gideon ask the angel as evidence that God was present with Israel? (Wonderful deeds—The Lord Himself—An army of angels—A vision from God)
4. How many men were used by God to defeat the Midianites? (22,000—300—32,000—10,000)
5. When did Gideon and his men go to the camp of Midian? (Noon—Morning—Night—Afternoon)
6. Who caused the Midianites to turn on one another? (Gideon—The Israelite army—Midian—God)

Thinking about God's Word

1. How does the opening of this story remind you of the beginning of the story of Deborah the Prophetess?
(Once again, the Israelites began to do evil in God's sight, God gave them over to an enemy nation, and the people called out for deliverance.)

2. Why did Gideon have trouble believing that God was with Israel?
(Israel was under Midian's control, and it had been many years since the people had seen God do miracles among them.)

3. With what was Gideon clothed?
(He was clothed with the Spirit of the Lord.)

4. Why did the Lord reduce Gideon's army from 32,000 men to 300 men?
(The Lord wanted the Israelites to understand that they would defeat Midian not by their own size or strength but only by God's power.)

5. What tactic did Gideon's men use?
(They surrounded the camp in the middle of the night, blew their trumpets, broke jars to reveal torches, and let out a battle cry.)

6. How did the LORD give Israel victory?
(He caused the Midianites to panic so that they turned their swords on one another. Then they were easily pursued by Gideon and his men.)

7. In the words of their battle cry, how did Gideon's men show that they believed God would help them?
(They shouted, "A sword for the LORD and for Gideon!")

Applying God's Word

1. Gideon doubted God's presence because he hadn't seen the "wonderful deeds" he expected from God. What is the most wonderful deed that God has done to assure us completely of His presence among us? See Matthew 1:23.
(God put on human flesh to come to earth in the form of a man and work out our salvation. Jesus is Immanuel, which means "God with us." And as if this wasn't enough reassurance that God is with us, God still comes to us with His real presence of body and blood in the Lord's Supper. What more wonderful deeds could we ask for?)

2. Gideon was clothed with the Spirit of the LORD. With what were you clothed in your Baptism?
(In Baptism, we are clothed with Christ Jesus. Galatians 3:27 says, "For as many of you as were baptized into Christ have put on Christ.")

3. In the New Testament, 1 Corinthians 1:25 records, "For the foolishness of God is wiser than man's wisdom, and the weakness of God is stronger than men." How does this Old Testament account exemplify the truth of these New Testament words?
(God demonstrates His power through human weakness. The Israelites had a weak army of just a few men, and it seemed like a foolish strategy to send most of those men home. But through this seeming weakness and folly, God demonstrated His great wisdom and strength!)

35

God Makes Samson Strong (Judges 13; 15–16)

Reviewing God's Word

Fill in the blanks, using the words below. Some words will not be used.

1. Samson's work was to begin to save **Israel** from the Philistines.
2. The **Spirit** of the Lord gave Samson strength.
3. Samson fell in love with **Delilah**.
4. The **lords** of the Philistines told Delilah to find the secret of Samson's strength.
5. When Samson lost his **hair**, he lost his strength.
6. The Philistines sacrificed to **Dagon**.
7. Samson's **family** buried him.

Delilah	The Lord	Spirit
commanders	shirt	friends
Dagon	lords	Israel

Thinking about God's Word

1. Why did the Lord give Israel over to the Philistines?
   (Israel once again did evil in the eyes of the Lord.)

2. What message did the angel of the Lord bring to Manoah's wife?
   (She would have a son who would begin to save Israel from the Philistines. No razor could be used on his head.)

3. What miraculous thing did God empower Samson to do when the men of Judah bound him?
   (The ropes fell off him, and he struck down 1,000 Philistines with a donkey's jawbone.)

4. What did the Philistines want Delilah to find out for them about Samson?
   (They wanted to know the secret of Samson's great strength.)

5. What was the secret of his strength?
   (He had great strength as long as his hair was never cut.)

6. What did the Philistines do to Samson?
   (After his hair was cut, they seized him, gouged out his eyes, bound him, and put him in a work prison.)

7. How do you know the Philistines didn't worship the Lord?
   (They sacrificed to their god Dagon and gave him credit for allowing them to capture Samson.)

8. Who gave Samson the strength to bring down the house of the Philistines?
   (God gave him the power.)

Applying God's Word

1. What pattern are you noticing in these stories from Judges?
   (Over and over, the people of Israel fell away from God until He sent another judge to rescue them.)

   How is this like us?
   (Despite all that God has done in our lives, we continue to fall into sin and do what is evil in the sight of the Lord.)

2. How did the Philistines break the First Commandment? How did Samson break the First Commandment?
   (The Philistines worshiped the false god Dagon. Samson allowed his relationship with Delilah to interfere with his relationship with God.)

   What people or things are you tempted to put before God?
   (Answers will vary.)

3. Compare Samson with Jesus, the ultimate Deliverer.
   (Samson possessed amazing physical strength, yet he also demonstrated human weakness and sinfulness. Samson gave his life to defeat the Philistines. Jesus was the perfect, sinless Deliverer. He single-handedly defeated the enemies of sin, death, and the devil's power so that we might be saved.)

36

Ruth
(The Book of Ruth)

Reviewing God's Word

Circle Yes or No for each statement.

1. Naomi was from Moab.	YES	(NO)
2. Naomi wanted Orpah and Ruth to return to Judah with her.	YES	(NO)
3. Ruth insisted on going with Naomi.	(YES)	NO
4. Boaz was from Bethlehem.	(YES)	NO
5. Ruth stole from the field of Boaz.	YES	(NO)
6. Boaz praised Ruth for the way she had taken care of Naomi.	(YES)	NO
7. Boaz was a family redeemer who took care of Naomi and Ruth.	(YES)	NO
8. Ruth was an ancestor of King David.	(YES)	NO

Thinking about God's Word

1. Why did Elimelech and his family go to Moab?
(There was a famine in the land of Judah.)

2. Whom did Elimelech's sons marry?
(They married Moabite women—Ruth and Orpah.)

3. What happened to Naomi's family?
(Her husband died, and then her sons died.)

4. How does the narrative describe the end of the famine?
(The famine ended when the LORD gave His people food.)

5. How did Ruth answer when Naomi told her daughters-in-law to return to their own homes while she went back to Judah?
("Where you go I will go, and where you lodge I will lodge. Your people shall be my people, and your God my God.")

6. Why must it have been difficult for Ruth to go with Naomi?
(She left her homeland, her family, and her friends to be a foreigner in a strange land.)

7. How did Ruth provide for Naomi?
(She worked in the field of Boaz, gathering what had been left after the reaping. God's law required Israelites to leave the edges of their fields for the poor and for foreigners.)

8. What blessing did Boaz speak to Ruth?
(He prayed that God would reward her for her service to Naomi and her trust in God's protection.)

9. Why did Naomi send Ruth to Boaz?
(Boaz was a relative and a family redeemer who was legally responsible to buy the property of Naomi and Ruth and protect their inheritance since they were widows.)

10. What did Boaz do in addition to buying the land?
(He also married Ruth.)

Applying God's Word

1. How was Boaz like Christ?
(Boaz was a willing redeemer for Ruth and Naomi when they were poor and helpless. He returned their inheritance to them. We were poor and helpless in our sin, but Christ, our willing redeemer, bought us back. He restored to us an inheritance of eternal life in heaven. Just as Boaz married Ruth, Christ is the Husband of the Church, and He loves us perfectly.)

2. How did Ruth show through her actions the connection between faith and loving service toward others?
(Ruth declared that Naomi's God would be her God. She took refuge in the Lord. This faith led her to love and serve Naomi unselfishly. True faith results in genuine love for others. We love because God first loved us [1 John 4:19].)

3. Every single person we meet is someone for whom Christ died. Boaz went above and beyond the law to care for and provide for Ruth and Naomi. What can we learn from His example?
(We are called to love and care for our neighbors—especially those in need—with the same unselfish love God has shown to us.)

37

Hannah and Samuel
(1 Samuel 1–2)

Reviewing God's Word

Draw a line through the sentences that are not true.

1. Elkanah had a wife by the name of Hannah.
2. Peninnah was the wife of Elkanah.
3. ~~Peninnah had pity on Hannah.~~
4. Hannah made a vow to the Lord.
5. ~~Hannah was drunk when she prayed in the temple.~~
6. ~~Hannah named her son Eli.~~
7. Hannah kept her vow to the Lord.

Thinking about God's Word

Answer each question.

1. Why was Hannah so upset that she wept and didn't eat?
   (She had no children and desperately wanted a son.)

2. What did Hannah do about her problem?
   (She went to the temple and prayed to God for a son.)

3. What vow did Hannah make to the LORD?
   (She said that if God would give her a son, she would give him to the Lord.)

4. How did the LORD remember Hannah?
   (He gave her a son.)

5. How did Hannah keep her promise to the LORD?
   (She brought young Samuel to Eli so he could serve with him in God's house.)

6. How else did Hannah thank God for His gift of Samuel?
   (She prayed a song to the LORD, praising Him for all His goodness, mercy, and strength.)

Applying God's Word

1. Hannah describes her prayer as "pouring out [her] soul before the LORD." God wants us to tell Him about all our pain, excitement, worry, distress, and joy, and He promises to hear all our prayers. What joys or sorrows can you share with God today?
   (Answers will vary.)

   Take a moment and pour out your soul in prayer.

2. Hannah realized that Samuel was a gift from God, and so she gave him to the LORD to serve in His house. What gifts has God given you that you can use to serve in His kingdom?
   (Specific answers will vary. Everything we have is a gift from God. All our time, talents, and possessions should be used first and foremost to serve others and further God's kingdom.)

3. The birth of Samuel was a sign for Hannah and Elkanah of God's grace. What special baby was born a thousand years later as a perfect expression of God's grace?
   (The birth of Jesus shows perfectly that God loves us and has mercy on us. God sent His own Son to be born as an infant and live and die as a man in order to deliver us from death, restore our relationship with God, and win for us eternal life!)

38

God Calls Samuel
(1 Samuel 2–4)

Reviewing God's Word

Draw lines to match each word to its definition.

1. Perceive	To mock and show a lack or respect for God
2. Blaspheme	To hold back from action
3. Minister	To serve by fulfilling priestly duties
4. Restrain	To realize

Thinking about God's Word

1. Why does the account say Eli's sons were worthless?
(They didn't know or believe in the LORD, and they showed contempt for the temple offerings.)

2. Who did Samuel think was calling him when he heard his name?
(Eli)

3. Who was really calling Samuel?
(God)

4. What did Samuel say when he realized the LORD was calling him?
(He replied, "Speak, for Your servant hears.")

5. What did God tell Samuel?
(He said that He was going to punish Eli's house because his sons had no respect for God and Eli had not restrained his sons.)

6. What was Eli's response when he heard what was going to happen?
(Eli said, "It is the LORD. Let Him do what seems good to Him.")

7. How did God bring about the punishment He had promised?
(Israel fought against the Philistines. Eli's sons were killed in battle. When Eli heard the news, he fell over backward and died.)

8. What did the Philistines capture in battle?
(They captured the ark of the covenant.)

Applying God's Word

1. The Bible says that Samuel did not yet know the Lord because the Word of the Lord hadn't been revealed to him. How do we come to know God?
(We, too, come to know God through His Word. He has given us the precious gift of Scripture, and through this perfect and complete Word of God, the Lord reveals Himself to us.)

2. What can we learn from Samuel's example about how to respond to God's Word?
(Samuel said to the LORD, "Speak, for Your servant hears." Each time we read the Bible or hear God's Word preached, we may be moved by God to respond in the same way. When God speaks, we are eager to listen.)

3. Samuel heard the voice of the LORD call out, "Samuel!" When did God call you by name to know Him and be His child?
(In your Baptism, the pastor [speaking for God] said, " [Your name] , I baptize you in the name of the Father and of the Son and of the Holy Spirit." Your name has been written in the Book of Life.)

39

Saul Becomes King (1 Samuel 8–11)

Reviewing God's Word

Of whom do you think when you read each of the following sentences?

1. The elders of Israel came to speak to him. **Samuel**
2. He chose the man to be anointed as king. **God**
3. He was the son of Kish and the first king of Israel. **Saul**
4. They shouted, "Long live the king!" **People of Israel**
5. He hid among the baggage. **Saul**
6. He led the people to defeat the Ammonites. **Saul**
7. He said, "Let us renew the kingdom." **Samuel**

Saul	God	Samuel
Benjamin	Kish	People of Israel

Thinking about God's Word

1. Why did the elders tell Samuel they wanted a king?
(Samuel was getting old, and his sons were not following his example or faithfulness to God. Israel wanted to have a king as the other nations did.)

2. Why was it a sin to ask for a king?
(The people were rejecting God as their king.)

3. How did God use natural events to send Saul to Samuel?
(Saul and his servant were searching for lost donkeys and went to Samuel to ask if he could help them find their animals. When Saul arrived, God told Samuel that Saul was the one God had chosen to be the king.)

4. What did God promise that Saul would do?
(He would save Israel from the Philistines.)

5. Why were the people so impressed with Saul?
(He was tall and handsome.)

6. How did God bless Saul in battle?
(The Israelites fought against the Ammonites and struck them down.)

7. What two things did the Israelites do to celebrate their victory in battle and renew the kingdom?
(They made Saul the king before the LORD and made peace offerings to God.)

Applying God's Word

1. What does this account teach us about the relationship between God and our governing authorities?
(Our governing authorities are God's gifts to us.)

What does this account teach us about how we treat our rulers?
(We should honor and respect our rulers, because their authority comes from God.)

2. Saul was in the midst of an ordinary search for lost donkeys when God led Samuel to anoint him king of Israel. What does this occurrence suggest about the ordinary moments of your life?
(No moments in life are too ordinary for God. Our God works through the simple, natural things of life to do His will. Nothing in your life is accidental!)

3. Saul was the first in a line of kings who were supposed to lead and deliver the people of Israel, but no king was able to do this perfectly. Whom did God ultimately send to lead and deliver His people?
(God sent Jesus as king, not over an earthly kingdom like Israel, but over all of God's people forever. He delivered us from our enemies of sin, death, and hell; He leads us in God's ways; and He reigns in heaven at the right hand of God.)

40

Samuel Anoints David
(1 Samuel 15–16)

Reviewing God's Word

Write the name of the speaker next to each quote. Names may be used more than once or not at all.

1. "Why did you not obey the voice of the LORD?" **Samuel**
2. "Do not look on his appearance." **God**
3. "There remains yet the youngest. He is keeping the sheep." **Jesse**
4. "I have sinned. Please pardon my sin and return with me." **Saul**
5. "I regret that I have made Saul king." **God**
6. "You have rejected the word of the LORD, and the LORD has rejected you from being king over Israel." **Samuel**
7. "Strike Amalek and destroy all that they have. Do not spare them." **God**

David	Jesse	Eliab
Saul	God	Samuel

Thinking about God's Word

1. In what way did Saul disobey God after defeating the Amalekites?
(Saul and the Israelites spared Agag the king, the best sheep and oxen, and other good plunder, even though God had told Saul to destroy everything.)

2. Why did God regret making Saul king?
(Saul turned his back on God and disobeyed His commandments.)

3. Why did Samuel refuse to excuse Saul's sin and return with him?
(Saul had rejected God's Word, and consequently, God had rejected him as king over Israel.)

4. Why did the Lord send Samuel to Jesse?
(God had chosen one of Jesse's sons to be king.)

5. Where did Jesse and his family live?
(They were from Bethlehem.)

6. What did God tell Samuel when Samuel was sure Eliab was the Lord's choice for the next king?
(God said, "Do not look on his appearance, because I have rejected him. For the LORD sees not as man sees. Man looks on the outward appearance, but the LORD looks on the heart.")

7. Whom had God chosen to be king?
(He had chosen Jesse's youngest son, a shepherd boy named David.)

Applying God's Word

1. In disobedience to God's command, Saul and his men greedily kept the best spoils for themselves. When have you acted selfishly in your use of God's gifts to you?
(Answers will vary.)

2. The LORD says that He looks at the heart. What is the condition of our hearts?
(By nature, our hearts are filthy and sinful [Jeremiah 17:9]. But through Baptism into Jesus' death and resurrection, our hearts are washed clean [Psalm 51:10]. Now when God looks at our hearts, our appearance is pleasing to Him because we have been given Jesus' righteousness!)

3. What similarities can you already see between David and Jesus?
(David came from Bethlehem, where Jesus was born. He was a shepherd, and Jesus is the Good Shepherd over all of God's people. Both David and Jesus were chosen by God to lead His people.)

41

David Fights Goliath
(1 Samuel 17)

Reviewing God's Word

Underline the word or phrase that answers each question.

1. Whom were the Israelites fighting against in this story? (Amalekites—Midianites—Philistines—Bethlehemites)
2. Who had followed Saul to battle? (David—Jesse's three oldest sons—Saul's brothers—Jesse)
3. From what had the LORD already delivered David? (Lions and bears—Many armies—Deadly disease—A poisonous serpent)
4. What did Saul try to give David? (Money—A javelin—A sling—His armor)
5. How did David kill Goliath? (With a spear—With a sling and a stone—With a curse—With an army)
6. Whose battle was this? (Saul's—Goliath's—The Lord's—David's)

Thinking about God's Word

1. What kind of battle did Goliath call for?
(Goliath said each side should send out their strongest man for a fight. The loser's army would become servants to the winner's people.)

2. Why were the Israelites so afraid to fight?
(Goliath was strong and skilled, and the people of Israel forgot that the LORD was with them.)

3. Why did David go to the battlefield in the first place?
(His father sent him to bring food to his brothers and to see if they were well.)

4. With what words did David show that he was not frightened by the giant?
("Who is this Philistine, that he should defy the armies of the living God?")

5. Why was David willing to fight Goliath?
(He had experienced God's protection in the past as a shepherd facing wild animals, and he knew that the LORD would deliver him again.)

6. What did David take with him to fight the giant?
(He took his staff, a sling, and five stones.)

7. With what did Goliath arm himself?
(He brought a sword, a spear, and a javelin.)

8. Who did David say would deliver Israel?
(God)

9. How did David kill Goliath?
(He killed him with a sling and one stone—by the power of God!)

10. What happened when the Philistines saw that Goliath was dead?
(They fled in fear, and the Israelites pursued them.)

Applying God's Word

1. God told Paul, "My grace is sufficient for you, for My power is made perfect in weakness" (2 Corinthians 12:9). How does the account of David and Goliath demonstrate this?
(David was a small shepherd boy who was barely armed, but God gave him power to defeat a mighty warrior. In David's weakness, God made His strength known to all the Israelites and Philistines.)

2. How does it change our attitude toward our own weaknesses to know that God's power is made perfect in weakness?
(Not only do we not have to be ashamed of our weaknesses, but we also can boast in them! When we admit that we struggle and fail, then we can tell others about God's power and the wonderful things God does through us and despite our sinfulness.)

3. What can we learn from David about facing difficulties and battles in our own lives?
(We often face enemies that seem too great for us to handle, but we can trust—as David did—that the LORD fights for us. We are too weak to battle sin and Satan, but God is strong enough. Jesus was victorious on the cross for us, and we can trust that He will deliver us from every enemy and every danger of life.)

42

David and Jonathan

(1 Samuel 18; 20)

Reviewing God's Word

Fill in the blanks.

1. The soul of Jonathan, Saul's son, was **knit** to the soul of David.
2. But as David won battles, Saul sought to **kill** him.
3. David said of Saul, "If he is **angry**, then know that he is determined to harm me."
4. Saul said to Jonathan, "For as long as the son of Jesse lives on the earth, neither you nor your **kingdom** shall be established."
5. Jonathan knew that his **father** was determined to put David to death.
6. Jonathan said to David, "The LORD shall be between me and you, and between my offspring and your offspring, **forever**."

Thinking about God's Word

1. Who was Jonathan?
(He was the son of King Saul.)

2. Who usually takes over the throne when a king dies?
(The king's son, the prince, is usually next in line for the throne. Jonathan should have been king after Saul.)

3. Whom had Samuel already anointed to be king after Saul? (See previous two stories.)
(Samuel, at God's direction, had anointed David to be the next king.)

4. How does the Bible describe the way Jonathan loved his friend David?
(He loved him "as his own soul.")

5. When did Saul begin trying to kill David?
(Saul became angry and ready to kill David when he saw his success in battle.)

6. How did Jonathan test his father to find out his attitude toward David?
(He told him that David had gone to Bethlehem to make a sacrifice. When Saul got angry, Jonathan knew he was ready to kill David.)

7. What reason did Saul give when he told Jonathan he was going to kill David?
(He told Jonathan that David was going to take the throne and the kingdom from him.)

8. With what action did Jonathan tell David that he needed to flee from Saul?
(He went out to shoot arrows with a young boy. He said to the boy, "Is not the arrow beyond you?" This was the signal to David that Saul was trying to kill him and he needed to leave.)

9. Who was at the center of Jonathan and David's friendship?
(The LORD was always between them, at the center of their friendship.)

Applying God's Word

1. Jesus taught that the second greatest commandment is "You shall love your neighbor as yourself" (Matthew 22:39). How did Jonathan follow this command?
(Jonathan loved David as his own soul. He gave David his robe, armor, and weapons. Jonathan wasn't jealous that David was chosen by God to be the next king, but he was a true friend to David and protected him from Saul.)

2. The name Jonathan means "gift of God." Truly, Saul's son was a gift of blessing and protection for David. What people in your life are God's gifts to you?
(Specific answers will vary. God has graciously given us family and friends. Each one of these people is a gift from God to us for our own blessing and protection. LORD)

3. God had promised Abraham that kings would come from his descendants. How does this account show God at work to keep His promise?
(Both Saul and David were descendants of Abraham. Although Jonathan was supposed to be heir to the throne and Saul was trying to kill David, God protected David and used Jonathan to keep him safe until he could be publicly made king over Israel.)

43

God's Covenant with David (2 Samuel 7)

Reviewing God's Word

Circle Yes or No for each statement.

1. David had a permanent dwelling, while the Israelites worshiped in a tent.	**(YES)**	NO
2. The Lord told David to make Him a temple.	YES	**(NO)**
3. David rose from a shepherd to a king through hard work and determination.	YES	**(NO)**
4. The Lord promised to give the throne to David's offspring.	**(YES)**	NO
5. God said David's son would build the temple as a house for the Lord.	**(YES)**	NO
6. The Lord promised that David's throne would be established forever.	**(YES)**	NO
7. God said David's son would follow His commands perfectly.	YES	**(NO)**
8. David went into the tabernacle tent and praised God for all His blessings.	**(YES)**	NO

Thinking about God's Word

1. How did God bless David in battle?
   (God gave David victories until all his enemies were defeated.)

2. Why did David go to Nathan the prophet?
   (David was concerned about the fact that he had a house of cedar, while the nation of Israel was still worshiping in a tent.)

3. What did the LORD say He had done for David?
   (God made David king, He was with David at all times, and He gave him rest from his enemies.)

4. What did God promise to do for David's son?
   (God said He would give David's son the throne, let him build the temple, be a father to him, and show him steadfast love.)

5. What did the Lord say He would do when David's son sinned?
   (He said he would discipline him but never stop loving him as a son.)

6. Did God bless David because David was a really good person?
   (No)

7. What did David say about why the Lord had given him greatness?
   (He said God had blessed him because of God's promise and the love God had in His heart for David.)

Applying God's Word

1. Who in this account did all the action: made David king, brought an end to battle, gave Israel a place to live, established David's kingdom, promised to bring success to David's son?
   (God did all of this.)

   What does this mean for the events of our lives?
   (God is always in control. David came to God looking to serve Him, and instead God pointed David to everything He had already done for him. Our focus should always be on God and His wonderful, gracious actions not our own actions toward God.)

2. What does this account teach us about why God gives us blessings?
   (God blessed David because He loved David and had promised to bless him. God blesses us because of His fatherly love for us His children and because He has promised good gifts to us. We can't earn His grace or take credit for receiving it. God's blessings are a result of His own mercy!)

3. God promised that He would establish David's throne forever. Who is reigning on David's throne today?
   (Jesus, David's descendant, reigns in heaven over all of God's people. His throne and His glory will never end.)

44

Solomon Becomes King
(1 Kings 2–3)

Reviewing God's Word

Draw lines to match each quote to the person who spoke it. More than one quote may be matched with the same speaker.

1. "Keep the charge of the LORD your God, walking in His ways."
2. "I give you a wise and discerning mind."
3. "Who is able to govern this Your great people?"
4. "I give you also riches and honor."
5. "Be strong. Show yourself a man."
6. "I am but a little child. Your servant is in the midst of Your people."
7. "If you will walk in My ways . . . then I will lengthen your days."

Solomon

God

David

Thinking about God's Word

1. What commands did David give his son Solomon before he died?
   (David told Solomon to be strong and show himself a man. Most important, he told him to walk in God's ways and keep His commandments.)

2. What does it mean that David "slept with his fathers"?
   (It means that David died. This use of the word "slept" reminds us that death for believers is only momentary until we wake to eternal life in heaven.)

3. What did the Lord say to Solomon when He appeared to him in a dream?
   (God invited Solomon to ask for anything.)

4. For what did Solomon ask the Lord?
   (Solomon asked God for an understanding mind to govern the people of Israel with discernment.)

5. What did God give Solomon in addition to wisdom?
   (God also gave King Solomon riches and honor and promised him a long life if he followed in the LORD's ways.)

6. What did Solomon do when he awoke?
   (He sacrificed offerings to God in thanksgiving.)

7. Why did two women come to Solomon?
   (One woman's baby had died, and the two mothers were arguing about whose baby was alive and whose was dead.)

8. What was Solomon's solution to their conflict?
   (He offered to cut the baby in half so each woman could have one half. He knew that the real mother would rather give up her child than let him be killed.)

9. Why were the people amazed at Solomon?
   (They saw that God had given Solomon divine wisdom to bring about justice.)

Applying God's Word

1. What does it mean to walk in the Lord's ways? How do we know what God's ways are?
   (God wants every moment of our lives to be lived in accordance with His will and in a way that glorifies Him. We learn God's ways from His Word and from the life of Jesus.)

2. How is it possible to walk in the Lord's ways?
   (It is not possible as sinful human beings to walk in God's ways. We continually disobey God's commands and fall short of His glory. But Jesus walked in the Lord's ways perfectly, not only as an example but also to fulfill the Law for us. His death and resurrection paid the price for all our sins and failures. By faith in Jesus Christ, our sins are washed away, and the Holy Spirit gives us power to live a new life and follow God's ways.)

3. Where does the world say wisdom comes from? Where does true wisdom come from?
   (The world says that we can become wise by studying, reading, thinking, and learning information. True wisdom comes from God alone. As Proverbs 9:10 reminds us, "The fear of the LORD is the beginning of wisdom.")

45

Solomon Builds the Temple
(1 Kings 5–6; 8)

Reviewing God's Word

Underline the word or phrase that answers each question.

1. Whom did Solomon ask to provide cedar and cypress wood? (The tribe of Judah —The tribe of Benjamin—The Egyptians—Hiram, king of Tyre)
2. How many years had Israel been out of Egypt before Solomon began building the temple? (200—77—480—600)
3. With what did Solomon cover the altar in the inner sanctuary? (Gold—Nickel—Copper—Silver)
4. How many years did Solomon spend building the temple? (10–12—2—7)
5. Where was the ark of the covenant placed? (In the palace—In the Most Holy Place—In the court—In the courtyard)
6. By what name did Solomon call God in his prayer? (Jehovah—God—Almighty—Lord, God of Israel)
7. What specifically did Solomon ask God to do in the very end of his prayer? (Give all the people wisdom—Grant Israel wealth—Defeat his enemies—Forgive the people)

Thinking about God's Word

1. What deal did Solomon make with Hiram, king of Tyre? **(Hiram provided Solomon with wood, and Solomon gave Hiram food for his household.)**
2. What was the wonderful result of this treaty? **(There was peace between Israel and Tyre.)**
3. How did the temple demonstrate Solomon's love for God? **(He spent seven years working on this beautiful, ornate house of worship in order to honor the Lord.)**
4. How did God show that He was present in the temple? **(He filled the building with His glory in the form of a cloud.)**
5. What did Solomon do to dedicate the temple? **(He prayed before the altar in front of all the people.)**

Applying God's Word

1. Solomon acknowledged that even heaven couldn't contain God, yet God chose to be present in the temple. How do we know that God is present with us in worship? **(Jesus promised, "Where two or three are gathered in My name, there am I among them" [Matthew 18:20]. Not only is God present at all times and in all places, but He also promises especially to be present in Word and Sacrament and among gathered believers.)**
2. What can you learn from Solomon about how to view your church? **(It is important to show honor and respect to your place of worship. Putting time, money, and energy into creating and maintaining your church is an act of worship and a way of thanking and praising God for all His gifts to you.)**
3. Solomon said to the Lord, "Listen in heaven Your dwelling place, and when You hear, forgive." How can we be certain that when God hears our prayers He will forgive our sins? **(Every sin we have committed and will commit was laid upon Jesus on the cross, and He took the suffering and death we deserve. Because of Christ's sacrifice, we are forgiven. The apostle John writes, "If we confess our sins, [God] is faithful and just to forgive us our sins and to cleanse us from all unrighteousness" [1 John 1:9].)**

46

God Provides for Elijah
(1 Kings 16–17)

Reviewing God's Word

Fill in the blanks, using the words below. Some words will not be used.

1. Ahab sinned against God by worshiping **Baal**.
2. **Elijah** the prophet told Ahab there would be years with neither dew nor rain.
3. **Ravens** brought Elijah bread and meat.
4. The Lord told Elijah to go to the city of **Zarephath**.
5. God used a **widow** to care for Elijah.
6. After some time, the widow's **son** died.
7. **The Lord** brought the widow's child back to life.

Zarephath	Elijah	Baal
daughter	maiden	Ahab
Dogs	The Lord	Ravens
widow	son	Samaria

Thinking about God's Word

1. What did Ahab do that showed he was a wicked king? **(He worshiped Baal and Asherah, false gods. He did more to make God angry than all the kings before him.)**

2. What did the Lord do to call Ahab to repentance? **(He sent a drought.)**

3. Why was having "neither dew nor rain" a terrible punishment? **(Soon there would be no food.)**

4. How did the Lord miraculously take care of Elijah? **(God sent ravens to bring Elijah bread and meat in the morning and at night.)**

5. Why did Elijah go to Zarephath? **(The brook he was relying on for water dried up. God commanded him to go to a widow in Zarephath.)**

6. Why was it unusual for God to command a widow to feed Elijah? **(Usually, widows were the people in need of care and assistance. Here, God used a widow to care for His prophet.)**

7. Why did Elijah tell the widow not to be afraid? **(Elijah told her that God would provide for her and her son. She could feed Elijah and her family, and she would not run out of flour or oil until the drought was over.)**

8. How did the widow show that she believed God would provide? **(She fed Elijah first and trusted that God would provide enough food for her and her son as well. All three of them ate for many days.)**

9. What tragedy happened while Elijah was staying with the widow? **(The widow's son died.)**

10. How did God provide in this situation too? **(God provided healing and new life to the widow's son. In answer to Elijah's prayer, God raised the boy back to life.)**

Applying God's Word

1. In this account, what powerful things did the Lord do by His Word? **(The Word of the Lord brought drought and would eventually bring rain. God's Word caused ravens to provide bread and meat for Elijah. God's Word provided food for the widow, her son, and Elijah. The Word of the Lord worked through Elijah to raise the widow's son from the dead.)**

   What power does the Word of the Lord (the Bible) have in your life? **(The Word has the power to forgive and bring salvation. It heals, restores, revives, and transforms lives.)**

2. How does God's care for Elijah compare with God's care for us? **(God daily provides us with everything we need for the care and support of our bodies. Rather than using miraculous means such as messenger ravens and supplies of flour and oil that never run out, God uses people and jobs to provide for us. All that we have is a gift from God.)**

3. What other Bible accounts show God's power over death? **(Possibilities include Jesus' raising of the widow's son in Nain, the daughter of Jairus, and Lazarus, as well as Jesus' own resurrection from the dead.)**

   What does God's power over death mean for us? **(Because God has power over death and raised Jesus from the dead, by faith in Christ we can be sure that on the Last Day, we will be raised from the dead too!)**

47

Elijah and the Prophets of Baal

(1 Kings 18)

Reviewing God's Word

Draw a line through the sentences that are not true.

1. Elijah told King Ahab to gather 450 prophets of Baal and 400 prophets of Asherah.
2. Elijah proposed a contest to see who the true god was.
3. ~~The prophets called to Dagon to bring down fire.~~
4. ~~A voice called from heaven to the prophets of Baal.~~
5. Elijah built an altar with twelve stones.
6. ~~Elijah tried to make it easier for the bull on his altar to burn.~~
7. God sent fire to consume the offering, the wood, the stones, the water, and the dust.
8. After God sent fire for His altar, the people worshiped the Lord.
9. ~~The prophets of Baal repented and believed in God.~~

Thinking about God's Word

1. Whom were the people worshiping besides God?
   (They were worshiping the false gods Baal and Asherah.)

2. How did Elijah put the idol Baal to a test?
   (Two altars with sacrifices were prepared, one for Baal and one for the true God. The god who set fire to his sacrifice would be regarded as the true God.)

3. What showed that the idol Baal had no power?
   (Baal's altar remained without fire.)

4. What did the twelve stones of Elijah's altar represent?
   (The twelve stones represented the twelve tribes of the sons of Jacob.)

5. Why did Elijah drench his altar with water?
   (He wanted to make it harder for the bull to burn so that the people would know it was truly God who sent fire for the sacrifice.)

6. How can you tell that the fire that fell from heaven was sent by God?
   (It was supernatural fire; it even consumed the water and stones.)

7. With what action and words did the people confess that Elijah had won the test?
   (They fell on their faces and cried, "The LORD, He is God. The LORD, He is God.")

8. What did the people do with the prophets of Baal at Elijah's command?
   (They seized and killed the prophets of Baal.)

Applying God's Word

1. Elijah asked the people how long they would "limp between two different opinions." God wants us to love Him with all our heart, soul, and mind (Matthew 22:37). What things in your life steal some of your trust and focus?
   (Answers will vary.)

2. Elijah mocked the prophets of Baal by asking them if their god was sleeping and needed to be woken up. Why do we never have to worry about the true God needing to be awoken?
   (The Bible promises that "He who keeps you will not slumber. Behold, He who keeps Israel will neither slumber nor sleep" [Psalm 121:3–4]. God never sleeps, and He is always present to hear our prayers.)

3. Elijah prayed to the God of Abraham, Isaac, and Israel. Is Elijah's God the same as ours? Explain.
   (There is and always has been only one true God: Father, Son, and Holy Spirit. The God of Abraham, Isaac, and Israel is also our God. The same God who miraculously brought down fire on Elijah's altar hears and answers our prayers as well!)

48

God Takes Elijah to Heaven
(1 Kings 19; 2 Kings 2)

Reviewing God's Word

Underline the word or phrase that makes each sentence true.

1. After Elijah killed the prophets of Baal, (Ahab—Elisha—Asherah—Jezebel) threatened to kill him.
2. Elijah traveled forty days to Mount (Sinai—Horeb—Carmel—Shepher).
3. God spoke to Elijah in a (whisper—wind—earthquake—fire).
4. Elijah asked Elisha to (follow him—lead him—stay behind—wander), but Elisha refused.
5. Elisha asked for a (single—triple—half—double) portion of Elijah's spirit.
6. Elisha called Elijah his (brother—friend—father—master).
7. Elisha used Elijah's (shoe—cloak—staff—scroll) to part the Jordan River.

Thinking about God's Word

1. Why did Elijah run into the wilderness?
(He heard that Jezebel wanted to kill him, and he was afraid.)

2. How did Elijah get food and water?
(An angel brought him food and water.)

3. How did God come to Elijah?
(God came to him in a low whisper.)

4. Why did Elijah seek out the Lord?
(He felt as though He was the only prophet left, and Jezebel was seeking to kill him.)

5. What did the Lord tell Elijah to do?
(God told Elijah to appoint Elisha to be the prophet after him.)

6. How did Elijah and Elisha cross the Jordan?
(Elijah struck with water with his cloak, and it parted in two.)

7. What did Elisha ask for from his teacher Elijah before he took over as prophet?
(Elisha asked for a double portion of Elijah's spirit.)

8. How was Elijah taken up into heaven?
(A chariot of fire and horses of fire took Elijah up to heaven in a whirlwind.)

9. By what miracle did the Lord show Elisha that He was with him as He had been with Elijah?
(God divided the Jordan River when Elisha used Elijah's cloak to strike the water.)

Applying God's Word

1. When Elijah felt completely discouraged and alone, God sent him Elisha to assist him and learn from him. What other Christians has God placed in your life to remind you that you aren't the only one left?
(Answers will vary.)

2. How do you know that you have received the Holy Spirit? See 1 Corinthians 12:3.
(If we have faith, we have the Holy Spirit. No one comes to faith outside of the working of the Holy Spirit.)

3. When Elijah went up on the mountain to wait for the Lord to pass by, God wasn't in the wind, earthquake, or fire, but He was in a low whisper. How does God show Himself to you in seemingly quiet and insignificant ways?
(We rarely see God at work in our lives today in such things as parting rivers or chariots of fire, but this doesn't change the fact that God is always present. He works in our lives through His Word and Sacraments and through the comfort and encouragement of others. Even the "low whisper" of an uplifting Bible passage or a friend's love is evidence of God's presence and blessings.)

49

Naaman and Elisha
(2 Kings 5)

Reviewing God's Word

Write the name of the speaker next to each quote. Names may be used more than once or not at all.

1. "Let Naaman come to me, that he may know that there is a prophet in Israel." **Elisha**
2. "It is a great word the prophet has spoken to you." **Naaman's servants**
3. "Go now, and I will send a letter to the king of Israel." **King of Syria**
4. "Are not the rivers of Damascus better than all the waters of Israel? **Naaman**
5. "Am I God, to kill and to make alive?" **King of Israel**
6. "Go in peace." **Elisha**
7. "Would that my lord were with the prophet who is in Samaria!" **Israelite servant girl**
8. "Behold, I know that there is no God in all the earth but in Israel." **Naaman**

Naaman	Elijah	Elisha
Kind of Syria	Naaman's servants	Jezebel
King of Israel	Baal	Israelite servant girl

Thinking about God's Word

1. Who was Naaman?
   (He was the commander of the army of the king of Syria.)
2. What was wrong with him?
   (He had leprosy.)
3. What did the servant girl say?
   (She said that if Naaman went to the prophet in Samaria, he could be healed.)
4. Why did the king of Israel tear his clothes?
   (He knew he couldn't heal Naaman, and he didn't want to anger the king of Syria. He didn't remember Elisha or trust God to use Elisha to bring Naaman healing.)
5. How did Elisha humble Naaman?
   (He sent a messenger to tell Naaman to wash seven times in the Jordan River.)
6. Why was Naaman upset?
   (He wanted Elisha to come out and wave his hands over him. He felt disrespected because the prophet only sent a messenger out to him with rather ordinary instructions.)
7. What happened when Naaman followed Elisha's instructions?
   (He was completely healed of his leprosy.)
8. With what words did Naaman admit that God of Israel had cured him?
   ("Behold, I know that there is no God in all the earth but in Israel.")
9. Why do you think Elisha refused Naaman's present?
   (Elisha knew that it was God who had healed Naaman, and he didn't want to take any credit for the miracle.)

Applying God's Word

1. How did the servant girl act as a missionary?
   (As a servant in a foreign land, she told her mistress about Elisha the prophet and the great things God could do through him.)
2. What evidence does the witness of the servant girl provide of God's love and grace for all people?
   (God blessed Naaman with His healing grace, even though Naaman was not one of the people of Israel. God doesn't distinguish between people, but He loves all people and wants all people to be saved.)
3. Naaman was upset that he had to wash in the Jordan River rather than the waters of Damascus, but his servants said to him, "It is a great word the prophet has spoken to you." Where did the power come from for Naaman's healing? How is this like Baptism? **(The power wasn't in the specific water but in the Word of God spoken through the prophet Elisha. The power in Baptism for forgiveness and eternal life doesn't come from the water itself, but from the Word of God working through the water to bring faith.)**

50

Jonah

(The Book of Jonah)

Reviewing God's Word

Fill in the blanks.

1. The **Word** of the Lord came to Jonah.

2. Jonah found a ship going to **Tarshish**, away from the presence of the Lord.

3. The mariners were afraid, and each cried out to his **god**.

4. Jonah said, "I am a Hebrew. I fear the LORD, the God of **heaven**."

5. The sailors hurled Jonah into the **sea**, and the sea ceased its raging.

6. The Lord appointed a great **fish** to swallow up Jonah.

7. "When my life was fainting away, I **remembered** the LORD."

8. The people of Nineveh **believed** God.

9. God **relented** of the disaster that He had said He would do to the people of Nineveh.

Thinking about God's Word

1. What did the Lord tell Jonah to do?
   (He told Jonah to preach to Nineveh because the people of Nineveh were doing evil.)

2. What did Jonah do instead?
   (He tried to run away from God by sailing to Tarshish.)

3. What did the sailors do when God sent a great storm?
   (They called out to their own gods. Then they cast lots to find out who had brought the storm upon them.)

4. What did Jonah tell the sailors to do when they discovered he had caused the storm by trying to run away from God?
   (Jonah told the sailors to throw him into the sea.)

5. How did God use Jonah's disobedience to bring other people to faith?
   (When the sailors saw how God calmed the storm, they stopped praying to their gods and sacrificed to the LORD.)

6. How did God show mercy to Jonah?
   (He sent a great fish to swallow up Jonah so he wouldn't drown.)

7. How long was Jonah in the belly of the fish?
   (He was there three days and three nights.)

8. What did Jonah do while he was in the belly of the fish?
   (He prayed to God and praised Him for being the source of salvation.)

9. What did the people of Nineveh do when they heard Jonah's message?
   (They believed God, fasted, dressed in sackcloth, and repented. Even the king of Nineveh put on sackcloth and sat in the dust.)

10. How did God respond to their repentance?
    (He forgave them and didn't bring disaster on Nineveh.)

Applying God's Word

1. Do you ever try to avoid doing what you know God wants you to do?
   (Answers will vary.)

   What did Jonah learn about running away from God?
   (It's not possible to run away from God, and it's certainly not wise. God will bring about His will in spite of us.)

2. The people of Nineveh seemed completely lost in their sin, but God worked repentance and faith in their hearts. When have you assumed people are too lost to be worth witnessing to?
   (Answers will vary.)

   Why is it that no one is too lost for the Gospel?
   (Jesus died to forgive and save all people.)

3. How is God's salvation for the people of Nineveh like the salvation He offers to us? **(Like the people of Nineveh, we deserve nothing but punishment and eternal destruction because we are caught up in our sin. But God has rescued us through Jesus, our Savior.)**

51

Isaiah Sees the Lord (Isaiah 6–7; 9; 53)

Reviewing God's Word

Draw lines to match each word to its definition.

1. Seraphim	To hold someone in high regard
2. Atone	Sins
3. Immanuel	Six-winged angels created by God
4. Esteem	Punishment
5. Smitten	Name of Jesus, means "God is with us"
6. Transgressions	To pay for
7. Chastisement	Struck, as with a hard blow

Thinking about God's Word

1. How did Isaiah describe the Lord, as he saw Him in his vision?
   (The Lord was sitting on a throne in an exalted place. His robe filled the temple. The Lord was great and majestic!)

2. What did the seraphim call out?
   ("Holy, holy, holy is the Lord of hosts. The whole earth is full of His glory!")

3. What did the seraphim do after flying to Isaiah?
   (The angel took a burning coal and touched Isaiah's lips with it. He told Isaiah that his sins were forgiven.)

4. How did Isaiah answer when God asked whom He should send?
   (Isaiah said, "Here am I! Send me.")

5. What kind of sign did God promise to Israel?
   (God said He would send a child born of a virgin who would be Immanuel or "God with us.")

6. What other names did God give for the promised Savior?
   (He would also be called Wonderful Counselor, Mighty God, Everlasting Father, and Prince of Peace.)

7. According to the last prophecy, what terrible things would Jesus have to suffer and what good things would His suffering mean for us?
   (Jesus would carry our grief and sorrows and be struck down by God. He would be wounded, crushed, and punished. But this suffering would bring us peace and healing!)

Applying God's Word

1. Isaiah had to have his sins taken away before he was ready to worship God or serve as God's messenger. How do we follow his example in our church services?
   (We begin church with Confession and Absolution. Because we recognize our sin and unworthiness, we first confess our sins before God and receive His merciful forgiveness. Then we are ready to worship God in His house.)

2. Isaiah gave five names for Jesus: Immanuel, Wonderful Counselor, Mighty God, Everlasting Father, and Prince of Peace. What does each of these names tell us about God?
   (Immanuel means that Jesus is true God who came to dwell with us on earth. Wonderful Counselor reminds us of the wisdom of Christ. Jesus is Mighty God, fully divine and omnipotent [all powerful]. The Savior is an Everlasting Father to the family of believers, a Father who loves and cares for His children. And He is the Prince of Peace, bringing to us through His death and resurrection forgiveness of sins and peace with God.)

3. Why did Jesus suffer in the brutal way Isaiah describes? And what does this suffering mean for us?
   (Jesus willingly endured all of this pain and punishment because of our sins. And in the most beautiful and unbelievable exchange ever made, Christ took our sin, our guilt, and the punishment we deserved, and in return He gave us peace and healing, forgiveness and eternal life!)

52

King Hezekiah Prays
(2 Kings 18–19)

Reviewing God's Word

Circle Yes or No for each statement.

1. Hezekiah followed the LORD's commands as king of Israel.	(YES)	NO
2. Sennacherib was the powerful king of Assyria.	(YES)	NO
3. All the cities of Judah were able to fight off the Assyrian army.	YES	(NO)
4. Hezekiah gave Sennacherib the silver and gold he requested.	(YES)	NO
5. The Assyrians respected and worshiped the LORD.	YES	(NO)
6. After the Assyrians' taunting, Hezekiah went into the house of the LORD .	(YES)	NO
7. Isaiah told Hezekiah that there was no hope for Jerusalem.	YES	(NO)
8. The army of Israel fought and defeated the Assyrians.	YES	(NO)

Thinking about God's Word

1. How was Hezekiah a good king?
(He trusted in the LORD and followed His commandments.)

2. Why did Hezekiah give silver and gold to the king of Assyria?
(The Assyrians had captured all the major cities of Judah. Hezekiah paid them in silver and gold to try to stop them from attacking Jerusalem.)

3. What did the leaders of the Assyrian army tell the people of Jerusalem?
(They told them that neither Hezekiah nor God could save them, because none of the gods of the other nations had been able to stop the Assyrians.)

4. What did the LORD tell Isaiah to say to Hezekiah?
(God said that Sennacherib, king of Assyria, would hear a rumor that would make him return to Assyria. Then Sennacherib would be killed in his own land.)

5. What did Hezekiah do when he received another threatening letter from Sennacherib?
(He spread out the letter before the Lord and prayed for deliverance.)

6. What did God promise to Hezekiah?
(Sennacherib would not enter Jerusalem or even shoot an arrow into the city.)

7. How did the LORD keep His promise to deliver Jerusalem?
(The angel of the LORD killed 185,000 people in the Assyrian army. Sennacherib returned home. While he was worshiping an idol there, he was killed by his own sons.)

Applying God's Word

1. How can we find comfort in this account when we face problems that seem unbeatable?
(The leaders of the Assyrian army told the people of Jerusalem that the LORD couldn't deliver them, because no other god had been able to stop the Assyrian army; yet, God did deliver Jerusalem. Even when nothing else can defeat the problems we have to deal with, we can be certain that God is strong enough to defeat any evil!)

2. What can we learn from Hezekiah about how to handle troubling situations?
(The first thing Hezekiah did with Sennacherib's threatening letter was spread it before the LORD and then pray. He took his problem straight to God and trusted that God could deliver the Israelites. We, too, can take every trial and struggle straight to God, knowing that He alone is our salvation.)

3. Hezekiah asked God to save Jerusalem "that all the kingdoms of the earth may know that You, O LORD, are God alone." How can this serve as a model for our prayers?
(We pray that God would save and deliver us ultimately so that other people will come to know God and find their salvation in Jesus Christ. In every situation, we can give honor and praise to God and share with others the great things God has done for us—especially how He has saved us through Jesus—so that others may know that the LORD is God.)

53

King Josiah (2 Kings 22–23)

Reviewing God's Word

Underline the word or phrase that makes each sentence true.

1. Josiah was only (12—10—<u>8</u>—9) years old when he became king.
2. The high priest when Josiah was king was (<u>Hilkiah</u>—Huldah—Asherah—David).
3. Josiah was (amused—<u>repentant</u>—angry—unconcerned) when he heard the words of the Book of the Law.
4. The Lord said He would bring disaster on Judah because the people had (not celebrated the Passover—taken too long repairing the temple—<u>worshiped other gods</u>—made Josiah king).
5. King Josiah commanded the people to celebrate the (<u>Passover</u>—Feast of Weeks—Day of Atonement—Feast of Booths).

Thinking about God's Word

1. What does it mean that Josiah walked in the way of King David?
   (King David followed God, and Josiah followed David's example of faithfulness to the Lord.)

2. What did King Josiah want done with the offerings collected from the people?
   (Josiah wanted the money given to the workmen who were repairing the temple so that they could buy the supplies they needed.)

3. What did Hilkiah find in the house of the LORD?
   (He found the Book of the Law, the Old Testament Books of Moses.)

4. What did Josiah do when he heard the Book of the Law read aloud?
   (He tore his clothes and commanded his officials to inquire of the Lord.)

5. Why was Josiah so upset?
   (He realized that the people of Israel hadn't been following God's commands for many years.)

6. What message did Huldah the prophetess give to Josiah from the LORD?
   (God said He would bring disaster upon Judah because the people had been worshiping other gods. But because Josiah repented, God promised to wait until after Josiah was gone to bring this destruction on the nation.)

7. Then to whom did Josiah read the Book of the Law?
   (He read it to all the people.)

8. What covenant did the people make before the LORD?
   (They made a covenant to keep God's commandments with all their heart and soul.)

9. What specific things did Josiah do to return the nation to following the LORD?
   (Josiah removed all worship of false gods from the temple and high places in the hills around Jerusalem, and He commanded the people to keep the Passover as God had instructed.)

Applying God's Word

1. Josiah did what was right in God's eyes, even as a young boy, by walking in the way of David and following the guidance of Hilkiah. Whom has God placed in your life to give you a godly example and godly instruction to follow?
   (Answers will vary.)

2. A wide variety of people were used to repair the temple, including carpenters, builders, and masons. What does this suggest about how God would have us understand and use our jobs and abilities?
   (Every job is a calling [or vocation] from God to serve Him through direct service to the church or through service to other people. God would have us value and respect all jobs and be eager to use our gifts and abilities to serve God.)

3. What comfort can we find in the Lord's response to Josiah's repentance?
   (Even though the nation of Judah would be punished for forsaking the Lord, God saw Josiah's repentance and forgave his sin. God promised Josiah that He wouldn't bring destruction during Josiah's reign. When we repent of our sins, God is eager to forgive us for Jesus' sake!)

54

God Calls Jeremiah
(Jeremiah 1; 23; 31)

Reviewing God's Word

Match each prophecy with its fulfillment by writing the correct letter next to each numbered statement.

1. God would give Jeremiah words to speak. **c**
2. God would use Jeremiah to break down and destroy and to build up and plant. **f**
3. God would send a righteous Branch of David. **b**
4. The Lord would be a shepherd to Israel. **a**
5. God would make a new covenant with His people. **e**
6. The Lord would forgive His peoples' sins. **d**

a. Jesus said, "I am the good shepherd" (John 10:11).

b. Jesus was born of David's descendants and lived a perfect, righteous life.

c. Jeremiah wrote two books (57 chapters) of the Bible.

d. Jesus died and rose again to pay for the sins of all people.

e. Jesus' blood sealed a new covenant and brought us peace with God (1 Corinthians 11:25).

f. Jeremiah prophesied God's judgment on the Israelites (Jeremiah 1–29; 34–52) and God's restoration of His people through Jesus Christ (Jeremiah 30–33).

Thinking about God's Word

1. What did the Lord tell Jeremiah He had appointed him to be?
   (God appointed Jeremiah to be a prophet to the nations.)

2. Why did Jeremiah think he couldn't do what God had asked?
   (Jeremiah thought he was too young.)

3. What two promises did God make to Jeremiah to reassure him and calm his fears?
   (God promised to give Jeremiah the words to say and to be with him wherever he went.)

4. How did the Lord show Jeremiah that the words he prophesied would be straight from God?
   (God touched his mouth.)

5. How did the Lord describe the "righteous Branch" of David?
   (God said the righteous Branch would be a wise king who would bring about righteousness and justice and would save Judah and Israel.)

6. What other name did the Lord give Jeremiah for this "righteous Branch"?
   (He would be called "The Lord is our righteousness.")

7. God promised to be a loving shepherd to His people. Then how did He promise to transform the people?
   (The Lord said He would turn their mourning to joy and their sorrow to gladness.)

8. What did the Lord promise about His Law?
   (He said He would write it on the peoples' hearts so they would have the Law within themselves.)

9. And what did God promise to do about the people's sins?
   (He said He would forgive all their sins and forget them completely.)

Applying God's Word

1. The Lord told Jeremiah that before he was born (and even before He formed him in the womb) He set Jeremiah apart for a specific purpose. What does this mean about how we view the life of an unborn child?
   (Because it is the Lord who forms a child in the womb and because, even before birth, God has plans for each child's life, every unborn baby is incredibly valuable! God desires us to value and protect each human life!)

2. Do you ever say to God "I'm only a youth" or "I'm only a kid"?
   (Answers will vary.)

   How does the account of Jeremiah assure you that you're never too young to serve the Lord?
   (God told Jeremiah that He would give him words to speak and be with him always. God promises the same thing to you! He will give you words to speak and be with you as you share with other people the Good News of the Gospel.)

3. To be righteous means to be right with God. If another name for Jesus is "the Lord is our righteousness," how do we enter into a right relationship with God? **(Our sin separates us from God. But on the cross, Jesus took all our sin and gave us His own righteousness in exchange. It is God who gives us a right relationship with Himself.)**

55

Israel and Judah in Exile (2 Kings 17; 24–25)

Reviewing God's Word

Fill in the blanks, using the words and numbers below. Some words will not be used.

1. Hoshea was king over **Israel**.
2. God used the nation of **Assyria** to bring judgment on Israel.
3. The Israelites had ignored the warnings God gave through the **prophets**.
4. Jehoiachin was an evil king of **Judah**.
5. Judah was taken into captivity by **Babylon** as a result of God's judgment.
6. **Zedekiah** was blinded, bound, and taken into exile.
7. The king of Babylon freed Zedekiah from prison after **37** years of exile.

Judah	Zedekiah	Josiah
Jerusalem	55	scribes
Assyria	Babylon	prophets
kings	Israel	37

Thinking about God's Word

1. What was Hoshea like as a king?
   (He did what was evil in the sight of God.)

2. Why did God let the Assyrians carry the Israelites into captivity?
   (Israel had repeatedly sinned against God, worshiped other gods, and ignored the prophets' warnings.)

3. In what way did God warn Israel and Judah about their sin and the exile that would occur as a judgment against their sin?
   (He sent many prophets to tell the people to turn from their sin and follow God's commands.)

4. How does the account describe Jehoiachin as a king?
   (He, too, did evil in God's sight.)

5. What did Nebuchadnezzar and the Babylonians do to Judah?
   (They took Jehoiachin as a prisoner, robbed the temple and the palace, and took everyone except for the poorest people into captivity.)

6. In what way was Zedekiah like Hoshea and Jehoiachin?
   (He also did what was evil in God's eyes.)

7. What happened as a result of Zedekiah's sin and God's further judgment on Judah?
   (The Babylonians blinded and captured Zedekiah; destroyed the temple, palace, homes, and walls of Jerusalem; and carried even more people into exile.)

8. How did the king of Babylon show kindness to Jehoiachin?
   (He let him out of prison, gave him a seat at the king's table, and gave him an allowance to live on.)

Applying God's Word

1. What does this account tell us about God's attitude toward sin?
   (God is very serious about sin. Because God is perfect and just, He cannot tolerate or ignore sin. The Israelites' disobedience and idolatry had to be punished.)

2. Since God is just and cannot tolerate sin, our sin requires punishment as well. Why will we not receive the punishment, exile, and death we deserve?
   (Jesus took our sins upon Himself. He was punished, He was forsaken by God, and He died. By faith in Jesus, our sins are pardoned, and we are assured that we will never have to face exile from God.)

3. God showed mercy and patience toward Israel by warning the people over and over to repent and turn from their sin. How does God show mercy and patience with unbelievers now? See 2 Peter 3:9. **(As with Israel, God continues to remind people through His Word and His servants that we are all sinful and need to repent. God is patiently waiting for all to have a chance to hear the Good News of salvation through Christ before He brings the world to an end.)**

56

God's Promises to the Exiles (Ezekiel 8; 36)

Reviewing God's Word

Draw a line through the sentences that are not true.

1. The people of Israel were committing great abominations.
2. God left the temple.
3. ~~God refused to punish Israel's sin because they were His people.~~
4. The Israelites had acted just like the sinful nations around them.
5. ~~Once the Israelites were exiled, God had forsaken them forever.~~
6. ~~God told the Israelites to fix their own hearts of stone.~~
7. God promised to give the Israelites His Spirit.
8. The Lord promised to restore Israel to a land like the Garden of Eden.

Thinking about God's Word

1. What drove God from the temple?
   (He was driven away by the terrible sinfulness of the people.)
2. How would the LORD act toward His people in their sin?
   (He would not spare or pity any of them. No matter how loud the people cried out to God, He would refuse to hear them.)
3. What did Ezekiel see in a vision that showed God's judgment on Israel?
   (The glory of the LORD left the temple.)
4. What was the LORD's purpose in giving Israel over to foreign nations?
   (His goal was that the people of Israel would know that He is the LORD.)
5. How would the LORD later show all the nations that He is God?
   (He would gather the people from everywhere they had been scattered and restore the people of Israel to their own land.)
6. What two things did God say He would use to cleanse His people, renew their hearts, and restore them to a life of following His commandments?
   (God said He would sprinkle them with clean water and give them His Spirit.)
7. How did the Lord describe the new land He would give to Israel?
   (It would have an abundance of fruit and crops, include newly rebuilt and inhabited cities, and be like the Garden of Eden.)
8. What did God say to assure Ezekiel that these prophecies would really happen?
   (He said, "I am the LORD. I have spoken, and I will do it.")

Applying God's Word

1. The LORD told Ezekiel that He was exiling the people in hope that they would repent and realize He is God. How does this help make sense of some of the difficult things you go through?
   (God's deepest desire is to save us. Sometimes, He uses difficult times to bring us to repentance and remind us that He is the Lord.)
2. How does God bring us the sprinkling with water and gift of the Spirit that He promised in Ezekiel?
   (In Baptism, God uses water to cleanse us from all our sins and idolatry. He removes our stony, sinful hearts and gives us hearts of faith. He gifts us with the Holy Spirit, who gives us the strength to walk in God's ways.)
3. Do you ever wonder how we can know that God will keep His promises to be with us always, to forgive our sins, and to take us to heaven when we die?
   (Answers will vary.)

What comfort do you find in God's final words to Ezekiel?
(God said, "I am the LORD. I have spoken, and I will do it." This is all the assurance we need. God cannot lie, and He is all-powerful to accomplish what He wills. What He has spoken, He will do.)

57

The Three Men in the Fiery Furnace (Daniel 3)

Reviewing God's Word

Draw lines to match each quote to a speaker. Names may match more than one quote.

1. "Blessed be the God of Shadrach, Meshach, and Abednego."
2. "When you hear the music, you are to fall down and worship."
3. "Our God whom we serve is able to deliver us."
4. "Who is the god who will deliver you out of my hands?"
5. "These men, O king, pay no attention to you."
6. "O king, we will not serve your gods or worship the golden image."

- The herald
- The Chaldeans
- Nebuchadnezzar
- Shadrach, Meshach, and Abednego

Thinking about God's Word

1. How did Nebuchadnezzar sin against the First Commandment?
   (He made an idol out of gold.)

2. How did the king force the people to commit idolatry?
   (He commanded the people to worship the image whenever they heard music.)

3. What punishment did the king use to threaten the people if they refused to worship the idol?
   (They would be thrown into a blazing furnace.)

4. Who did not obey the command of the king?
   (Shadrach, Meshach, and Abednego)

5. What did Shadrach, Meshach, and Abednego say when Nebuchadnezzar threatened to throw them into the furnace?
   (They said that their God could deliver them, and whether God wanted to deliver them or not, they would never worship the idol.)

6. How do we know the furnace was very hot?
   (The king ordered his men to make it seven times hotter than usual. It was so hot that even the men putting Shadrach, Meshach, and Abednego into the furnace died.)

7. Why was Nebuchadnezzar astonished?
   (When he looked into the furnace, there were four men instead of three and all the men were unbound and walking around unhurt.)

8. How did Nebuchadnezzar and the people know that God had completely protected the three men?
   (Not only were they still alive, but the fire hadn't burned a hair of their heads or a thread of their cloaks. They didn't even smell like fire!)

9. How did the king change as a result of this event?
   (Instead of worshiping his idol, Nebuchadnezzar realized that the Lord was the true God, because only He could deliver so powerfully.)

Applying God's Word

1. When the music played, "all the people" bowed down and worshiped the idol. Shadrach, Meshach, and Abednego could have used the excuse that "everyone is doing it," but they chose to follow God instead. What sinful things does it seem like "everyone is doing," and how can you bring God glory by following Him instead?
   (Answers will vary.)

2. God didn't stop Shadrach, Meshach, and Abednego from entering the fire, but He did save them while they were in the fire. What does this suggest about difficult times in our lives?
   (Even as followers of God, we still face fiery furnaces. God doesn't promise that we'll never experience difficulties. But He does promise that when we walk through fire, He will be with us there and deliver us from eternal death through Christ.)

3. Why did Shadrach, Meshach, and Abednego say they would still love and thank God even if He didn't rescue them from the furnace?
   (These men knew that God had given them more important blessings than physical life. They knew that even if it wasn't God's will to deliver them from the flames [as with many martyrs of the Church], God's gifts of forgiveness and eternal life were theirs, and God would remain faithful.)

58

Daniel in the Lions' Den (Daniel 6)

Reviewing God's Word

Underline the word or phrase that makes each sentence true.

1. The king made Daniel (a servant—a king—a prince—a president) in the land.
2. The king signed (an ordinance—a book—a petition—a dominion).
3. It said that no one was to pray to anyone except (God—the king—Daniel—the princes) for thirty days.
4. Daniel prayed (10—3—20—5) times a day.
5. The king let Daniel be thrown to the lions because he (wanted Daniel killed—could not change the law—hated Daniel—wished to please the princes).

Thinking about God's Word

1. How did Daniel become distinguished in the land?
   (He had "an excellent spirit," God's Spirit, in him. The king noticed that Daniel was different because he followed the Lord.)
2. Why did the presidents and satraps want to get Daniel in trouble?
   (They were jealous of Daniel because the king wanted to place him over the whole kingdom.)
3. What ordinance did the presidents and satraps persuade the king to sign?
   (They made a law that for thirty days whoever prayed to any god or man other than the king would be thrown into a lions' den.)
4. How did the new law appeal to the king's pride and at the same time break the First Commandment?
   (The new law made the king a god to whom people should pray.)
5. How did Daniel respond to the ordinance?
   (He continued to faithfully pray to the true God in his home, three times a day.)
6. Who reported Daniel's worship to the king?
   (The presidents and satraps reported him.)
7. How can you tell that the king thought highly of Daniel?
   (He was greatly distressed when he heard of Daniel's situation and was determined to rescue him.)
8. How did God protect Daniel?
   (God sent His angel to shut the mouths of the lions.)
9. What happened to the men who had tried to get Daniel killed?
   (They were thrown into the lions' den and devoured.)

Applying God's Word

1. Daniel's godly actions and constant prayer caught the attention of the king, the presidents, and the satraps. How can your actions be a witness of your faith in God?
   (Answers will vary.)
2. God doesn't give us specific rules about when and how to pray; however, Daniel chose to pray on his knees, three times a day. What does Daniel's posture of prayer suggest about the nature of God and our relationship with God?
   (Kneeling is a good reminder of our humility before God. We are truly beggars when it comes to prayer. We are not worthy on our own to come before God but, through Christ, we have been blessed with an open invitation to approach the throne of God in prayer and thanksgiving.)
3. The Bible compares Satan to a roaring lion (1 Peter 5:8). God delivered Daniel from the lions. In what way has God delivered us from Satan?
   (Jesus' death and resurrection defeated Satan, who cannot stand against us if we are in Christ, and nothing—not even Satan—can separate us from the love of Christ.)

59

Daniel Sees Heaven (Daniel 7)

Reviewing God's Word

Fill in the blanks.

1. Daniel saw a **dream** as he lay in his bed.
2. The Ancient of **Days** took His seat.
3. A stream of **fire** issued and came out from before Him.
4. A **thousand** thousands served God.
5. The court sat in judgment, and the **books** were opened.
6. Behold, with the clouds of heaven there came one like a son of **man**.
7. All **peoples**, nations, and languages should serve Him, the Son of Man.
8. His dominion is an **everlasting** dominion, which shall not pass away.

Thinking about God's Word

1. Why did Daniel write down his visions?
(He knew that they were from God for all the people of God.)

2. Whom did Daniel see sitting upon the throne?
(He saw the Ancient of Days, God the Father.)

3. How did Daniel describe God?
(He was dressed in white with white hair. His throne was made of fire, and fire came out from before Him.)

4. Whom did Daniel see surrounding God?
(Thousands upon thousands of angels stood before God and served Him.)

5. What was the court of heaven doing?
(It was sitting in judgment.)

6. Whom did Daniel say would serve the Son of Man (Jesus)?
(All people of all nations and languages will serve Jesus.)

7. What comfort did Daniel receive when his vision alarmed him?
(An angel assured him that all the saints of God will inherit the kingdom forever.)

Applying God's Word

1. How does Daniel's description of God help you understand what God is like?
(Answers will vary. God is eternal and holy [white hair and white robes]. He is a mighty and powerful ruler. He is surrounded by angels who worship and serve Him. Truly, God is awe-inspiring and deserving of all our worship and praise!)

2. What does it mean for us that Jesus, the Son of Man, was presented before the throne of the Father?
(Jesus was presented as our Savior and our perfect substitute. Because of His atoning death and resurrection, we will stand before the awesome throne of God on the Last Day with complete joy and confidence, knowing that we have been made righteous through Christ. Then we will join the multitudes serving God.)

3. What does it mean to be one of "the saints of the Most High"?
(Saints are all those made holy and set apart for service to God. We have been made saints through Baptism into Christ, and so we will receive the kingdom prepared for us in heaven.)

60

A New Temple and a New Wall
(The Books of Ezra; Nehemiah)

Reviewing God's Word

Circle Yes or No for each statement.

1. God commanded King Cyrus of Persia to build Him a house in Jerusalem.	(YES)	NO
2. King Cyrus himself provided the goods for the building of the temple.	YES	(NO)
3. The people of God resisted the command to return and rebuild.	YES	(NO)
4. The Jews and their neighbors freely offered aid.	(YES)	NO
5. The dedication of the temple involved a joyful Passover festival.	(YES)	NO
6. Nehemiah asked for permission to rebuild the wall of Jerusalem.	(YES)	NO
7. It took nearly a year to rebuild the city wall.	YES	(NO)
8. The nations around Judah were afraid when they saw the new wall.	(YES)	NO
9. The people celebrated the completion of the wall with music and sacrifices.	(YES)	NO

Thinking about God's Word

1. Why did King Cyrus tell the exiles to return to Jerusalem?
(The Lord commanded Cyrus to rebuild the temple, so he sent God's people back to undertake this project.)

2. Who returned to Jerusalem?
(The heads of the tribes of Judah and Benjamin, the priests and Levites, and everyone whose hearts God moved to be part of the rebuilding returned to Jerusalem.)

3. How did the Israelites get the supplies they needed for the temple?
(Not only did the people of God give all they could, but all their neighbors contributed as well, by the command of King Cyrus.)

4. Why did Nehemiah ask to return to Jerusalem?
(He heard that the wall of Jerusalem was in disrepair, and he wanted to rebuild it.)

5. Why did Nehemiah tell the people they should rebuild the wall?
(With a restored wall, they would no longer suffer the mockery of their enemies, but Jerusalem would again be a prosperous and protected city.)

6. Why were the nations around Judah frightened?
(When the wall was rebuilt successfully and quite quickly, the enemy nations knew that the Lord was with Judah.)

Applying God's Word

1. King Cyrus probably didn't believe in the LORD, but God used him anyway to deliver the people of God from exile. What does this mean for how we view our rulers today?
(Whether or not the people in our government or other positions of authority are Christians, God can use them for His purposes. God works through all people to accomplish His will.)

2. Those "whose spirit God had stirred" worked to rebuild the temple. What does this tell us about why we do good works?
(It is the Spirit of God in us who moves us to serve God and to do good works. God gives us both the will to follow Him and the strength to do so [Philippians 2:13]. God moves in all believers to motivate works of love in response to the salvation we've received through Christ.)

3. How might reading about the joy of the Israelites as they worshiped in the new temple affect our attitude toward worship?
(We often take for granted our churches and the opportunity we have to worship freely. Truly, our churches and freedom to worship are gifts from God! Let us join the psalmist in responding with gladness to the invitation to go the house of the Lord.)

61

Esther and the King
(Esther 1–2)

Reviewing God's Word

Draw lines to match each name to the correct description.

1. Ahasuerus	Official in charge of the women
2. Esther	Jew who saved the king's life
3. Mordecai	High-ranking official to whom everyone had to bow
4. Vashti	Young Jewish woman who won the king's favor and became queen
5. Haman	King in Susa
6. Hegai	Queen who refused to appear before the king at his feast

Thinking about God's Word

1. Why did King Ahasuerus want Queen Vashti to appear before him and his officials?
   (He wanted to show all the people and princes her beauty.)

2. How were both the king and queen acting sinfully?
   (Ahasuerus only wanted to show off his wife's beauty, as if she was just his possession. Vashti didn't respect her husband.)

3. What did the king do with Queen Vashti?
   (He sent her away and sought a new queen to replace her.)

4. Why is it important that both Mordecai and Esther were Jews?
   (The Jews were God's people. Mordecai had been part of the people of Judah who were exiled. The Jews were foreigners in the land of Persia.)

5. What happened to Esther in the palace?
   (She won the king's favor, and he made her queen. King Ahasuerus even gave a feast in her honor.)

6. What did Mordecai do to earn himself a place in the king's record?
   (Mordecai found out about a plot to kill the king and told Esther so she could warn the king. The criminals were found and hung. The king made note of the fact that Mordecai saved his life.)

7. Why did Haman want to destroy the Jews?
   (Mordecai refused to bow down to Haman, even though everyone else in the land did. Haman was angry and wanted to get rid of Mordecai and all of his people.)

Applying God's Word

1. The story of Esther is a beautiful example of how God directs events to accomplish His will. How does this account show God using even sinful actions to bring about His will?
   (Ahasuerus and Vashti were both acting sinfully, but God used the removal of Vashti to make room for Esther to become queen. It can be discouraging to see how our world is so full of sin, but we can find comfort in the knowledge that God works even through sinful people and sinful actions.)

2. How did Mordecai show godly care for Esther?
   (Mordecai took care of his cousin Esther because both her parents had died. He raised her and tried to protect her when she went to the palace by warning her not to let others know she was a Jew.)

   Whom has God placed in your life to care for you?
   (Answers will vary. Take a moment to thank God for those people who take care of you!)

3. Haman wanted to destroy all the Jews. Why could Mordecai and Esther be sure his plan wouldn't succeed?
   (God had promised that even in exile He would protect a remnant of His people and bring them home. Because the Jews worshiped the Lord, they could trust in His deliverance.)

62

God Saves His People
(Esther 3–8)

Reviewing God's Word

Draw a line through the sentences that are not true.

1. ~~King Ahasuerus came up with a plan to get rid of the Jews.~~
2. Mordecai asked Esther to go to the king and plead for the Jews.
3. Most people who went to the king uninvited were killed.
4. ~~The king was angry that Esther came before his throne.~~
5. Esther told the king about Haman's wicked plot.
6. ~~The king spared Haman because he was a powerful man.~~
7. Mordecai took over Haman's position in the king's court.

Thinking about God's Word

1. Why would it have taken great courage for Esther to approach the king?
   (Anyone who approached the king's throne without being summoned was killed unless the king held out his scepter.)
2. How did Mordecai convince Esther to go to the king?
   (He told her that perhaps she was placed in the palace "for such a time as this.")
3. What was Esther's first request of the king?
   (She asked the king and Haman to join her for a feast.)
4. What did Esther ask for from the king the second time he offered to grant any request?
   (She asked for her own life and for the lives of her people.)
5. Why would it have taken special courage for Esther to plead for her people at this feast?
   (While Haman himself was present, Esther told the king about Haman's wicked plot.)
6. How was Haman punished?
   (He was hanged.)
7. How did God bless Esther and Mordecai?
   (Esther received Haman's house, and Mordecai was given Haman's position.)
8. How did God deliver His people?
   (The king wrote a new edict protecting the Jews from being destroyed, and all the Jews rejoiced.)

Applying God's Word

1. God placed Esther in the palace in order to deliver the Jews. In what way might God have placed you in your home or school or church "for such a time as this"?
   (Answers will vary.)
2. Esther was afraid to approach the king because she knew she might be killed for coming before the throne uninvited. Why can you approach God's throne through prayer with joyful confidence?
   (Jesus has taken the punishment for our sin and made us righteous in God's sight through His death and resurrection. Because we are forgiven, we have no reason to fear God's wrath. Instead, we can have confidence when approaching God with any and every concern and know that He hears all our prayers.)
3. Romans 8:34 says "Christ Jesus . . . is at the right hand of God . . . [and] is interceding for us." How is Esther's role in this account like Christ's role of intercessor?
   (Esther went before the king to plead for her people and speak on their behalf. Jesus is our intercessor who speaks on our behalf before the Father. God grants us forgiveness and salvation for the sake of Christ Jesus.)

63

Waiting for God's Messenger (The Book of Malachi)

Reviewing God's Word

Draw lines to match each image to the idea it represents.

1. Incense	Strong cleansing from sin
2. Refiner's fire	Christ / warm light of the Gospel
3. Fuller's soap	Joy and excitement over our salvation
4. Stubble	Prayers
5. Sun of righteousness	Protection and healing
6. Wings	All the arrogant and evildoers
7. Leaping like calves	Purifying nature of God's judgment

Thinking about God's Word

1. Where and when does Malachi say people will glorify God's name?
   (Everywhere and at all times, God's name will be glorified.)

2. What does God mean when He compares Christ to a person who purifies metals?
   (Jesus takes away our sins and makes us spiritually pure and clean before God.)

3. How did the LORD show that He would remember those who believed in Him?
   (He wrote their names in a book of remembrance to mark them as saved and heirs of heaven.)

4. To what relationship does God compare His relationship with those who believe in Him?
   (He says He is like a father and we are like His sons [children].)

5. How does God make it clear in Malachi that He does punish sin?
   (He says that the wicked who don't fear God's name will be destroyed by the fire of His judgment.)

6. What does God promise to those who do fear His name?
   (He says the sun of righteousness [Christ] will come and bring healing and the joy of salvation.)

Applying God's Word

1. What does this section from Malachi say about how God views sin?
   (God is serious about sin. He will punish those who live in wickedness. Everyone who doesn't fear God's name will face God's judgment.)

2. Why can we face Judgment Day with all the carefree joy of a leaping calf?
   (Jesus, our Sun of Righteousness, has taken the judgment we deserve upon Himself and suffered in our place. By faith in His death and resurrection, we are spared the death we deserve and given healing and salvation.)

3. After the end of the Old Testament, God's people had to wait and trust Him for over four hundred years for the coming of the Messiah. What coming are we waiting for, and how can we be sure it will happen?
   (We are waiting for the second coming of Christ, when Jesus will return and take us home to heaven. As the people of the Old Testament found comfort in God's Word and in the knowledge of God's faithfulness in the past, we look to the promises of Scripture and the history of God's goodness to know that He will come again, as He has promised.)

64

The Birth of John Foretold (Luke 1)

Reviewing God's Word

Answer each question with names or words below. Some names will not be used.

1. Who was Zechariah's wife? **Elizabeth**
2. In what building was Zechariah burning incense? **Temple**
3. What was the name of the angel God sent to Zechariah? **Gabriel**
4. What was Zechariah's child to be named? **John**
5. The child would have "the spirit and power" of what prophet? **Elijah**
6. Who was unable to speak until the child was born? **Zechariah**
7. Name one other Bible woman who was blessed with a child in her old age. **Sarah**

Gabriel	Elijah	Palace
Temple	John	Zechariah
Elizabeth	Sarah	Joseph
Jesus	Michael	Mary

Thinking about God's Word

1. What great event was drawing near at the time of this lesson?
(The birth of Jesus, the promised Savior)
2. Which words tell that Zechariah and Elizabeth were God-fearing?
("They were both righteous before God, walking blamelessly in all the commandments of the Lord.")
3. Why was Gabriel sent to tell Zechariah that his wife would give birth to a son?
(Zechariah's wife, Elizabeth, had not been able to have children. Gabriel told Zechariah that he would soon have a son and that this boy had been chosen by God to call people to repentance and speak of the Messiah who was about to walk among them.)
4. Which words show that Gabriel came from God in answer to Zechariah's prayer?
("Your prayer has been heard.")
5. Why did Zechariah ask, "How shall I know this?"
(The angel's words seemed unbelievable. His wife was old and had not been able to have children up to that point. The fact that his son would be "great before the Lord" probably seemed both wonderful and overwhelming.)

Applying God's Word

1. What is a messenger? How does John fit in this role?
(A messenger is one who brings news. John told the people to repent and be ready to receive Jesus at His coming.)

Can we be messengers for Jesus too? Explain.
(Yes, but in a different way than John. He spoke about Jesus coming into the world to answer the need for a Messiah. We speak about our Savior, who has given eternal life to people who trust by faith in His work. In our messages to the world, it is important to tell that Jesus is coming again to unite to Himself all who believe.)

2. The angel came to bring Zechariah good news. How does the angel's message relate to the greatest Good News of all?
(Gabriel said that John would prepare the people for the coming of the Savior who would die on a cross to pay for the punishment of all mankind's sin. Like the Old Testament prophets, John spoke of Jesus' work before it was complete. As New Testament Christians, we can rejoice in all that God has fulfilled in His Son.)
3. Why is it sometimes hard for us to believe what God says? Can we trust that He will always keep His promises?
(God's words about forgiveness, salvation, and eternal life may seem so great and gracious that it does not appear possible that they could happen. God now "has spoken to us by His Son," [Hebrews 1:2] and all of Christ's words are found in the Bible. The Word made flesh is trustworthy as He fulfilled His purpose on earth and all prophecies about Him. He is "the faithful God who keeps covenant and steadfast love" [Deuteronomy 7:9].)

65

The Birth of Jesus Foretold
(Luke 1; Matthew 1)

Reviewing God's Word

Draw lines to match the words to their meanings.

1. virgin	title given to Jesus
2. favored	to see; notice
3. Behold	a promise of marriage
4. conceived	woman who has not had sexual relations
5. betrothed	greatly honored
6. Savior	place in a woman's body where a baby develops
7. womb	to become pregnant

Thinking about God's Word

1. Why was Mary afraid of the angel at first?
(Mary was probably scared because she had never seen an angel before. She was also troubled by the angel's high praise for her because she wondered what the greetings could mean.)

2. In which words did Mary say she did not understand how everything would happen that the angel had said?
("How will this be, since I am a virgin?")

3. With which words did Mary say that she would submit to God's plans for her?
("I am the servant of the Lord. Let it be to me according to your word.")

4. How does the angel make clear that God, not Joseph, was to be the true Father of Jesus?
(He tells Joseph, "That which is conceived in her is from the Holy Spirit.")

5. What did the angel tell Joseph that Jesus would do while on earth?
(Jesus was coming to save His people from their sins.)

6. What was the Savior to be named, according to the angel's words?
(Jesus)

Find three other names for Jesus from this lesson.
(Son, Son of the Most High, Son of God)

Applying God's Word

1. Which words of the Apostles' Creed are clearly referenced in Gabriel's message to Mary?
("Conceived by the Holy Spirit")

2. Which words of the lesson show that the Savior was to be true man, born of a woman?
("You will bear [give birth to] a son. You shall call His name Jesus.")

3. Why was it necessary for the world's Savior to be a human?
(God's plan of salvation included two stages for His Son to carry out—humiliation and exaltation. Jesus' humiliation means that He "emptied Himself, by taking the form of a servant, being born in the likeness of men" [Philippians 2:5–8] so He could die a physical death. Jesus died a blameless man and perfect God, and His suffering was in our place.)

66

The Birth of John
(Luke 1)

Reviewing God's Word

Underline the word or phrase that answers each question.

1. On which day after the baby was born was he circumcised? (Eighth—Fifth—Seventh—First)
2. What did the neighbors want to name the baby? (John—Joseph—David—Zechariah)
3. What did the Elizabeth insist that the baby should be named? (Zechariah—John—Jesus—David)
4. For whom was this child to prepare the way? (Jesus—Moses—His servant David—John)
5. Who asked for a writing tablet? (Elizabeth—The relatives—Zechariah—The angel)
6. Where was John until the day he appeared to Israel? (In the wilderness—In his father's house—In the temple—In prayer)

Thinking about God's Word

1. How did God's promise to Zechariah and Elizabeth come true?
(Elizabeth had a son.)

2. Why did Elizabeth's neighbors and relatives question whether the child should be named John?
(John was not a name common to their family, and it was tradition to pass on names from one generation to the next.)

3. In the naming of their son, how did the parents show that they had learned to obey and trust God without question?
(They insisted he be named John, as the angel had said.)

4. How did Zechariah settle the matter of naming the child?
(He wrote, "His name is John.")

After that, how were the angel's words fulfilled?
(Zechariah spoke when the child was named.)

5. How did Zechariah use his loosed tongue, which once had spoken words of doubt at God's promise?
(He began to praise God and prophesy.)

6. What did Zechariah prophesy about his son?
(He would be called a prophet of the Most High, for he would go on before the Lord to prepare the way for Him to give God's people the knowledge of salvation through the forgiveness of their sins.)

Applying God's Word

1. Which words, prophesied by Zechariah, refer to the work of Jesus, our Savior?
("He has visited and redeemed His people.")

2. When our sinful doubt and personal understanding seems to advise us to follow the plans of our heart, to whom should we be really listening?
(God)

Why?
(God knows and desires what is best for us. "All things work together for good, for those who are called according to His [God's] purpose" [Romans 8:28]. These words were true for Zechariah and they are meant for us today too.)

3. How can you show your thankfulness to God for having kept His promises?
(We can joyfully thank, praise, serve, and obey Him.)

67

The Birth of Jesus

(Luke 2)

Reviewing God's Word

Underline the word that makes each sentence true.

1. (Caesar Augustus—Quirinius—Julius) was the governor of Syria when Jesus was born.
2. Everyone had to go to (Rome—his own town—Bethlehem) to be registered.
3. Mary and Joseph traveled to Bethlehem from the city of (Syria—Jerusalem—Nazareth).
4. Mary and Joseph belonged to the line of (Joseph—David—Mary).
5. (Jerusalem—Nazareth—Bethlehem) was the city of David.
6. When the angel appeared, the shepherds in the field were (excited—terrified—curious).
7. Mary treasured up all these things and (buried—gave thanks—pondered) them in her heart.
8. (David—Joseph—God) was the true Father of the Child Jesus.

Thinking about God's Word

1. How did God use Caesar Augustus to bring Mary and Joseph to the place where Jesus was to be born?
   (Mary and Joseph had to return to Bethlehem because Caesar ordered that all people be registered in their own town.)

2. Which simple words tell how the Savior of the world was born at Bethlehem?
   ("While they were there, the time came for Mary to give birth. And she gave birth to her firstborn son. She wrapped Him in swaddling cloths and laid Him in a manger, because there was no place for them in the inn.")

3. What kind of birth announcement did God send when Jesus was born?
   (Angels announced the birth to shepherds.)

4. How do you know the shepherds believed the angels?
   (They went immediately to see Jesus.)

5. Which words show that Mary, the mother of Jesus, remembered all these events?
   ("Mary treasured up all these things, pondering them in her heart.")

6. What difference would it make to us if Jesus had not been born?
   (We would not have forgiveness, life, and salvation in His name.)

7. Who gave the Christ Child to us as a gift of love? Find the answer in John 3:16.
   (God)

Applying God's Word

1. Of what should the giving of presents at Christmas remind Christians?
   (God's gift of the Savior)

2. Why is the birth of Jesus such a significant event?
   (God became a human so that as both man and God, He could save us from our sins.)

3. Who told you the good news of how Jesus was born for you?
   (Answers will vary.)

   How can you show your appreciation for having been told these wonderful things?
   (Besides rejoicing and saying "thank you" to these confessors of Jesus' story, you can look to their example and learn to share with others the account of the incarnation and birth of Christ.)

4. How will Jesus' second coming be similar to and different from His first entrance into the world?
   (Similar: Jesus will descend from heaven, not as a spirit, but again in the flesh. He will not be coming as an earthly king. Different: Instead of entering the world to save mankind, Jesus will arrive to gather into His heavenly kingdom those who believe in Him and to condemn those who do not.)

68

The Visit of the Wise Men (Matthew 2)

Reviewing God's Word

Answer each question with words or phrases from below. Some words will not be used.

1. From where did the Wise Men originally come? **The East**
2. At which city did they stop for information? **Jerusalem**
3. What did the Wise Men call Jesus? **King of the Jews**
4. Who was troubled about the Wise Men's question? **Herod**
5. What was the age of the oldest boys that Herod killed? **Two**
6. Where was Joseph to flee with Mary and Jesus? **Egypt**
7. To what city in Israel did Joseph bring his family after trouble passed? **Nazareth**

Two	The East	Persia
Four	Egypt	King of the Jews
Jerusalem	Herod	Messiah
Nazareth	Bethlehem	Scribes

Thinking about God's Word

1. Why did the Wise Men need a star to guide them from their land to the Holy Land?
(They didn't know where the Savior was.)

2. How did the chief priests and scribes of Jesus' time discover where the Savior was to be born? See Micah 5:2.
(They studied the Old Testament prophecies.)

3. Why was Herod disturbed at the words of the Wise Men?
(He was the earthly king of the Jews, and he didn't want any threat to his power.)

What was the lie Herod told regarding what he would do after Jesus was found?
(He said he wanted to worship Him.)

4. Why did Herod ask the Wise Men to let him know where Jesus was to be found?
(He wanted to kill the newborn king.)

Why did God warn the Wise Men not to tell Herod where Jesus was?
(God wanted to prevent Herod from killing Jesus.)

5. How did the Wise Men show they believed Jesus is God?
(They brought Him gifts fit for a king and bowed down to worship Him.)

6. Jeremiah prophesied the "Slaughter of the Innocents" (see Jeremiah 31:15), which took place at this time. In what respect were the young boys in Bethlehem innocent?
(They were killed although they had never committed a crime.)

7. Why are God's children happy to know that the angels are always near them?
(Angels are God's helpers and representatives.)

How did God use angels in this story?
(He had them bring His messages from God to Joseph. These words of warning were part of God's plan to preserve and continue the plan of salvation He had set out to accomplish in Jesus.)

Applying God's Word

1. What did Herod not understand about Jesus' kingship? See Jesus' words to Pilate in John 18:33–37. **(Jesus is not a king in the political use of the term. Rather, Jesus is the ruler of the universe, the Lord of all who love and trust in Him.)**

2. The Wise Men brought Jesus gifts with a lot of earthly value. As we gather in church to worship Jesus, what can we remember about everything we are and possess?
(There is nothing we own, materially or otherwise, that God has not given to us as a blessing: "Every good gift and every perfect gift is from above" [James 1:17]. So, everything we could give is really an offering of thanks. God does ask that we give to Him in whatever way we are able [e.g., time, talents, money] and be in constant service to others. We are serving our king Jesus when we are helping those around us. And, as we gather to receive His Word and Sacrament during worship, we are filled with joy and relief to bring our confession of sins to Jesus.)

3. How did God defend Jesus against all danger and guard and protect Him from all evil when He was a baby?
(God told Joseph to take Mary and Jesus to Egypt.)

How does God do the same for you daily?
(He guards and protects us from evil. This doesn't mean that nothing bad ever happens to God's people, but we can trust that God's plan for our life is good—whether in life or death, He is with us.)

69

The Boy Jesus in the Temple (Luke 2)

Reviewing God's Word

Draw a line through the sentences that are not true.

1. ~~Each year, Jesus' parents traveled back to Bethlehem for the Feast of the Passover.~~
2. Even though Jesus wasn't with them, His parents left with their group to go home at the end of the feast.
3. At the time of this story, Jesus was twelve years old.
4. ~~Mary and Joseph assumed that Jesus would start walking home eventually.~~
5. Jesus' parents returned to Jerusalem because they could not find Him in the group.
6. ~~After three hours of searching, they finally found Him at the temple.~~
7. ~~Mary was glad that Jesus was talking to teachers in the temple.~~
8. The teachers were amazed by the way Jesus interacted with them—questioning, listening, and understanding.
9. ~~After His mother greeted Him, Jesus said, "I should have told you that I wanted to stay here."~~
10. Jesus obeyed His parents by leaving the temple with them to return to Nazareth.

Thinking about God's Word

1. Which words tell that Jesus' parents were obeying a requirement that God had put in place for the Israelites? Hint: see Deuteronomy 16:6.
("Jesus' parents went to Jerusalem every year at the Feast of the Passover.")

2. Why did Jesus study Scripture even though "all the treasures of wisdom and knowledge" (Colossians 2:3) are to be found in Him?
(According to His human nature, He grew in knowledge through the study of God's Word.)

3. Which words tell that Mary and Joseph were very worried over the thought of losing Jesus?
("Your father and I have been searching for You in great distress.")

4. How did Jesus reply to His mother when she shared about her concern about Him?
("Did you not know that I must be in My Father's house?")

What did Jesus mean when He said this?
(Jesus is the Son of the Most High God. He respectfully communicated to His mother that the temple was not only a place He wanted to be in order to learn and grow, but it was also where He judged He needed to be at that time.)

5. In what other recent story did Luke record that Mary treasured in her heart the events of Jesus' life?
(In the account of Jesus' birth. After the shepherds went through the countryside spreading the news, it is written that "Mary treasured up all these things, pondering them in her heart.")

Applying God's Word

1. What details of this account show Jesus to be true God? What details of this account show Jesus to be truly human?
(Jesus showed Himself to be caring for the business of His Father in heaven. Jesus was obedient also to His earthly parents; He grew and learned as other children do.)

2. How have you come to learn and know Scripture? Name people and things that have helped your spiritual growth.
(Answers will vary.)

3. Two commandments of God were clearly obeyed by Jesus in this lesson. What are they? How did Jesus obey them? How can we follow God's laws in these ways?
(The Third Commandment ["Remember the Sabbath day by keeping it holy"] and the Fourth Commandment ["Honor your father and your mother"]. Jesus studied God's Word, and He was obedient to His heavenly Father and His earthly parents. We, too, can worship God and obey God and our parents. We can't keep these commands perfectly, as Jesus did, but by the Spirit's power, we are moved to desire to keep the commandments.)

70

John Baptizes Jesus
(Matthew 3; John 1)

Reviewing God's Word

Underline the word or phrase that answers each question.

1. What was the theme of the message John preached? (Repentance—Rejoicing—Waiting—Forgiveness)
2. John baptized with water; what did he say Jesus would baptize with? (Water—God—Incense—Holy Spirit)
3. Whom did John feel unworthy to baptize? (Citizens of Jerusalem—Jesus—A Pharisee—Mary)
4. Which Old Testament prophet did John quote? (Isaiah—Malachi—Jeremiah—Ezekiel)
5. Read 1 Peter 3:18–21. Our Baptism is (a removal of dirt—a symbol of the start of our Christian life—salvation through Christ's death and resurrection—a promise of eternal life someday).

Thinking about God's Word

1. In his preaching, John said that it was time to repent. Why? **(Because "the kingdom of heaven is at hand.")**
2. Some priests and Levites asked John who he was, and John clarified that he was neither Elijah nor Christ. How did he describe himself? **("I am the voice of one crying out in the wilderness, 'Make straight the way of the Lord.'")**
3. Why was John angry when the Pharisees and Sadducees came to him to be baptized? **(These teachers of the law had no desire to confess their sins and live in repentance.**
4. How can you tell that John recognized Jesus as the Christ? **(John said, "I need to be baptized by You, and do You come to me?")**
5. What reason did Jesus give John for being baptized by him? **(Jesus said, "Let it be so, for thus it is fitting for us to fulfill all righteousness.")**
6. How did God show Jesus as the Savior whom He had promised to send? **(He spoke from heaven after Jesus had been baptized, saying, "This is My beloved Son, with whom I am well pleased.")**
7. How was each person of the Trinity revealed at this Baptism? **(Jesus was baptized, the Father spoke from heaven, and the Spirit descended like a dove to rest on Jesus.)**

Applying God's Word

1. Why did Jesus not need to be baptized as a sign of repentance? **(Jesus committed no sin and therefore had no need to repent.)**

   Why, then, was He baptized? **(He was baptized because He was obedient to God in our place. He was washed with water to show His oneness with the sinners He would later die for on the cross.)**
2. Three years later, after Jesus rose from the dead, He instructed His disciples to baptize "all nations" (Matthew 28:19). Does this command include babies too? Explain. **(Yes. Babies are by nature sinful and need forgiveness. Baptism is water and the Word of God together, and God is the creator of new life and faith at any age.)**
3. When we were baptized, the sign of the cross was made on our forehead and over our heart. What does this mean? Why is this sign a continual reminder of our Baptism? **(Making the sign of the cross reminds us of God the Holy Trinity's presence and saving work when we were called His child at the time of our Baptism. Jesus was killed on a cross, enduring the punishment for the same sins that He promises to forgive in Baptism.)**

71

The Temptation of Jesus (Matthew 4)

Reviewing God's Word

Fill in the blanks, using the words below. Some words will not be used.

1. Jesus was led into the wilderness by the **Spirit**.
2. He fasted **forty** days and nights.
3. The devil asked Jesus to turn **stones** to bread.
4. Jesus said, "You shall not put the **Lord your God** to the test."
5. The devil showed Jesus all the **kingdoms** of the world.
6. The devil asked Jesus to fall down and **worship** him.
7. Jesus said, "Be gone, **Satan**."
8. Three times Jesus said, "It is **written**."
9. Angels came and **ministered** to Jesus.

written	ministered	forty
kingdoms	Spirit	gold
Satan	stones	protected
worship	Lord your God	twenty-five

Thinking about God's Word

1. Into whose power had man fallen when Adam sinned? **(Satan's)**

   Why had Jesus come into the world? **(To save fallen humanity)**

2. With what words did the devil first try to plant the seed of doubt into Jesus, as he once had done to Adam and Eve? **(He said, "If You are the Son of God . . .")**

3. According to Jesus' words, by what shall man really live? **("Every word that comes from the mouth of God")**

4. When Satan tempted Jesus the second time, how did he try to twist God's Word to lead Jesus into sin? **(He told Jesus to throw Himself off the temple because God has promised in His Word that the holy angels will protect God's people. But, Jesus knew it was wrong to test His Father with that senseless act.)**

   How did Satan twist God's Word in the Garden of Eden? **(He asked Eve if God really said they should not eat from any tree of the garden, which was twisting what God actually said. He said all trees were for them, except the tree in the middle.)**

5. In the third temptation, how did the devil use humankind's love for honor and possessions to try to lead Jesus into sin? **(He showed Jesus all the kingdoms and splendor of the world, promising them to Jesus if Jesus would worship him.)**

   How had he used the same kind of temptation against Adam and Eve? **(He led Adam and Eve to believe that they could be like God if they ate the middle tree's fruit.)**

6. Satan tried to tempt Jesus my misquoting God's Word. How did Jesus respond? **(He quoted God's Word correctly.)**

7. What was Jesus' final answer to the devil's temptations? **("Be gone, Satan! For it is written, 'You shall worship the Lord your God, and Him only shall you serve.'")**

8. Why did Satan want to keep Jesus from doing His work? **(All humanity would remain in his control if Jesus failed.)**

   How did the devil plan to spoil what Jesus had come to do? **(He wanted to entice Jesus to sin.)**

Applying God's Word

1. What was the difference in outcome between Satan's attempt to lead Adam into sin and his attempt to lead Jesus into sin? **(Adam fell into sin; Jesus resisted temptation.)**

2. This account shows how Jesus obeyed God's Law in our place. Explain. **(The devil was unable to entice Jesus to sin. Jesus resisted temptation in our place, but He understands the pressure that His children are up against. "We do not have a high priest who is unable to sympathize with our weaknesses, but one who in every respect has been as tempted as we are, yet without sin." [Hebrews 4:15].)**

3. In facing and resisting temptation, Jesus pointed us to the means through which the Holy Spirit strengthens us to resist temptations. What is that means? **(Jesus resisted the devil through His use of the Word of God. Through the same Word of God, the Holy Spirit strengthens and encourages us for the new life He has called us to live in Him.)**

72

Jesus Calls Disciples
(John 1; Luke 5)

Reviewing God's Word

Draw lines to match each name to the actions that fit the person.

1. Jesus	• was introduced to Jesus by Philip.
2. Nathanael	• heard John speaking of Jesus.
3. Andrew	• was from Bethsaida.
4. Levi	• spoke of "catching men."
5. Simon	• said, "Behold, the Lamb of God!"
6. Philip	• was a tax collector.
7. John the Baptist	• wrote about Jesus before His coming.
8. Moses	• was given the name "Cephas" by Jesus.

Thinking about God's Word

1. Why do you think the first thing Andrew told his brother Simon was "We have found the Messiah"?
(God's people had been waiting for Him to send the Anointed One, who would save them from sin. By communicating this simple message, Andrew was sharing the good news that the promised Savior had finally come.)

2. How do you think Philip felt when Jesus turned to him and said, "Follow Me"?
(He probably had many emotions. He was probably excited to be called by the Messiah, but he was also likely scared about what it would be like to leave and follow the Lord.)

3. How do you know that people in this story were eager to hear God's Word?
(People were crowding around Jesus.)

What do you think Jesus talked about to the people?
(The people's sin and God's love, grace, and forgiveness)

4. Why did Simon not seem to think they should try fishing again?
(They had fished all night and caught nothing.)

What was it that made him willing to let down the net, nevertheless?
(Jesus' command)

5. How did Peter show that he knew he had seen a miracle?
(He fell down at Jesus' knees and said, "Depart from me, for I am a sinful man, O Lord.")

6. After the large number of fish was caught, why might Jesus have told Simon not to be afraid?
(Simon Peter was initially unsure how Jesus could be of any help with their fishing. Then he was overwhelmed as the boats began to sink and ashamed in the presence of Jesus' power.)

7. How did the disciples show that they believed and trusted in Jesus?
(They left everything and followed Him.)

Applying God's Word

1. Even though the disciples had not known Jesus for very long at the time He called them, what knowledge did they have of Him that allowed them to trust Him and follow?
(Because they had been told that Jesus was the Messiah, they knew that His power did not come from human strength. Although it was not completely clear to them that He was equally man and God, they knew they were safe with their Savior.)

Why do we have peace by knowing that Jesus is the Savior?
(We know that Jesus died in our place and that His new life gives us the promise of eternal life. Trusting in Him is made possible by the Holy Spirit.)

2. Simon Peter's exclamation of doubt—"Master, we toiled all night and took nothing!"—sounds like something we would say. Explain. **(We frequently doubt God's ability to provide for us. And yet, God remains at work, giving us just what He knows we need, which is not always what we hope for or want.)**

3. What does the amount of fish in the catch show about the growth expected in God's kingdom?
(Just as Peter and the other disciples caught a large catch of fish at Jesus' command, the apostles later brought large numbers of people into God's kingdom as the Holy Spirit worked through their preaching. God also asks us to be "catching men" as we share His Word about the Savior so that they might believe.)

73

Jesus Changes Water to Wine (John 2)

Reviewing God's Word

Fill in the blanks, using the words below. Some words will not be used.

1. There was a wedding in the city of **Cana**.
2. Mary, Jesus, and His **disciples** were among some of the guests.
3. The people ran out of **wine**.
4. Jesus said, "My **hour** has not yet come."
5. Mary told the **servants** to do whatever Jesus might command.
6. By His power, Jesus turned the **water** into good wine.
7. Jesus' **glory** was revealed during this miracle.

servants	day	guests
Nazareth	wine	water
hour	Cana	father
forgiveness	glory	disciples

Thinking about God's Word

1. Why was it not hard for Jesus' followers to believe that He was a true man?
(He was born into a human family and did things as other people did, such as attend weddings.)

2. Who went to Jesus for help when the wine had run out?
(Jesus' mother, Mary)

Why should we go to Jesus in prayer when we need help?
(He is the only real source of help.)

3. Why might Jesus have told His mother "My hour has not yet come"?
(He did not believe it to be the right time to reveal His power.)

4. How did Jesus show Himself to be true God before the people at Cana?
(He turned water into wine.)

5. What did Jesus use to turn water into wine?
(Only the power of His Word)

6. To whom was some water taken after it had been changed to wine?
(The master of the feast)

7. Which words tell how the disciples reacted after Jesus performed this miracle?
("And His disciples believed in Him.")

Applying God's Word

1. Tell how this account shows Jesus as both true man and true God.
(As true man, Jesus went to celebrate at a wedding with His disciples. He also listened to His mother's plea for help. As true God, Jesus performed a miracle, changing water into wine.)

2. Mary had great faith in Jesus' power, as seen in her statement "Do whatever He tells you." Read Hebrews 11:1 and explain what faith means.
(Jesus' promise of eternal life in heaven someday is nothing that we can see right now, but the gift of faith the Holy Spirit has given allows us to know that Christ is with us now, will fulfill our earthly needs, and will reveal heaven when He knows it is the right time.)

3. What does this account indicate about the scope of human problems about which Jesus is concerned?
(Jesus is concerned about all the things that trouble, inconvenience, embarrass, or threaten to harm us. Nothing that we are experiencing is too insignificant to bring to God in prayer. Jesus hears us and acts according to His will—which is always good.)

74

Jesus Clears the Temple (John 2)

Reviewing God's Word

Circle Yes or No for each statement.

1. The Jews in the temple welcomed Jesus when He arrived for the Passover.	YES	(NO)
2. Jesus made a whip to drive the sellers out of the area.	(YES)	NO
3. God's house had been turned into a "house of trade."	(YES)	NO
4. Jesus told the people they had to leave as soon as they finished their sales.	YES	(NO)
5. Jesus was angry because the Jews in the temple were disrespecting His Father's house.	(YES)	NO
6. The temple that Jesus promised to raise in three days would be made of stone.	YES	(NO)

Thinking about God's Word

1. Why would Jesus, who was called the Prince of Peace by the prophet Isaiah (9:6), make a whip to drive people out of the temple?
(**Jesus was not trying to be violent; He made a whip to restore order to the holy place of worship. Being one with the Father, He was deeply upset that the people abused His dwelling place, and He firmly emphasized that such behavior was not to be tolerated.**)

2. Selling livestock is not a sinful occupation. What reason did Jesus give the sellers and traders as to His just anger? (**The people in the temple had made God's house "a house of trade." Jesus was not angry about the buying and selling of animals, but rather where it was taking place.**)

3. The Jews asked, "What sign do You show us for doing these things?" What does this tell about their opinion of Jesus and His actions?
(**They did not believe that Jesus had the power and authority to decide what should happen in the temple.**)

4. Why might Jesus have spoken about His coming resurrection in order to answer the Jews? (**He wanted to point out the direct connection between the physical temple of the people and His body—God dwells in both. Christ had to die so that God could bless His people with forgiveness when they gathered in His house.**)

5. Which parts of this story indicate that the disciples paid close attention to the words of the prophets and their Teacher, Jesus? (**"Jesus' disciples remembered that it was written, 'Zeal for Your house will consume me,'" and "When therefore He was raised from the dead, His disciples remembered that He had said this."**)

Applying God's Word

1. The sinfulness of God's people was very visible in the temple—they were buying and selling in a place that God had declared holy and set aside for worship. They stopped caring about God's order and commands. In what ways is our body similar to the temple in this story? (**Our bodies are God's temples, since He has sent His Spirit to dwell in us.**)

2. When the Jews asked Jesus for a sign in order to understand His actions, it was almost as if they were saying, "Who do you think You are?" Later in Jesus' ministry, He asked Simon Peter, "Who do people say that the Son of Man is?" (Matthew 16:13). Why is it important that we know exactly who Jesus is? (**If Jesus wasn't who He said He was—that is, fully God and man—we would not have salvation in Him.**)

3. After clearing out the temple, Jesus took the opportunity to address the Jews' doubts about Him by pointing to His resurrection. The Jews could not make sense of His prophesy, but the disciples committed these words to heart. If we interact with nonbelievers, what can we learn from Jesus' eagerness to point to His new life? (**If Jesus had not been raised from the dead, He would not have had victory over sin, the devil, and the grave. The apostle Paul says that "if Christ had not been raised, then our preaching is in vain" [1 Corinthians 15:14]. This message needs to be at the center of our discussions with people who are skeptical about Jesus. The resurrection is at the heart of our faith!**)

75

Jesus Teaches Nicodemus (John 3)

Reviewing God's Word

Fill in the blanks, using the words of Jesus below. Some words may be used more than once or not at all.

1. "Unless one is born of **water** and the Spirit, he cannot enter the kingdom of God."
2. "We speak of what we **know**."
3. "As Moses **lifted** up the serpent in the wilderness, so must the Son of Man be **lifted** up."
4. "Whoever **believes** in Him should not perish but have eternal life."
5. "For God did not send His Son into the world to **condemn** the world."
6. "The **light** has come into the world, and people loved the darkness."
7. "Whoever does what is true comes to the light, so that it may be clearly seen that his **works** have been carried out in God."

believes	fail	perish
light	know	water
works	lifted	actions
strength	condemn	express

Thinking about God's Word

1. Why did Nicodemus decide to visit Jesus at night?
(He might have been busy during the day. Or, because Pharisees were often looked to for religious answers, Nicodemus may not have wanted people to see him talking to Jesus. It could have looked as though he didn't understand God's Word.)

2. With which words does Nicodemus show he recognizes that God's power is at work in Jesus?
("For no one can do these signs that You do unless God is with him.")

3. What Means of Grace is Jesus referring to when He tells Nicodemus that one must be "born of water and the Spirit" to enter the kingdom of God?
(Holy Baptism)

4. The story of Moses raising up the image of a bronze snake on a pole in order to heal God's dying people is found in Numbers 21:4–9. Tell about the connection between this story and Jesus' crucifixion.
(Moses lifted up a bronze snake on a pole, and God promised to preserve the life of all who looked at it. When Jesus was lifted up to die on the cross, God promised to give eternal life to all who trust in Jesus' act as the sacrifice for their sin.)

5. What (or who) is "the light" that Jesus speaks of? Hint: see John 8:12.
(Jesus says, "I am the light of the world.")

What does He mean by "the darkness"?
(The darkness is sin.)

6. At the end of this story, by whom does Jesus say that our works have been carried out?
(God)

Applying God's Word

1. Nicodemus confesses his understanding that someone can do the great miracles Jesus had performed only if "God is with him." Little did he know how much truth was in this insight! How would you explain to Nicodemus that God was more than just "with" Jesus?
(God sent His Son to earth, but He didn't just sit in heaven and watch Him. God is one with Jesus. Jesus is God. Along with the Holy Spirit, the Father and Jesus are part of the Holy Trinity—a divine mystery to us limited by our human reason. Jesus was called Immanuel by the prophets, meaning "God with us.")

2. What does Jesus' statement "the light has come into the world, and the people loved the darkness rather than the light" say about sinful people's reaction to God's Son walking among them? See also John 1:9–11. **(Jesus is the light who came to earth, and the sinful people around Him loved their sinful way of life. No one would ever seek Christ by his or her own choosing.)**

3. If our good works are carried out in God, should we be prideful when we serve others? Explain. **(No. God gives us the ability to do good works in His kingdom, so our attitude should not be prideful. Instead, we should rejoice in how He has equipped us for service and give all glory to Him.)**

76

Jesus and the Samaritan Woman

(John 4)

Reviewing God's Word

Draw a line through the sentences that are not true.

1. ~~Jesus' disciples told Him about Jacob's well near Samaria, and they set out to sample the water.~~
2. While He was waiting at the well for His disciples to return from the city, Jesus met a woman.
3. ~~It was not uncommon for a Jewish man and a Samaritan woman to have a conversation in public.~~
4. Jesus told the woman that He could give her living water that quenches thirst forever.
5. The Samaritan woman told Jesus that she had no husband to bring to Him.
6. ~~Once Jesus revealed He knew the woman's past, she exclaimed "Messiah!"~~
7. Samaritans from the town believed in Jesus both because of the woman's testimony and Jesus' teaching.

Thinking about God's Word

1. If Jewish people were not supposed to interact with Samaritans, why might Jesus have talked to the woman at the well?
(The fact that these two groups did not associate with each other did not matter to Jesus. As the One who had come into the world to extend salvation to all people, it was not in His nature to avoid spending time with people from certain backgrounds. Cultural boundaries didn't matter to Him.)

2. The woman did not immediately understand that she was talking to the Messiah. Why then is it reasonable that she was confused by a description of "living water"?
(Her understanding of Jesus' words was limited to what she thought was physically possible when drawing water, such as using a bucket, ropes, and jug. Jesus spoke of the blessing of water received spiritually—a concept she could not yet grasp.)

3. Which words of Jesus tell what happens to those who are given this special water?
("The water that I will give him will become in him a spring of water welling up to eternal life.")

4. When the woman eagerly asks for the water that Jesus speaks about, how does He respond?
(Jesus says to her, "Go, call your husband, and come here.")

5. From Scripture, it is clear that God is omnipotent (all powerful), omniscient (all knowing), and omnipresent (all present). Which of these attributes is made obvious during Jesus' interaction with the woman?
(God's omniscience is revealed when Jesus tells the woman about her past, and it has been only minutes after they first met. He says, "You have had five husbands, and the one you now have is not your husband.")

6. How does Jesus reveal His messianic identity to the woman?
(After they had talked about the Savior to come, Jesus shared: "I who speak to you am He.")

Applying God's Word

1. Against cultural norms, Jesus began talking to the Samaritan woman because she was dear to His Father in heaven. What can this teach us as we look for opportunities to share the Good News?
(We must not limit sharing our confession of the truth about Christ only to people like us—who understand us and of whom we are familiar. Jesus died for all, and God desires all to hear this news. God's definition of loving people may extend beyond our comfort zone, but He will equip us to speak.)

2. Which Sacrament involves being washed with God's life-giving water? Which person of the Holy Trinity is poured out on God's children at that time?
(The Sacrament of Holy Baptism takes place when ordinary water joins with God's Word to become living water that washes away sins. When we are baptized, God the Holy Spirit is "poured out on us richly through Jesus Christ" [Titus 3:6].)

3. One of three ways that God uses His Law is to lead us to recognize our sin. In which part of this story is Jesus using the Law in this way?
(Jesus asks the woman to bring her husband to Him because He knows her past involves multiple husbands. He perceives that the command "Go, call your husband, and come here" will convict the woman of her sin.)

77

Jesus Rejected at Nazareth (Luke 4)

Reviewing God's Word

Circle Yes or No for each statement.

1. Jesus went to the synagogue in Nazareth because it was the Sabbath day.	(YES)	NO
2. All in the synagogue were impressed that Jesus recited Isaiah's words from memory.	YES	(NO)
3. Jesus said to the people, "This Scripture is soon to be fulfilled before you."	YES	(NO)
4. The people remembered Jesus only as Joseph's son, and they were amazed by His words.	(YES)	NO
5. According to Jesus, "Only a prophet who speaks in his hometown is acceptable."	YES	(NO)
6. When Jesus spoke of Elijah and Elisha's time, he mentioned only Gentile believers.	(YES)	NO
7. In this story, God protected His Son from death before it was His time.	(YES)	NO

Thinking about God's Word

1. Why do you think Luke makes a point of mentioning that Nazareth was where Jesus "had been brought up"?
(This becomes significant as the story progresses. Those who were at the synagogue were especially amazed by Jesus' words because they had watched Him grow up and knew Him as simply "Joseph's son." The wrath that they later displayed proves Jesus' point that "no prophet is acceptable in his hometown.")

2. Considering that Jesus was fully God as well as man, what seems unusual about the fact that He read from the scroll of the prophet Isaiah?
(Because Jesus is the Word made flesh, He was present while Isaiah prophesied and so knew what had been written about His coming before He read the scroll.)

3. According to Jesus, who is "He" and who is "Me" in the prophetic phrase "He has sent Me to proclaim liberty"?
("He" is God the Father; "Me" is God the Son, Jesus. Isaiah received these words from God and wrote them down long before the Messiah came, but in the context of Jesus speaking them, the Scripture is fulfilled.)

4. Which words tell that Jesus had a captive audience when He began preaching?
("The eyes of all in the synagogue were fixed on Him.")

5. Jesus' message to the people at the synagogue that day was that God does not withhold mercy from those who are Gentiles, or non-Jewish. What two Old Testament examples did He share to show this truth?
(He pointed to the prophet Elijah's care by a widow of another land, as well as the cleansing of Naaman, a foreign man, at a time when other Israelites were sick.)

6. When Jesus had finished teaching, the people were angry and attempted to kill Him by throwing Him off a cliff. How did He escape this danger?
(He simply passed through the people who were plotting His death and went to another place.)

Applying God's Word

1. Why did the people in the synagogue become "filled with wrath" after Jesus preached?
(Since the time when God first established a covenant with the Israelites, they had been waiting for their promised Savior. They believed this Messiah would bring salvation to them, the Jewish people. It did not make sense to these Jews that the Messiah would also desire to save those outside the Israelite community. John 3:16 tells that God's compassion extends to cover the entire earth.)

2. In what way is Jesus' passing through the people's midst similar to the event when an angel appeared to Joseph, telling him to flee with Mary and Jesus to Egypt?
(In both instances, God was at work preserving the life of His Son.)

3. Just as it is true that a prophet is not accepted in his hometown, it can also be difficult to confess our faith to people we know really well and who may have known us throughout our childhood. "What will they think of me if I tell about the truth?" How do Jesus' words in Matthew 10:22 respond to this fear?
(In this passage, Jesus acknowledges that the disciples will be hated by people, but they will receive eternal life as they hold firm in their faith. God does not promise that we will avoid persecution; rather, He tells us to accept it, defend the faith, and place our trust in Him.)

78

Jesus Heals a Paralyzed Man (Mark 2)

Reviewing God's Word

Underline the word or phrase that makes each sentence true.

1. Jesus was inside a (house—synagogue—temple) when the paralyzed man was brought to Him.
2. The first thing Jesus did for the man was to (ask his name—heal his sickness—forgive his sins).
3. (Jesus—The sick man—The scribes) said, "Who can forgive sins but God alone?"
4. Jesus called Himself (the Messiah—the Son of Man—the Savior) in this lesson.
5. The teachers spoke evil things of Jesus (in their hearts—so that all could hear—in a low voice).
6. Jesus told the sick man to pick up his (belongings—bed—scroll) and go home.
7. The people who saw this miracle (laughed at the scribes—told Jesus to leave their country—glorified God).

Thinking about God's Word

1. Why did the four men bring their sick friend to Jesus?
(Their friend was paralyzed, and on his own he could not walk to hear Jesus.)

2. How did these men show their faith in Jesus' power to help?
(They did not allow the large crowd to stop their efforts to bring their friend in front of Jesus; they persevered through the problem because they knew Jesus was the only answer. Together, they made an opening in the roof of the house and lowered their friend to Jesus.)

3. Which words of Jesus tell what the man actually needed more than the healing of his body?
("Son, your sins are forgiven.")

4. Why did the scribes think that Jesus had mocked God?
(Jesus forgave the man of his sins, and the scribes rightly thought that this action was something only God can do. However, they were missing the point of Jesus' divinity, which truly enabled Him to do such things.)

5. Answer the question that Jesus posed to the scribes: "Which is easier, to say to the paralytic, 'Your sins are forgiven,' or to say, 'Rise, take up your bed and walk'?
(It would be easier to tell someone that his or her sins are forgiven.)

6. What reason did Jesus give for deciding to physically heal the man of his paralysis?
(He performed this miracle so that all who were present, including the doubting scribes, would know that "the Son of Man has authority on earth to forgive sins.")

Applying God's Word

1. The friends of the paralyzed man went to great lengths to be in Jesus' presence in order that He might richly bless their friend with healing. Today, Jesus gives us good gifts of healing as we gather for worship in God's house. Give an example of a time when your attitude was not like that of the man's friends.
(Examples will vary.)

2. Jesus blessed the paralyzed man with two incredible acts of healing, one of body and one of spirit. Which of these do you think is more important? Why?
(More important is spiritual healing—the forgiveness of sins. Our physical body's problems may be frustrating, but they are only temporary. Spiritual healing brings us into heaven, which lasts forever.)

3. What connections can you make between this man's friends taking Him to Jesus and parents bringing their newborn child to the waters of Baptism?
(Like the man, newborn babies are paralyzed—not physically, but with sin. They cannot move anywhere without being carried by those who love them. As parents bring their child to be baptized, they do so in faith, trusting God's power to heal. It is the triune God who speaks over the little one, saying, "Child, your sins are forgiven.")

79

The Sermon on the Mount (Matthew 5–7)

Reviewing God's Word

Fill in the blanks, using the words below. Some words will not be used.

1. Blessed are those who **mourn**, for they shall be comforted.
2. Blessed are the pure in heart, for they shall **see** God.
3. Rejoice, for your **reward** is great in **heaven**.
4. Love your **enemies** and pray for those who persecute you.
5. Your Father knows what you need before you **ask** Him.
6. Give us this day our daily bread, and forgive us our **debts**.
7. Lead us not into temptation, but deliver us from **evil**.
8. He was **teaching** them as one who had authority.

fight	know	see	stupidity
enemies	debts	heaven	teaching
Christ	reward	ask	worshiping
strength	battles	call	rest
fail	mourn	evil	flee

Thinking about God's Word

1. The pattern of the first part of Jesus' sermon involves Him listing the blessings that are given to those who recognize their sin and turn to Him in faith. Name some of the blessings that are given to God's people.
(The kingdom of heaven, comfort, a wonderful inheritance, the title "Sons of God," a great reward in heaven.)

2. Where does "the light" come from that Jesus speaks of when He says His followers "are the light of the world?"
(According to John 8:12, we know that "the light of the world" is Jesus.)

3. Which words of Jesus tell that God loves and provides for believers and unbelievers alike?
("For He makes His sun rise on the evil and on the good, and sends rain on the just and on the unjust.")

4. What might Jesus mean by instructing the people to not pray "empty phrases as the Gentiles do"? Didn't He come to earth to bring salvation for Jews and Gentiles?
(Jesus did come to pay for the forgiveness of all people. He uses the Gentiles' behavior as a negative example of wrongdoing because many of them worshiped false gods. Their long prayers to idols were meaningless.)

5. Everyone who hears Jesus' words but "does not do them" will be like whom?
(A foolish man who built his house on the sand.)

Applying God's Word

1. When Jesus describes people as "poor in spirit" and "those who mourn," He is not talking about any physical problems or sadness but rather about our spiritual poverty and mourning that comes about as a result of sin. Does this mean He might forget about your physical needs?
(No, but He knows that addressing our spiritual sickness because of sin is the most important healing He can bring. As in the previous story of the paralyzed man, God will surely bless you beyond what you can imagine—both in body and soul.)

2. As you reflect on Jesus' teaching that our light shines so that others "see [our] good works and give glory to [our] Father who is in heaven," explain why the statement "I won some souls today" is incorrect. **(That statement points to confidence in our own accomplishments and the greatness of our work in confessing the faith. People may [or may not] thank you for witnessing to them, but the work of salvation was actually God's. He is the creator of faith.)**

3. Edward Mote wrote the line "My hope is built on nothing less Than Jesus' blood and righteousness" as the opening to a well-known hymn. Does this describe the man who built his house on the rock or the man who chose to build on the sand? Why?
(This describes the man who built his house on the rock. Jesus shed His blood so that we could be covered with His righteousness, and this truth is a central message of the Gospel. Having the hope of eternal life because of Christ is a foundation that can't be destroyed in this life and will carry us into the next.)

80

Jesus Calms a Storm
(Mark 4)

Reviewing God's Word

For the following statements in Mark's Gospel, circle T for true and F for false.

Statement	T	F
1. "Jesus was tired and fell asleep by the sea."	T	(F)
2. "Jesus said to His disciples, 'Let us go across to the other side'."	(T)	F
3. "And no other boats were with Him."	T	(F)
4. "A great windstorm arose."	(T)	F
5. "The disciples wondered if Jesus would wake up."	(T)	F
6. "Do You not care that we are perishing?"	T	(F)
7. "Has your faith not been strengthened?"	T	(F)

Thinking about God's Word

1. How can it be shown from this lesson that Jesus was true man?
(He fell asleep.)

2. Why did the disciples awaken Jesus?
(The storm had become so violent that they feared they would drown; they knew Jesus could save them.)

3. With what words did Jesus calm the storm?
(He said, "Peace! Be still!")

4. Why did the wind and sea obey Jesus?
(He is one with God the Father, and therefore He created them and controls their patterns.)

5. Show from this lesson that Jesus was true God and true man.
(Although He slept like a normal man, Jesus demonstrated His power over the wind and waves. With only His speech, He determined the behavior of creation.)

6. What words of the disciples suggest they may have doubted Jesus, even while they asked Him for help?
(They said, "Teacher, do You not care that we are perishing?")

7. Why might Jesus have responded to their fear by saying "Have you still no faith"?
(The disciples had already spent a significant amount of time with Jesus as He had been preaching of peace and hope for life in the kingdom of God. He had performed miracles in their presence, and yet in a moment of trouble, they seemed to forget all of this.)

6. Who permitted this great storm to come up?
(God)

Why does God let trials and temptations come to His children?
(To test our faith and to demonstrate His power, glory, and ability to provide for people in need)

Applying God's Word

1. Psalm 121:4 says God "will neither slumber nor sleep." What does this mean for you?
(It is comforting to know that our God is never asleep but always aware and attentive to our needs. When we call upon Him, He will always hear us and act in His time and according to His good plan.)

2. John 1:3 says, "All things were made through Him, and without Him was not any thing made that was made." Who is "Him" in this verse? How does this verse help us understand Jesus' command over the storm?
(Jesus is the one spoken of in this verse. In this passage of John, we are reminded that the "Word," Jesus, was with God when the world was made. He, too, controls creation.)

3. Why do you think the disciples ask one another "who then is this?" with regard to Jesus? Don't they know the identity of Him who called on them to follow?
(When Jesus called His disciples, many eagerly shared with one another joy over finding the Messiah. They had been waiting for the fulfillment of God's promise, but at this point they still didn't really understand what that meant and how Jesus would interact with men and creation.)

81

Jesus Heals Jairus's Daughter (Mark 5)

Reviewing God's Word

Underline the word or phrase that answers each question.

1. What was soon to happen to Jairus's young daughter? She would (become sick—die—prophesy—possess demons).
2. How did Jairus suggest Jesus could help his daughter? (Lay His hands on her—Bring living water to her—Cast the demon out of her—Talk to her)
3. What did the sick woman in the crowd do in order to be healed? (Called out to Jesus—Stopped Jesus' disciples—Touched Jesus' garment—Spoke to Jairus)
4. What did Jesus call death in this lesson? (Rest—Sleep—The end of everything—Heaven)
5. How did the people in Jairus's house show unbelief in Jesus? (They cast Him out—They laughed at Him—They left the room—They closed their ears)
6. How old was Jairus's sick daughter? (30—12—21—5—6)
7. What was Jesus' first instruction to those in the room who witnessed the miracle? (Tell no one—Spread the news—Feed the girl—Let the girl rest)

Thinking about God's Word

1. How did Jairus show his faith in Jesus?
(He pleaded with Jesus to come to his house because his daughter was dying. He was confident in Jesus' power to heal, even when the situation seemed to be hopeless, as seen in his words "lay Your hands on her, so that she may be made well.")

2. In what way was the sick woman's understanding of Jesus' ability to heal similar to that of Jairus?
(She knew that simply Jesus' body, His very presence, was more than enough to heal sickness.)

3. After the woman had already felt her healing take place, how did Jesus explain the way she had been cured?
(He said to her, "Daughter, your faith has made you well.")

4. When people from Jairus's house brought news of His daughter's death, what did they suggest Jesus should do?
(They did not see any point in Jesus traveling to the girl because they believed her death could not be reversed. They told Jairus, "Why trouble the Teacher any further?")

5. What did Jesus mean when He said, "The child is not dead but sleeping"?
(He could bring the girl to life as simply as if He were waking her from sleep.)

6. How did Jesus show the people of Jairus's household that His power over death meant resurrection was possible?
(He brought the young girl back to life.)

7. At what other time did Jesus prove that He had the ultimate victory over the grave?
(When He rose from His own death)

Applying God's Word

1. Even though Jairus's daughter was near death, Jairus didn't turn to despair. What did he do instead? How should we react when faced with a scary situation?
(Jairus found Jesus and asked Him to come home with him and help. He trusted in Jesus' power and knew He would act. When we are faced with problems, we can take all of our concerns to God in prayer. We might not understand how He is helping, but He is at work doing what is best for us.)

2. Jesus told the sick woman that her faith had made her well. Who gave her that faith?
(Her faith was a gift from God. Jesus heals His children as He works through this faith.)

3. Because of Jesus, the death of Jairus's daughter was really just a short sleep that had a joyful ending. Why does death mean the same thing for you too?
(When we believers die, our bodies perish but our souls will be alive in heaven and reunited with our bodies on the Last Day. That's a reason to rejoice!)

82

Jesus Feeds Five Thousand (John 6)

Reviewing God's Word

Draw a line through the sentences that are not true.

1. ~~A few people followed Jesus across the Sea of Galilee, and more joined when they heard about a meal.~~
2. At the time of this story, the Feast of the Passover was about to take place.
3. Jesus asked Philip where they should buy bread to feed the crowd as a way to test him.
4. ~~In response, Philip pointed out a young boy who already had loaves of bread and fish.~~
5. ~~Jesus said, "Have the people gather around me for the blessing."~~
6. All the people in the crowd were able to eat until they were full.
7. ~~When the crowd saw this sign, some inwardly questioned Jesus' authority.~~

Thinking about God's Word

1. Why did a large crowd follow Jesus when He crossed the sea and went up on a mountain?
("They saw the signs that He was doing on the sick," and probably out of curiosity and amazement, they desired to know more about this great miracle worker.)

2. What did Philip's answer show that he thought was of first importance in getting food for hungry people?
(He said, "Two hundred denarii [eight months' wages] would not buy enough bread for each of them to get a little.")

3. Why do you think Jesus tested Philip with a question about how to provide for Jesus' followers?
(Jesus "knew what He would do" to supply the bodily needs of the people who had come into the wilderness to hear Him teach. However, He wanted to hear from Philip the degree of trust that he had in His power. Although Jesus knows all things, He desired to hear an honest response from His disciple.)

4. What made Andrew's observation of the small boy seem at first like an impossible solution?
(Five small barley loaves and two small fish could never feed five thousand people. By human means, this is not doable and makes no sense.)

5. What did Jesus do before He distributed the bread to the crowd?
(He gave thanks to His Father for the food that the people were about to eat.)

6. In which prayer do we say, "Give us this day our daily bread"?
(The Lord's Prayer)

Why do we ask for it, even when we know we'll get it?
(So that we remember that all we have comes from the hand of our gracious God.)

Applying God's Word

1. Jesus' miracles led the people to see Jesus as a great prophet. But, Jesus is more than a prophet. Explain. **(Jesus is the very Son of God and Savior of the world. All the prophets in the Old Testament were equipped by God to lead His people and point to the coming of His Son. After His resurrection, Jesus appeared to two disciples "and beginning with Moses and all the Prophets, He interpreted to them in all the Scriptures the things concerning Himself" [Luke 24:27].)**

2. Jesus could have simply taken away the people's hunger. Instead, He satisfied their hunger by multiplying a meager lunch of bread and fish. In another meal, the Lord's Supper, Jesus also provides for His disciples (then and now). What do they receive with the bread and wine?
(With the bread and wine, recipients receive the very body and blood of Christ.)

What benefits are received?
(The forgiveness of sins, new life, and salvation)

3. After He fed the crowd and commanded the gathering of leftovers, Jesus withdrew, because He knew the people would want to "take Him by force to make Him king." Why would Jesus not have wanted this to happen?
(Jesus had not come to be an earthly king with political power but a heavenly king who forgives sins and gives grace to His people. All of Christ's authority came from His Father [John 13:3]; God the Father created and sustains His Son's kingship.)

83

Jesus Walks on Water (Matthew 14)

Reviewing God's Word

Answer each question with a word or phrase from below. Not all words will be used.

1. Whom did Jesus send away? **crowd**
2. What was Jesus doing while He was on the mountain alone? **praying**
3. During which watch did Jesus come to His disciples? **fourth**
4. What did the disciples think Jesus was when they saw Him? **ghost**
5. With which word did Jesus tell Peter to walk out to Him? **come**
6. What describes Peter's feelings when he saw the wind? **afraid**
7. With what name did the disciples acknowledge Jesus' identity? **Son of God**

crowd	afraid	come	Son of God
fourth	ghost	praying	follow
Peter	planning	last	Christ

Thinking about God's Word

1. Why were the disciples not waiting for Jesus when He came down the mountain from praying?
   (Jesus had previously asked them to continue on to the other side of the water.)

2. How did the disciples show that they didn't believe that it was Jesus when they saw Him coming toward them?
   (They said, "It's a ghost!" and were filled with fear.)

3. What did Jesus say to them?
   ("Take heart; it is I. Do not be afraid.")

   How did those words show why He had come to them?
   (He had come to be with them, to comfort them with His peace, both then in the temporal sense and for all eternity.)

4. Why could Jesus walk on water?
   (Jesus is fully God, and as evidenced in His earlier control of the waters, has command over creation.)

   Why could Peter walk on water?
   (Jesus gave him the power to walk on water through the faith that God had created in him.)

5. What did Peter cry out when he began to sink?
   ("Lord, save me.")

6. Which words of Jesus tell why Peter began to sink?
   ("You of little faith")

   How did Jesus show Peter that He was the merciful Son of God?
   (He reached out and caught Peter, rescuing him.)

7. What two things happened when Jesus climbed into the boat?
   (The wind ceased and Jesus' disciples worshiped Him.)

Applying God's Word

1. Jesus spoke to His disciples in their fear, saying, "Take heart; it is I. Do not be afraid." How do these words of Jesus apply also to us?
   (Jesus invites us to trust in Him. We, too, don't need to fear situations in life that seem unbelievable or harmful. On the cross, Jesus extended His hands in order to protect all mankind from sinking eternally into death.)

2. As soon as Peter began to look at the scary environment around him, he began to sink. In what way are we like Peter?
   (Peter began to sink when he was no longer looking at Jesus. When we take our eyes off our powerful and trustworthy Savior, we also begin to doubt and lose faith.)

3. This was not the first time the disciples had witnessed Jesus' power over the created elements, but their responses to Jesus' miracle of calming the wind was drastically different in this story. Compare their reactions. **(In the story of Jesus calming the storm, the disciples marveled at Jesus' identity and asked, "Who is this?" This time, the disciples eagerly confessed that Jesus is the Son of God, and they worship Him.)**

84

Jesus Is Anointed
(Luke 7)

Reviewing God's Word

Circle Yes or No for each statement.

1. Jesus was walking by a Pharisee's house, and He asked to eat with him.	YES	(NO)
2. The sinful woman began weeping as she stood in Jesus' presence.	(YES)	NO
3. The Pharisee took pity on the woman because of her repentant cries.	YES	(NO)
4. Jesus called the Pharisee by his name.	(YES)	NO
5. In Jesus' analogy with the debtors, the sinful woman at His feet is represented by the debtor who owed the most to the moneylender.	(YES)	NO
6. The Pharisee objected to Jesus' accusations regarding his lack of hospitality.	YES	(NO)
7. Jesus said, "He who is forgiven little, loves little."	(YES)	NO

Thinking about God's Word

1. In previous stories, the Pharisees were intrigued by Jesus, but they were often provoked to anger by His teachings and the way He used His authority. Name one action of Simon the Pharisee that makes him similar to others in his group.
(Like other Pharisees, Simon mentally doubted Jesus' power and truth.)

2. The woman did not say a word during this event. In what four ways did she show that she was deeply grieved by her sin?
(She not only cried, but she also wept in the presence of her Lord. With those tears, she washed Jesus' feet. She then proceeded to kiss His feet and pour expensive ointment over them.)

3. Which part of this story reveals Jesus' omniscience?
(Similar to other moments when Jesus sensed a Pharisee's smug doubt, Jesus told Simon that He had something to say to Him because He knew the judgment he had mentally passed on the woman.)

4. In Jesus' story about the moneylenders, what does the debt stand for? Think about the point that Jesus made.
(The debt represents the sin that a person carries with them. Like an amount of money not paid off, sin hangs over a human's head and heart like a great weight.)

5. According to Jesus' final words to the woman, why was she now clean to stand in His presence?
(Her forgiveness was on account of her faith. Jesus looked at her faith, a gift from Him, and cancelled the enormity of her sin.)

Applying God's Word

1. Recall the Beatitudes that Jesus taught during His sermon on the mount. Which of these promises especially speak to the woman who came to Jesus? Why?
("Blessed are the poor in spirit, for theirs is the kingdom of God" and "Blessed are those who mourn, for they shall be comforted." This woman recognized the depth of her sin and her inability to do anything to save herself. The only thing she knew to do was to go to Jesus with a confession of brokenness.)

2. In Mark 2:17, Jesus said, "I came not to call the righteous, but sinners." Did the Pharisee need to hear these words? Do you?
(If the Pharisee would have been able to hear and trust that these words are truth, he would have seen the error in his ways. He called the woman on the floor a "sinner," as if he had never done anything wrong. Romans 3:11 tells us that "none is righteous." We, too, need these reminders. Our sinful flesh can tempt us to think too highly of ourselves and ignore the sin that God came to forgive.)

3. What would you say to a person who shares a desire to be forgiven but is worried that he or she has done too much wrong for Jesus to love him or her?
(It is by God's gift of faith in the atoning death and resurrection of His Son that your sins are forgiven. The quantity or enormity of sin does not matter. God would have condemned all of us if Jesus had not provided forgiveness and salvation.)

85

Peter's Confession and Jesus' Transfiguration

(Matthew 16; Mark 9)

Reviewing God's Word

Fill in the blanks, using the words below. Some words will not be used.

Jesus asked His disciples who **people** thought the Son of Man was. "Some say John the Baptist, others say **Elijah**, and others Jeremiah or one of the **prophets**," they replied. Jesus said to them, "Who do **you** say that I am?" **Simon Peter** told Jesus their belief that He is the **Christ**. Jesus said that "flesh and blood" had not **revealed** that truth to him, but His Father in heaven. This knowledge has power over **hell**.

war	death	Elijah	flesh
people	Simon Peter	scribes	Christ
cripples	John	revealed	you
prophets	transfigured	hell	Pharisees

Fill in the blanks with words from below.

Jesus took **Peter**, **James**, and John up a mountain. He was **transfigured** before them. Two men, **Moses** and **Elijah**, appeared with Jesus. Peter offered to build **tents** for the three men. A voice came from a **cloud**, saying Jesus is God's **Son**. **Jesus** told the disciples not to tell what they had seen.

Moses	Jesus	Elijah	covered
two	six	Son	pillar
Peter	John	James	choice
cloud	transfigured	tents	fires

Thinking about God's Word

1. Which words show that the people on earth during Jesus' time had different ideas about who the Son of Man was? **(The disciples said, "Some say John the Baptist, others say Elijah, and others Jeremiah or one of the prophets.")**

2. According to Jesus, who was helping Peter answer Jesus' question about His identity? **(God the Father)**

3. When Jesus says "you," He is talking about all the disciples —those present with Him then and those throughout the world now. To what will Jesus' disciples be given the keys? **(The kingdom of heaven)**

4. What did Jesus look like in His transfiguration? **("His clothes became radiant, intensely white, as no one on earth could bleach them.")**

5. What did Peter want to do for Jesus? Why? **(Peter wanted to make three tents—one each for Jesus, Moses, and Elijah. He "did not know what to say," so this was what he came up with in his fear.)**

6. Why were the disciples terrified? **(They were seeing Jesus in His glorious, divine state. He was with two great Old Testament leaders whom the disciples had never seen but only heard about.)**

7. What did the voice from the cloud say? Who was speaking? **(God the Father spoke, saying, "This is My beloved Son; listen to Him.")**

8. When would the disciples be able to tell people what they had seen on the mountain? **(This experience was to be shared after Jesus had risen from the dead.)**

Applying God's Word

1. In the story of Jesus' transfiguration, the disciples heard God the Father's message that Jesus is His Son. Up until that time, they had not seen Jesus appear to them in His glory. Why, then, is Peter's confession (in the first story) so remarkable? How is our confession about Jesus like Peter's? **(When Peter confessed that Jesus is "the Christ, the Son of the living God," he was speaking not from having seen Jesus' divinity but from the faith given to him by God. We, too, confess that Jesus is the Son of the living God—not from having seen Him in His divinity, but because God's Spirit has given us faith to believe.)**

2. Jesus said, "On this rock I will build My Church." The "rock" He is talking about is the confession that Jesus is the Christ, the Son of God. What is wrong with the belief that all different religions can bring you into God's kingdom? **(Other religions have false gods, or they do not teach that Jesus was the Christ— God's Son, who paid for the sins of the world. Any church that does not teach that Jesus is the Christ is in error.)**

3. Tell the meaning of the words spoken from the bright cloud for the disciples and for you. **(God identified Jesus as His Son. Those witnessing the event saw Jesus in His glory and recognized Him as the promised Messiah. God tells believers of all time to listen to Jesus. We have God's message written for us in His Word, the Bible.)**

86

Jesus Sends the Seventy-Two (Luke 10)

Reviewing God's Word

Underline the word that makes each sentence true.

1. The Lord appointed (12—72—45) men to go ahead of Him to preach about the kingdom of God.
2. Before the men left, Jesus told them that "the (land—water—harvest) is plentiful, but the laborers are few."
3. "I am sending you out as lambs in the midst of (war—wolves—confusion).
4. "Say to them, 'The (kingdom—love—Law) of God has come near to you.'"
5. "The one who hears you (rejects—calls—hears) Me."
6. "I saw (God—rulers—Satan) fall like lightning from heaven."
7. "Rejoice that your (actions—names—hearts) are written in heaven."

Thinking about God's Word

1. Where did Jesus send the seventy two?
(The appointed men were to go ahead of Jesus "into every town and place where He Himself was about to go.")

2. The "harvest" that Jesus referred to was the task of calling human souls into His kingdom. The "laborers" are people who work to tell others about the kingdom of God. Which category do the seventy-two fall under—souls in need of salvation or laborers who preach God's word?
(They are laborers ready to work for the good and enlargement of God's kingdom.)

3. What three items are the men not supposed to bring during their travels?
(Moneybag, knapsack, or sandals)

4. How will the men be provided with food and drink along the way?
(Jesus said they are to extend His peace to a house upon arriving in a new town. Then, they will stay with that family during their whole time in the town, eating what is put in front of them.)

5. What are the men supposed to do if a town does not receive them?
("Go into its streets and say, 'Even the dust of your town that clings to our feet we wipe off against you. Nevertheless know this, that the kingdom of God has come near.'")

6. Jesus says that "the one who rejects Me rejects Him who sent Me." Rewrite this sentence in your own words. **(The one who denies Jesus denies God.)**

7. When the seventy-two return from their mission, they are excited about Jesus' power over demons. Jesus says there is a better reason to be joyful. Why should the men have rejoiced?
(Their names are written in heaven.)

Applying God's Word

1. The "laborers" that God sends out today are His people who have come to faith in Jesus by God's grace and who now tell others about the Gospel. Who are some people in your life who told you about the way to heaven?
(Answers may vary. Examples may include pastors, Sunday school teachers, parents, and friends.)

2. Jesus tells the men to bring few belongings on their journey, because they will be provided for by people they meet along the way. In this, Jesus emphasized being content with their living situation so they could focus on teaching about God's kingdom. According to these instructions, what should be our top focus in life?
(We should first and foremost be concerned that our confession of faith and eagerness to tell others about God's kingdom is not overshadowed by the things we own on earth or the environment in which we live.)

3. If we have a chance to tell someone what Jesus has done for him or her, should we expect that person to become a Christian? Explain. Hint: does Jesus say that all people will receive Him?
(No, we know that not all who are told about God's kingdom will come to faith, immediately or ever. If we share the Good News with someone and that person rejects it, he or she is rejecting God Himself. If the person receives this news, it is the work of God.)

87

The Good Samaritan (Luke 10)

Reviewing God's Word

For the following statements, circle T for true and F for false.

1. The lawyer's question about how to inherit eternal life was to test Jesus.	(T)	F
2. After the lawyer summarized the Law, Jesus said, "And you can never fulfill this to live."	T	(F)
3. While going to Jerusalem, a man fell into the hands of robbers.	(T)	F
4. The man called out for help, but no one came to him.	T	(F)
5. A priest tended to the man's wounds.	T	(F)
6. A Samaritan had compassion on the man.	(T)	F
7. The wounded man was the Good Samaritan.	T	(F)
8. A neighbor to others is one who shows mercy.	(T)	F

Thinking about God's Word

1. What two questions did the lawyer, the expert in the law, wish to have answered?
("What shall I do to inherit eternal life? Who is my neighbor?")

2. How did Jesus respond to the lawyer's first question?
(Jesus responded with a question: "What is written in the Law?")

3. According to Jesus, did the lawyer interpret the Law correctly? Explain. **(Yes, Jesus confirmed his answer and added that man will live if He keeps the Law.)**

4. Which words tell that the wounded man's condition was severe?
("Leaving him half dead")

5. How did the priest and the Levite react when they saw the injured man?
(They passed by on the other side of the road.)

6. By using a parable, what lesson did Jesus teach the lawyer?
(The meaning of the word "neighbor.")

7. In what ways was the Samaritan a neighbor, or one who showed mercy, to the wounded man?
(He came to where the man was, bandaged his wounds, took him to an inn, took care of him, and paid for his extended care.)

8. What did Jesus ask the lawyer, the expert in the law, at the end of His parable?
("Which of these three, do you think, proved to be a neighbor to the man who fell among the robbers?")

Applying God's Word

1. In response to the lawyer's summary of the Law (what God asks of us), Jesus told him that if he did this, he would live. This message is not very comforting to sinners like us. Why?
(If our salvation depended on our ability to love God and our neighbor perfectly, we would not have the gift of eternal life. We humans cannot do all that God asks of us because our very flesh is sinful.)

2. God instructs all of His people to show mercy to those around them; as a result, believers and unbelievers alike become our neighbors. List some specific tasks that involve showing compassion to other people.
(Answers may vary.)

3. How did Jesus prove Himself to be a good neighbor to us?
(Jesus did what we were unable to do for ourselves. He kept the Law perfectly in our place and died to pay the penalty we deserved for disobeying the Law.)

88

Jesus Heals a Blind Man (John 9)

Reviewing God's Word

Draw lines to match each name with the action that fits the person or place.

1. Jesus	disapproved of Jesus' miracle on the Sabbath.
2. Neighbors	was healed by Jesus and confessed Him as Lord.
3. Siloam	asked, "How were your eyes opened?"
4. Pharisees	said, "Who sinned, this man or his parents?"
5. Disciples	anointed the blind man's eyes with mud.
6. The man born blind	is the pool where the blind man washed.

Thinking about God's Word

1. What did Jesus' disciples think was the cause of the man's blindness?
(They believed that either the man or his parents had committed a sin that resulted in him being born blind.)

2. According to Jesus, why was this man blind?
(He was born this way so that "the works of God might be displayed in him.")

3. Describe the order of events when Jesus healed the man.
(First, Jesus spat on the ground to make mud from the dirt. Then He rubbed the mud in the man's eyes and instructed him to wash in the pool of Siloam. The man did as he was told and returned from the pool with his sight restored.)

4. What reason did the Pharisees give for not believing that Jesus was sent from God?
(Jesus healed the blind man on the Sabbath day.)

5. How did the man describe Jesus' identity when he was questioned by the Pharisees?
("He is a prophet.")

6. What happened after the man was cast out?
(Jesus found him and asked him if He believed in the Son of Man.)

Applying God's Word

1. In this story, Jesus reminds His disciples that He is "the light of the world." His light is needed by all people, not simply those who physically can't see. In what way are we blind without the light that Jesus brings?
(Without Jesus' light, we are left in spiritual darkness. Our sin is like blindness.)

2. The Pharisees accused Jesus of not keeping the Sabbath laws. Which of the Ten Commandments tells us God's law for how we should regard the day set aside for worship?
("Remember the Sabbath day by keeping it holy.")

What does this commandment mean?
(It means that we should gladly gather in church with God's people to hear His Word and be strengthened in our faith.)

3. Many people who knew the blind man were curious about how he was given sight. When they asked, the man told them all that Jesus had done for him. Jesus has done a lot for you too. Tell about His healing in your life.
(I was born blind in my sin, but the Holy Spirit has given me the gift of faith to know the light of Jesus' truth. His perfect life, death, and resurrection were meant for me.)

89

The Good Shepherd (John 10; Psalm 23)

Reviewing God's Word

Using the words below, fill in the blanks to make each Scripture quote correct. Some words will not be used.

1. The sheep follow him, for they know his **voice**.
2. The **thief** comes only to steal and kill and destroy.
3. The good shepherd lays down his **life** for the sheep.
4. I **know** My own and My own know Me.
5. He restores my **soul**.
6. Your rod and Your staff, they **comfort** me.
7. Surely goodness and mercy shall **follow** me.
8. I shall dwell in the house of the LORD **forever**.

faults	heart	convict	life
wolf	voice	remember	follow
comfort	hope	forever	know
protect	bless	soul	thief

Thinking about God's Word

1. Who is a thief and robber of the sheep?
   ("He who does not enter the sheepfold by the door but climbs in by another way.")

2. How, specifically, does the shepherd call his sheep?
   (By name)

3. In John 14:6, Jesus says, "I am the way, and the truth, and the life. No one comes to the Father except through Me." Which words in this story say a very similar message?
   ("I am the door of the sheep. If anyone enters by Me, he will be saved.")

4. What could happen if a hired hand takes care of the sheep?
   (Since he does not own the sheep, he will not be as concerned with their safety if danger arises. Instead, he will try to save himself. If he sees a wolf coming, he will leave the sheep and flee.)

5. Of whom does Jesus speak when He talks about "the sheep"?
   (All those who by faith believe in Him.)

6. Jesus compares His close relationship with His sheep (or, people) with that of His intimate connection to whom?
   (God the Father. Jesus said, "I know My own and My own know Me, just as the Father knows Me and I know the Father.)

7. Name some of the ways that Psalm 23 describes how the Lord provides abundantly for His people.
   (He makes us lie down in pastures, leads us beside still waters, restores our soul, prepares a table for us even when enemies are threatening, and has called us into His eternal kingdom. [Other answers may apply.])

8. Which words of Psalm 23 would be especially comforting if we or someone we know is close to death?
   ("Even though I walk through the valley of the shadow of death, I will fear no evil, for You are with me; Your rod and Your staff, they comfort me.")

Applying God's Word

1. Humans have a tendency to pride themselves in being independent; that is, being able to take care of matters on their own. Sheep are not known for being smart animals and are very dependent. Why, then, would we want to be like sheep?
   (Humans are always following something, and if it's not the voice of Jesus, then it's our sinful desires. Neither sheep nor humans can protect themselves from God's judgment. We can take joy in coming at our Good Shepherd's call, because He protects us and saves us.)

2. In Psalm 23, King David describes the peace he has even though the possibility of death is all around him. His comfort is that God is with him. We also have this comfort, as well as a promise sealed in a death that Jesus predicts in this story. Where is this prediction and how did this death take place? What does this mean for you?
   (Jesus says, "I lay down My life for the sheep." He was crucified. By trusting that His death means we have new life, we know we will be in heaven with Jesus when we die. This is the comfort that David speaks of.)

3. Isaiah 53:7 says, "Like a lamb that is led to the slaughter, and like a sheep that before its shearers is silent, so He opened not His mouth." This verse of Scripture is not comparing us to sheep. Who is being prophesied about and what event is being described?
   (Here the prophet Isaiah describes when Jesus will be condemned to death and nailed to a cross. According to this account, He will be obedient to those over Him and follow the path they mark for His death.)

90

Jesus Raises Lazarus (John 11)

Reviewing God's Word

Draw a line through the sentences that are not true.

1. ~~When Jesus learned that His friend Lazarus was ill, He rushed to go heal him~~.

2. Jesus first spoke to His disciples about Lazarus's death by saying that Lazarus was asleep.

3. Martha and Mary both said, "Lord, if You had been here, my brother would not have died."

4. ~~Jesus said, "Your brother may rise again."~~

5. Jesus wept with Martha, Mary, and the Jews who were gathered to mourn.

6. ~~After rolling away the stone, Jesus entered the tomb to lay His hands on Lazarus.~~

7. Some Jews who witnessed Lazarus's resurrection went to tell the Pharisees what He had done.

Thinking about God's Word

1. Why did the disciples misunderstand Jesus when He said Lazarus had "fallen asleep"? What did Jesus really mean?
   (They thought that Jesus was speaking about literal, physical sleep; therefore, it seemed silly to travel to see Lazarus when he seemed to be recovering on his own. For Jesus, who has power over the grave, death is no different than sleeping.)

2. Who was the first of Lazarus' sisters to greet Jesus?
   (Martha)

3. Which of Martha's first words to Jesus show that she still had hope even during her sadness?
   ("But even now I know that whatever You ask from God, God will give You.")

4. How does Mary's action upon greeting Jesus point to her trust in Him as One sent from God?
   (She fell at His feet—a posture used by those who are worshiping.)

5. Because Jesus knows that His Father always hears Him, why did He pray aloud in front of Lazarus's tomb?
   (Jesus thanked His Father that the people around Him could hear His prayer so "they may believe" He was sent by God.)

6. With what words did Jesus bring Lazarus back to life?
   ("Lazarus, come out.")

7. How did the Pharisees react when some Jews told them about Jesus raising Lazarus from the dead?
   (They began making plans to put Jesus to death.)

Applying God's Word

1. Why did Jesus delay in going to see Lazarus? We know He had the power to heal His friend before he died.
   (When Jesus shared with His disciples about Lazarus's death, He explained why He did not go to prevent it: "For your sake I am glad that I was not there, so that you may believe." His plan was to wait until Lazarus died so He could visit the mourners with the promise of resurrection and display His power in that very miracle.)

2. Are you ever like Martha and Mary—frustrated and confused by God's timing? Explain.
   (Yes, we are always anxious to have answers on our own time and are impatient when the situation doesn't make sense. Trusting that God is at work is an ability that we have through the work of the Holy Spirit.)

3. Jesus' power over death was certainly displayed as He resurrected the bodies of Lazarus and Jairus's daughter. But what resurrection is even more significant for us?
   (Jesus' resurrection is the truth that provides believers with the certain promise of their own resurrection and eternal life with Him in heaven.)

91

The Prodigal Son
(Luke 15)

Reviewing God's Word

Write the name of the speaker next to each quote. Some names will not be used.

1. "I am no longer worthy to be called your son." **younger son**
2. "Bring quickly the best robe, and put it on him." **father**
3. "Your brother has come." **servant**
4. "These many years I have served you." **older son**
5. "And the father divided his property between them." **Jesus**

servant	older son	mother
master	God	citizen
Jesus	father	younger son

Thinking about God's Word

1. What did the younger son do with his inheritance after he received it?
   (He squandered it in reckless living.)
2. What hardship did the foreign country, in which the younger son was living, begin to experience around the time that he had spent everything?
   (A severe famine)
3. Why did the son feed pigs?
   (He had no other way to live.)
4. How can you tell that the younger son was truly sorry for what he had done?
   (The story says that "he came to himself," meaning he realized the error of his ways.)
5. Find the words the son planned to use to say that he had sinned greatly and no longer deserved his father's love.
   ("Father, I have sinned against heaven and before you. I am no longer worthy to be called your son. Treat me as one of your hired servants.")
6. How can you tell that the father had been waiting for his son?
   (The father saw the son when he was still a long way off and ran out to meet him.)

   How did the father show that he had never stopped loving his son and that he had already forgiven him?
   (He welcomed him back and celebrated his return with a great feast, music, and dancing.)
7. What did the father mean when he said, "For this my son was dead, and is alive again"?
   (The son was dead in sin, but he was made alive through forgiveness and restored to the family.)
8. Why was the older son upset about the celebration being held for his brother?
   (He did not think that his brother was deserving of the loving kindness being shown by their father.)
9. Of whom is the father of this lesson a true picture?
   (God)

Applying God's Word

1. Did the father approve of his son's sin? How did he show that he loved him just the same?
   (No, but he forgave the son and welcomed him back.)

   How did the father's never-ending love help the son?
   (The father welcomed his son, restored him to the family, and allowed him a new beginning.)
2. When have we acted like the younger son?
   (We act like the younger son when we turn our back on Jesus by seeking comfort in our sin and neglecting to use our gifts to serve others in the kingdom of God.)

   the older son?
   (We act like the older son when we think that our worth or goodness means we are better than others.)
3. Will God ever turn away a repentant person because his or her sin is too great for forgiveness? Explain.
   (No, God always loves, forgives, and restores repentant sinners.)

92

Jesus Heals Ten Men (Luke 17)

Reviewing God's Word

Fill in the blanks, using the words below. Some words will not be used.

1. Jesus traveled along the border between **Samaria** and Galilee.
2. **Ten** men with leprosy met Him.
3. They called, "Jesus, **Master**, have mercy on us!"
4. Jesus told them to show themselves to the **priests**.
5. One of the men came back and **praised** God in a loud voice.
6. Jesus asked, "Were not ten **cleansed**?"
7. Jesus said to the Samaritan, "**Rise** and go your way; your **faith** has made you well."

Samaria	changed	Messiah	praised
priests	Ten	Nazareth	cleansed
Jesus	gatekeeper	younger son	faith
Master	welcomed	Five	knowledge

Thinking about God's Word

1. Where was Jesus going?
   (Jerusalem)

2. As Jesus entered a village, how did ten men alert Him to their need?
   (They "stood at a distance and lifted up their voices, saying, 'Jesus, Master, have mercy on us.'")

3. Why did the men want Jesus to have mercy on them?
   (They had leprosy.)

4. At what point during the story did the men realize they had been cleansed?
   (This healing took place while they were going down the road to find the priests.)

5. Who came back to praise God?
   (One leper who was a Samaritan)

6. What words describe how the man acted when he returned to see Jesus?
   (He was "praising God with a loud voice" and "he fell on his face at Jesus' feet.")

7. What did Jesus mean when He said, "Where are the nine?"
   (Why didn't the others also return to offer their thanks and praise?)

8. Why was the leper healed?
   (His faith made him well.)

Applying God's Word

1. Tell how this account shows Jesus as the Lord and Savior of all people.
   (Jesus demonstrated His desire to help and save those who were looked down on by society, including lepers and Samaritans.)

2. How have you acted like one of the nine men who did not return to give thanks to Jesus?
   (We often forget that our daily cleansing from sin and blessings of this life are gifts from God.)

3. What example does the Samaritan provide for those who love and trust in Jesus as Savior? Hint: think of the ways God has restored you to health.
   (The Samaritan praised Jesus for physically healing him. God often gives new health to our bodies as well, and this is a cause for thanksgiving. Even more than that, God healed us from the leprosy of our sin.)

93

Jesus and the Little Children (Mark 9–10)

Reviewing God's Word

Underline the word or phrase that answers each question.

1. What group was discussing who was the greatest in the kingdom of heaven? (Parents—Disciples—Priests—Scribes)
2. If someone receives a child in Christ's name, whom is that person really receiving? (Disciples—Peter—Their parents—Jesus)
3. What was the disciples' reaction when people brought children to Jesus? (Rebuking—Approving—Smiling—Worrying)
4. Why did Jesus say He wanted the children to be brought to Him? (They always chased Jesus—They were calling for Him—They were orphans—The kingdom of God belonged to them)
5. What did Jesus do for the children? (Healed—Taught—Blessed—Questioned)

Thinking about God's Word

1. Why might the disciples have kept silent when Jesus asked about their discussion?
(They had been arguing, and they might have assumed Jesus would not approve of this topic.)

2. What must a person do to be first in God's kingdom?
("He must be last of all and servant of all.")

3. According to Jesus, anyone who receives a child in His name is receiving Him too. If someone receives Jesus, who is that person ultimately receiving?
(The person receives the One who sent Jesus—God the Father.)

4. With which words did Jesus tell the disciples that they were not to keep the children away?
("Let the children come to Me. Do not hinder them, for to such belongs the kingdom of God.")

5. How does Jesus emphasize that all people, regardless of age, are to be like children in terms of their faith?
("Truly, I say to you, whoever does not receive the kingdom of God like a child shall not enter it.")

Applying God's Word

1. Jesus said that the greatest in His kingdom were those who were "last of all and servant of all." What does this say about people who believe they need to loudly proclaim their good works so others see what a "good" Christian they are?
(Jesus calls His people to live a life of humble service toward others. God blesses our good works, but drawing a lot of attention to them is not in line with Jesus' emphasis on humility.)

2. Though God is without sin, our relationship with Him has similarities to our relationship with our earthly father. How so? In what ways does God provide beyond our fathers' capabilities?
(Humans are completely dependent on God to provide for them. For both believers and unbelievers, He sustains life and health and gives material blessings. To those who respond to the Holy Spirit at work in His Word, He gives the gift of faith.)

3. What can this story tell us about the necessity to baptize babies, welcoming them into God's kingdom?
(Jesus clearly says that children have saving faith. They receive this gift and belong to the kingdom just like anyone else whom the Spirit has been poured out on.)

94

Jesus and Zacchaeus
(Luke 19)

Reviewing God's Word

For the following statements, circle T for true and F for false.

Statement		
1. Jesus passed through Jericho.	(T)	F
2. A man named Zacchaeus was a chief tax collector.	(T)	F
3. Zacchaeus climbed into a tree so he could mock Jesus as He passed by.	T	(F)
4. Jesus looked up in the tree and told Zacchaeus He would be staying at his house.	(T)	F
5. Zacchaeus showed that he was sorry for his sins by returning four times as much as he had gotten dishonestly.	(T)	F
6. Jesus said, "Today salvation has passed by this man."	T	(F)
7. Jesus came to save what was lost.	(T)	F

Thinking about God's Word

1. Why did Zacchaeus decide to climb a tree when he heard Jesus was passing through?
(He "was seeking to see who Jesus was," but because he was not a very tall man, he could not see above the crowd that had gathered.)

2. How do we know that Jesus was looking for Zacchaeus when He came to the tree?
(He looked up to where Zacchaeus was.)

3. Why did some people grumble?
(Jesus was going to be the guest of a "sinner." Many people did not think highly of tax collectors because of their dishonesty, and the crowd thought it strange that Jesus would spend time with tax-collector Zacchaeus.)

4. Was Jesus the guest of a sinner? Explain.
(Yes. Zacchaeus was a sinner just like every person Jesus encountered during His ministry. He was completely forgiven by Jesus.)

5. Tell how the Holy Spirit was at work in Zacchaeus's life after he was found by Jesus and received Him as his Savior.
(Zacchaeus promised to give half of his goods to the poor, and if he had cheated anybody out of anything, he would pay back four times the amount.)

6. Why did Jesus go with Zacchaeus?
(To bring salvation to Zacchaeus and his house)

7. In which words did Jesus give the reason for His coming into the world?
("For the Son of Man came to seek and to save the lost.")

Applying God's Word

1. Isaiah 55:6 tells us to "seek the Lord while He may be found; call upon Him while He is near." This is an instruction to listen to God's Word. How did Zacchaeus, against some obstacles, respond to this? How do you?
(Because of his physical limitations, Zacchaeus could have easily given up on seeing Jesus. Still, he sought to be in His presence, and the result was that he received faith and believed in the truth Jesus taught. Many things can distract us from Jesus. But, as the Holy Spirit works in us, we desire to remain close to Jesus through His Word.)

2. How did those who grumble show that they did not understand why Jesus had come to them?
(Jesus came for repentant sinners—those who recognize their sinfulness. Those who suppose themselves righteous apart from Him do not belong to Him, since they do not recognize their need for the Savior.)

3. What does Jesus' message of salvation for Zacchaeus mean for us?
(We are among those who were lost. God sent His Son to earth to pay for our sins, seek us out of our sinful wandering, and draw us to Him.)

95

The Triumphal Entry (Matthew 21; Mark 11; Luke 19)

Reviewing God's Word

Underline the word or phrase that answers each question.

1. Toward which city were Jesus and His disciples going? (Capernaum—Bethlehem—Jerusalem—Jericho)

2. Which sad part of Jesus' life was soon to begin? (Hiding—Preaching—Suffering—Ascension)

3. What animals did Jesus send two disciples to find? (Donkey and colt—Horse and pony—Sheep and goat—Watch dog and tabby cat)

4. What did the disciples tell those who questioned them about taking the animals? ("Your king has come"—"It is the cause"—"The Lord needs them"—"Please, sir")

5. Who spoke the words "Say to the daughter of Zion"? (Pharisee—Moses—A prophet—The disciples)

6. What name did the multitude apply to Jesus? (Hosanna—Son of David—Rabbi—Savior)

7. If the people had not praised Jesus upon His entrance, what did He say would cry out? (Babies—Fields—Stones—Donkeys)

8. What did Jesus show Himself to be in this lesson? (Savior—Mighty—Rich—Government official)

Thinking about God's Word

1. Why did Jesus send two disciples ahead to the next village? **(To get a donkey and her colt)**

2. Why did Jesus want a donkey instead of another animal? **(Jesus planned to fulfill the prophecy that described His arrival in Jerusalem, and specifically that He would be on a donkey.)**

3. What were the words of the prophecy that was fulfilled? **("Say to the daughter of Zion, 'Behold, your king is coming to you, humble, and mounted on a donkey, and on a colt, the foal of a beast of burden.'")**

4. Who is the daughter of Zion? Hint: what city was Jesus entering? **(Jerusalem)**
   Who was the king who came to the daughter of Zion? **(Jesus)**

5. How did the disciples prepare the donkey for Jesus? **(They put their cloaks on it to make a saddle.)**

6. What did the crowd do to honor Jesus as their King? **(They spread their cloaks and tree branches on the road and praised Him.)**

7. What did the people shout? **("Hosanna to the Son of David! Blessed is He who comes in the name of the Lord! Hosanna in the highest!")**

8. How did the Pharisees react to all of the commotion? **(They told Jesus to "rebuke" His disciples.)**

Applying God's Word

1. Horses were used by soldiers and kings for delivering messages and appearing before the people. Donkeys were used in the everyday life of the people. Besides fulfilling the prophecy, how did Jesus' entrance on a donkey indicate the kind of king He was? **(Throughout His ministry, Jesus preached [among other things] a message of humility and service to others. He said of Himself that "the Son of Man came not to be served but to serve, and to give His life as a ransom for many" [Matthew 20:28]. He was a heavenly king, establishing His Father's kingdom.)**

2. The people shouted, "Hosanna to the Son of David!" *Hosanna* means "save us now." Why did they give Jesus the name "Son of David"? In what way would Jesus provide an answer to their cry during the week ahead? to your cry? **(The "Son of David" refers to Jesus' lineage [see page 154 of *120 Bible Stories*]. The people of the city knew He was a descendant of King David, and they also trusted in God's promise to provide a Messiah through this line of people. Jesus answered their request for salvation by dying for their sins on that Friday. His death is the atonement for our sins today too.)**

3. Jesus' entrance into Jerusalem marked the start of a very important week in His life; we call it "Holy Week." We remember this story with a celebration called "Palm Sunday." Name any other holy days you can think of that are commemorated in the days immediately following Palm Sunday. **(Maundy Thursday [Jesus instituted the Lord's Supper], Good Friday [Jesus died on the cross], Easter Sunday [Jesus rose from the dead].)**

96

The Widow's Coins
(Mark 12)

Reviewing God's Word

Draw a line through the sentences that are not true.

1. ~~Jesus was talking to a Pharisee when one of His disciples pointed to the widow.~~

2. The rich people at the temple put in large sums of money.

3. ~~A widow put in one piece of silver, which was her last day's wage.~~

4. ~~Jesus said, "This poor widow has put in the same amount as all those who are contributing."~~

5. Others who had contributed to the offering simply gave out of their abundance.

Thinking about God's Word

1. How do you think the rich people felt about their contributions?
   (They were able to "put in large sums of money." Perhaps they felt proud of their offering to God and happy about their ability to give an amount that would make a difference.)

2. Why did the widow give an offering of only two coins?
   (That was the most she could give because it was all the money she had.)

3. What do the widow's actions communicate about her faith in God?
   (Since "all she had to live on" was put into the offering box, it seems that the widow simply trusted that God would provide for her. She likely knew that her daily bread came from Him and He would be faithful to supply her needs.)

4. What did Jesus mean when He said that the others at the temple "contributed out of their abundance"?
   (Their offering was very little compared to all the wealth they had.)

Applying God's Word

1. Why might Jesus have explained to His disciples His understanding of the widow's giving?
   (Humans naturally think that whoever has the most of something [wealth, intellect, possessions] is better than those who have very little. Jesus wanted His disciples to know that this is not God's attitude toward abundance and giving. It's a matter of one's heart and not the amount in one's hand.)

2. "The LORD sees not as man sees: man looks on the outward appearance, but the LORD looks on the heart" (1 Samuel 16:7). These words were spoken when one of Jesus' ancestors, David, was anointed as king. But this truth applies in many situations. What can this verse tell you about the widow's giving? your own?
   (The widow did not give with selfish intentions in mind, but she gave up her personal riches out of faith in God. God saw her sacrifice as commendable because her heart was in the right place. God is not concerned with what an offering [of money, time, etc.] looks like to others, but He cares that it is sincere and given out of trust.)

3. What are the greatest riches you have been given?
   (The gift of faith, and with that, the forgiveness of sins and salvation through Christ)

97

The Lord's Supper (Luke 22)

Reviewing God's Word

Draw lines to match each name to the action that fits the person.

1. Judas	sought a way to kill Jesus.
2. John	instituted the Lord's Supper.
3. Satan	agreed to betray Jesus in return for money.
4. Chief priests	claimed he was ready to die with Jesus.
5. The disciples	helped Peter prepare the Passover.
6. Peter	entered into Judas Iscariot.
7. Jesus	allowed Jesus to host the Passover in his home.
8. The man with a jar	were the first recipients of the Lord's Supper.

Thinking about God's Word

1. Which great Jewish festival was drawing near at this time?
(Passover)

2. The chief priests took their time in devising the best way to put Jesus to death because "they feared the people." What, exactly, was their fear regarding the people?
(They were afraid that Jesus' followers would be outraged or even revolt if He was put to death.)

3. From whom did Judas receive motivation to go to the chief priests?
(Satan)

4. What message were Peter and John supposed to tell the man with the jar of water?
("The Teacher says to you, Where is the guest room, where I may eat the Passover with My disciples?")

5. How did Jesus tell His disciples that this would be the last Passover meal they would all share?
("I have earnestly desired to eat this Passover with you before I suffer.")

6. What did Jesus do with the bread before He broke it and gave it to His disciples?
(He gave thanks.)

When was Jesus' body broken for us?
(Although none of His bones were broken, Jesus' body was physically broken by His death on Calvary.)

7. Tell what Jesus said about the bread and the cup of wine.
(Of the bread, He said, "This is My body, which is given for you." He said the cup, meaning the wine, "is poured out for you" and "is the new covenant in My blood.")

With what words does Jesus indicate that this meal, His Supper, is to be received by His people in generations to come?
("Do this in remembrance of Me.")

8. Who is the "you" that Jesus was talking about when He said His body and blood were given for "you"?
(The disciples, and by extension, all who put their faith in Him.)

9. What did Peter tell the Lord he was ready to do with Him?
(He said he was prepared to go to prison and to death with Jesus.)

Applying God's Word

1. Exodus 12 describes God's instructions for the Passover meal. A lamb "without blemish" was sacrificed—its blood on the Israelites' doorposts sealed the safety of the people, and its flesh was eaten for their nourishment. Why was Passover a fitting time for Jesus to die for the sins of the world?
(At the Feast of the Passover, a lamb was slaughtered in remembrance of God's deliverance of His people from bondage in Egypt. The slaughtering of the Passover lamb prefigured the sacrifice of Jesus, the "Lamb of God," for all the world's sins.)

2. For what purpose did Jesus pour out His blood?
(To earn our salvation.)

3. What else is received with the bread and wine at the Lord's supper?
(The true body and blood of Jesus under the bread and wine)

Why should God's people receive the Lord's Supper often?
(We should receive the Sacrament often in obedience to Christ, to receive forgiveness of our sins, life and salvation, and the strengthening of faith His promise provides.)

98

Jesus in the Garden
(Matthew 26; Mark 14; Luke 22)

Reviewing God's Word

Circle Yes or No for each statement.

1. When Jesus and the disciples arrived at the garden, He said, "Come pray with Me."	YES	(NO)
2. Jesus told three disciples to keep watch with Him.	(YES)	NO
3. While Jesus suffered greatly, the disciples kept falling asleep.	(YES)	NO
4. Jesus said to them, "The spirit is not willing, and the flesh is also weak."	YES	(NO)
5. God sent an angel to Jesus to strengthen Him during His agony.	(YES)	NO
6. Judas betrayed Jesus with a common greeting of that time—a kiss.	(YES)	NO
7. Jesus said to Judas, "Friend, why do you come now?"	YES	(NO)
8. The disciples remained with Jesus as He was led away.	YES	(NO)

Thinking about God's Word

1. What instructions did Jesus give to all of His disciples upon arriving at Gethsemane?
("Sit here, while I go over there and pray.")

What did He specifically ask of Peter, James, and John?
("Remain here, and watch with Me.")

2. Which words describe the change that the disciples saw coming over Jesus?
("Jesus began to be sorrowful and troubled.")

3. What did Jesus ask His Father to let pass from Him?
("This cup")

What was Jesus speaking about?
(His suffering and death)

4. In your own words, tell what Jesus was praying about when He said, "My Father, if it is possible, let this cup pass from Me. Nevertheless, not as I will, but as You will."
(God, if it is possible, please do not require Me to suffer on a cross. However, I will carry out Your plan and not My own.)

5. How does knowing that Jesus was fully man help in understanding what He was praying about?
(Jesus knew that His death on a cross would be horribly painful. Not only would He physically suffer, but His Father would also leave Him to bear the world's sins alone. As a man, He felt the terror of this pending experience and wanted to avoid it, if possible.)

6. What were Jesus' great drops of sweat like that fell to the ground?
(Drops of blood)

7. What happened to a servant of the high priest?
(One of the disciples struck him with a sword, cutting off his ear.)

8. Summarize Jesus' explanation for why swords and violence were not necessary during His arrest. **(Jesus said that His Father could have sent a countless number of angels to protect and deliver Him. And yet, this was not God's plan. Jesus came in peace to sacrifice Himself and fulfill the Scriptures.)**

Applying God's Word

1. What example do Jesus' actions upon arriving in the garden provide for us for times when we are scared, worried, or nervous?
(Jesus turned to His Father in prayer when He was overwhelmed and filled with sorrow. He told God what was burdening Him, but He stated His trust in God's ultimate plan. When we experience agony about difficult situations, the best thing we can do is present these concerns to our Father. He may not take away our suffering, just as He did not take away Jesus' suffering, but He will strengthen us so we may endure it.)

2. When Jesus saw Judas approaching, He said, "The Son of Man is betrayed into the hands of sinners." In what way are we, two thousand years later, part of that description?
(Our Savior was put to death by people who are just as sinful as we are. Even though we didn't physically help nail Him to the cross, our sin was the reason He died there.)

3. How and why did the disciples react when Jesus was arrested? When might it be easy for us to act in the same way?
(The disciples "left Jesus and fled" after they realized what was happening to Him and the great danger He was in. They knew that if His life would be taken, their lives would be threatened too. It is tempting to consider abandoning our faith when other people don't like us because of it.)

99

Peter Denies Jesus (Matthew 26)

Reviewing God's Word

Fill in the blanks, using the words or phrases below. Some words will not be used.

1. Peter followed Jesus to the courtyard of the **high priest**.
2. "The whole Council were seeking **false** testimony against Jesus."
3. Jesus remained **silent** when the high priest asked Him about rebuilding the temple.
4. The high priest said Jesus spoke **blasphemy** and therefore deserved death.
5. Two **servant** girls claimed that Peter had been with Jesus.
6. The third time Peter was confronted, he said of Jesus, "I do not **know** the man."
7. After the rooster crowed, Peter left the courtyard to **weep**.

Pilate	evil	unchanged	know
pray	like	blasphemy	high priest
good	servant	understand	remember
promises	silent	weep	false

Thinking about God's Word

1. Which words indicate that Caiaphas and the Council didn't want to give Jesus a fair trial but had already made up their minds to put Him to death?
("The whole Council were seeking false testimony against Jesus that they might put Him to death.")

2. It was actually not possible for Jesus to have a fair trial. Explain how this fit into God's plan for His Son. **(Jesus was without sin, but it was God's plan for His Son to be condemned to death. There was no true reason for His death sentence; however, God understood that sinful men would kill Jesus out of fear.)**

3. Two witnesses quoted Jesus as saying that He could "destroy the temple of God" and rebuild it in three days. The people thought He was speaking literally, but what was Jesus really talking about? Hint: see page 170 of *120 Bible Stories.* **(He was speaking of the death of His body, "the temple of God." The rebuilding pointed to His resurrection on the third day after He was crucified.)**

4. What was Jesus' response when the high priest asked if He was the Christ? **("You have said so.")**

5. What is the meaning of the sin of blasphemy, which brought a fateful judgment on Jesus?
(Jesus claimed to be God.)

   Was He guilty of this sin? **(No, Jesus is God.)**

6. In what part of the story do they mock Jesus' divinity?
(They mocked Him and called His claim to be the Son of God blasphemous. They asked Jesus to identify who was slapping Him—poking fun at His omniscience.)

7. What did Peter deny (not admit or confess)?
(He denied ever being with Jesus or knowing Him or that he was one of Jesus' disciples.)

8. How is Peter's remorse over his denial clearly shown?
(When he suddenly remembered Jesus' prediction of his denial, he left the courtyard and "wept bitterly.")

Applying God's Word

1. The Council determined that Jesus was deserving of death because they decided His claim to be God was blasphemous. From what you yourself have learned of Jesus' life, cite four or five actions or proclamations that indicate Jesus was the Christ.
(Various answers may include the angel's message to Mary; Jesus' fulfillment of prophecies, starting with His birth; John the Baptist's description of Jesus; God the Father's proclamation at Jesus' Baptism; Jesus' miracles; Jesus' confession to the Samaritan woman.)

2. In what ways did Peter disobey the commandments "You shall have no other gods" and "You shall not misuse the name of the Lord your God"?
(Honoring oneself before God breaks the commandment to have no other gods. Peter acted out of fear for his life and failed to trust in the one true God. The third time someone questioned him, he "began to invoke a curse on himself and to swear." Peter was not using God's name in a way that was pleasing to Him but, rather, for a false testimony.)

3. How do God's people today deny Jesus as their Savior?
(Answers will vary. Possibilities include people pretending they are not followers of Christ in order to fit in with a certain group or in other ways failing to live as a child of God.)

   Does God forgive everyone who repents of their denial? Explain. **(Yes, God fully forgave Peter, and He pours His grace on all of His repentant children.)**

100

Jesus' Trial
(Matthew 27; John 18)

Reviewing God's Word

Underline the word or phrase that makes each sentence true.

1. Pilate was the Roman (high priest—governor—king—authority).
2. Pilate asked Jesus if He was a (God—king—Christian—Roman).
3. Jesus answered that His "(kingdom—love—leadership—Father) is not of this world."
4. "Pilate said to Jesus, "What is (hope—the way—Your purpose—truth)?"
5. Pilate told the Jews that he found in Jesus no (guilt—divinity—innocence—hope).
6. To show that he did not claim responsibility for Jesus' blood, Pilate (spit on the ground—washed his hands—summoned the guard—wept).
7. The crown that Jesus wore was made of (thorns—gold—purple—reeds).
8. When Pilate brought Jesus forth, the crowd said, ("Flog Him!"—"Here is the man!"—"Condemn Him!"—"Let Him be crucified!")

Thinking about God's Word

1. Why did Pilate ask Jesus if He was the King of the Jews?
(This was the charge that had already been brought against Jesus by the religious authorities who had turned Him over to Pilate. He wanted to see if Jesus would confirm this accusation.)

2. The duties of a king that Pilate probably thought of—ruling a people with laws, justice, and wise decisions to keep the peace—were not the descriptions that Jesus provided of His kingship. What was Jesus' purpose in His kingdom?
(Jesus said that His kingdom is not of the world. In the world, His purpose is "to bear witness to the truth" so that He could bring others into His heavenly kingdom.)

3. What did Pilate mean when he told the crowd that he found no guilt in Jesus?
(After examining Jesus with questions about His kingship, He did not see any fault or threat in Jesus, based on the testimony that He gave.)

4. How did Pilate plan to release Jesus?
(It was his custom to release one prisoner during the Feast of the Passover. He hoped that the people would call for Jesus' release rather than that of Barabbas—a robber.)

5. Explain how Pilate knew that "it was out of envy that they [the religious leaders] had delivered Jesus to him."
(Pilate may have known of Jesus' great following, and he also could clearly see that the temple authorities did not approve of His popularity. He knew that it was not guilt that prompted Jesus' arrest, but rather the leaders' dislike of His teaching.)

6. What unfair treatment did Pilate let the soldiers give Jesus, even when he knew that Jesus was without fault?
(Pilate allowed Jesus to be scourged, tortured, mocked, and humiliated. He had the soldiers clothe Him like a king and pretend to honor Him.)

7. Did all of the Jews in Jerusalem want to see Jesus crucified?
(It is recorded that only the crowd that had gathered for Jesus' trial wanted to see Him dead. Many of the jealous religious authorities probably made up this group. It's likely that most of Jesus' followers were not present.)

Applying God's Word

1. In response to one of Pilate's questions, Jesus said that "everyone who is of the truth listens to My voice." How does Jesus' trial highlight the multitudes that were deaf to His voice or resisted His words?
(Jesus' trial provides an ultimate example of humanity's blindness to the work of the Messiah in their midst and deafness to His words. Though He had faithful followers at the time of His death, He still remained somewhat of a mystery. The religious leaders who supposedly knew the Old Testament prophecies did not recognize God's Son. "He came to His own, and His own did not receive Him" [John 1:11].)

2. The prophet Isaiah wrote of Jesus' suffering before death: "He was oppressed and He was afflicted, yet He opened not His mouth" (53:7). How were Pilate's actions part of God's plan of salvation for the world?
(Although Pilate seemed like a wicked man for condemning Jesus to death, this trial and mocking had been allowed by God as part of Jesus' agony in our place. Pilate did not understand the full weight of his decision to crucify Christ, but God was behind this process every step of the way.)

3. Pilate delivered Jesus to be crucified, but his decision to condemn Jesus was not why Jesus went to the cross. Who is really responsible for Jesus' death?
(All people of all time are the reason for Christ's death. Our sinfulness would condemn us to death if Christ's cross had not become our salvation. We are the reason God sent His Son into the world to die.)

101

The Crucifixion (Matthew 27; Luke 23; John 19)

Reviewing God's Word

Draw a line through the sentences that are not true.

1. ~~As the soldiers led Him to be crucified, Jesus asked God to bring revenge upon His enemies.~~
2. The sign that Pilate made for Jesus' cross read, "Jesus of Nazareth, the King of the Jews."
3. Jesus told one of the two criminals crucified with Him that he would enter Paradise.
4. ~~Jesus said to His mother, "Woman, you shall see Me again."~~
5. From the cross, Jesus called out, "Father, into Your hands I commit My spirit."
6. ~~The soldiers broke Jesus' legs because they were not sure if He was dead.~~
7. ~~Joseph of Arimathea had never heard of Jesus, but he decided to give Him a proper burial.~~
8. Jesus' body was placed in a new tomb that had not yet been used.

Thinking about God's Word

1. Where was Jesus crucified?
   (The Place of the Skull, also known as Golgotha)

2. What words did Pilate write on the sign that was placed above Jesus on the cross?
   ("Jesus of Nazareth, the King of the Jews")

   Why did he choose this phrase?
   (It named the claim about which Jesus had been tried and condemned to death.)

3. Two criminals were crucified on either side of Jesus. The first one labeled Jesus as "the Christ," but then he taunted Him. What did he not understand about Jesus' death?
   (This man failed to recognize that Jesus came into the world for the very purpose of this death.)

4. Which words of the other criminal show his faith in Jesus' saving work?
   ("Jesus, remember me when You come into Your kingdom.")

   What certain promise did Jesus give him?
   ("Truly, I say to you, today you will be with Me in Paradise.")

5. What did Jesus do when He saw His mother standing at the foot of His cross?
   (He told her that "the disciple whom He loved," likely John, would now be her son. That meant that this disciple would care for Mary's needs.)

6. What words did Jesus call out in a loud voice before He bowed His head and died?
   ("Father, into Your hands I commit My spirit.")

7. One reason why Jesus' legs were not broken was because the soldiers could tell that He was already dead. Name another explanation for why His bones were not broken.
   ("These things took place that the Scripture might be fulfilled." As commanded by God, the Passover lamb's bones were never broken. Jesus is the Lamb of God.)

8. Toward the beginning of Jesus' ministry, Nicodemus had asked Jesus about His kingdom (see page 172 of *120 Bible Stories*). What might Nicodemus's presence at Golgotha mean?
   (Nicodemus's arrival to prepare Jesus' body for burial seems to indicate that he was not like other teachers of the law who supported Jesus' condemnation. Perhaps he was a believer.)

9. Jesus had predicted His resurrection numerous times before His disciples and groups of Jewish followers. How did the actions of Joseph of Arimathea and Nicodemus show that they did not grasp this prophecy?
   (They bound Jesus' body in linen and anointed it with spices because they thought He would be dead forever.)

Applying God's Word

1. How does Jesus' prayer that God would forgive those who sentenced Him to death relate to His purpose in dying?
   (Jesus hung on the cross to pay the punishment for the sins of all people. Everyone who looks to the cross and in faith believes that Christ's death was for them will receive forgiveness for their sin. Jesus intercedes for us, saying, "Father, forgive them.")

2. In Psalm 22:1, King David laments, "My God, my God, why have You forsaken me?" Jesus says these same words while crying out from the cross. As His children, do we need to fear being forsaken by God? Explain.
   (Jesus felt the pain of separation from God because He was carrying our sin. Because Christ stood in our place, God will never abandon us. We may feel lonely or far from Him, but He promises to always be near to us. "I will not leave you or forsake you" [Joshua 1:5].)

3. Jesus' death was both physically excruciating (crucifixion is a brutal process) and spiritually agonizing (He felt the weight of the world's sins and God's wrath). And yet, Hebrews 12:2 says that Jesus died "for the joy that was set before Him." What was the source of this joy?
   (Jesus knew that His death was the atoning sacrifice necessary to take away the sins of people from all time. He went to the cross willingly because He knew that His death meant forgiveness and eternal life for all who believe in Him.)

102

The Resurrection (Luke 24; John 20)

Reviewing God's Word

For the following statements, circle T for true and F for false.

1. When the women arrived at the tomb at early dawn, the stone was not yet rolled away.	T	(F)
2. Two men (angels) said to the women, "Why do you seek the living among the dead?"	(T)	F
3. The angels reminded the women that Jesus had predicted His resurrection while He was still teaching in Galilee.	(T)	F
4. All the apostles rejoiced upon hearing the news of Jesus' resurrection.	T	(F)
5. When Jesus appeared to Mary Magdalene, she was outside the tomb by herself weeping over His absence.	(T)	F
6. It was not until Jesus spoke her name that Mary Magdalene recognized Jesus.	(T)	F
7. Jesus said to Mary Magdalene, "Do not cling to Me, for My kingdom is not of this world."	T	(F)
8. Jesus broke the chains of death for us.	(T)	F

Thinking about God's Word

1. How soon after Jesus' burial did the women travel to the tomb?
(They went to the tomb "on the first day of the week." This was Sunday—the third day after Jesus' burial.)

2. Were the women expecting Jesus' resurrection? Explain.
(No, they were carrying spices to the tomb so that they could anoint Jesus' body. This was the final stage of burial.)

3. Why did the angels who appeared to the women mention that Jesus had already predicted His resurrection?
(They were showing the women that there was no need to be surprised at Jesus' disappearance from the tomb. If they had taken His words to heart, perhaps they would not have been so perplexed.)

4. To whom did the women run to tell the news of Jesus' resurrection? What was the reaction from this group?
(Jesus' eleven disciples [Judas had hung himself] were the first to hear of the good news, "but they did not believe them.")

5. Which disciple showed by his actions that he had faith in the words of the women and this act of God?
(Peter ran to the tomb. He found just what he had been told. The tomb was empty with only the linens remaining.)

6. Why was Mary Magdalene weeping outside the tomb?
(She thought that someone had stolen the body of Jesus.)

7. Who did Mary Magdalene think Jesus was when He first appeared to her? When did she recognize Him as her Lord?
(At first, she thought He was the gardener. When Jesus spoke her name, her eyes were opened to the identity of Jesus.)

8. What did Jesus want Mary Magdalene to do rather than stay with Him?
(She was to go to Jesus' brothers, meaning His disciples, and tell them that He would soon be ascending to the Father.)

Applying God's Word

1. In 1 Corinthians 15:14, the apostle Paul says that "if Christ has not been raised, then our preaching is in vain and your faith is in vain." What would you say to someone who claims to trust in Jesus as the Savior but does not believe in His resurrection?
(Answers will vary. There is no Good News of forgiveness and salvation if Jesus remained in the grave. The Gospel writers and many others were eyewitnesses of Jesus' defeat of death, and they give a clear historical testimony of the resurrection's truth.)

2. Mary did not acknowledge the risen Jesus until He spoke to her. How does Jesus speak to people today to bring them to recognize Him as their Lord?
(Jesus works through the Word and Sacraments [Baptism and the Lord's Supper]. As people hear God's Word and receive the gifts of His Means of Grace, the Holy Spirit imparts and strengthens faith in Him as their only Savior from sin.)

3. Jesus said to Mary Magdalene, "I am ascending to My Father and your Father, to My God and your God." What does this statement tell us about our relationship with God because Jesus conquered death?
(By faith, we have the joy of being "fellow heirs with Christ" [Romans 8:17] in God's kingdom. "For in Christ Jesus you are all sons of God, through faith" [Galatians 3:26].)

103

Jesus Appears on the Emmaus Road (Luke 24)

Reviewing God's Word

Fill in the blanks, using the words below. Some words will not be used.

1. While two disciples were walking to a village called **Emmaus**, Jesus began walking alongside them.
2. Jesus said, "What are you **talking** about as you walk?"
3. Cleopas asked if Jesus was the only visitor to **Jerusalem** who was not aware of what happened.
4. The disciples said, "We had **hoped** that He was the one to redeem Israel."
5. Jesus said, "O **foolish** ones, and slow of heart to believe all that the **prophets** have spoken!"
6. The disciples said to each other, "Did not our **hearts** burn within us while He talked to us on the road?"
7. Jesus was known to them in the breaking of the **bread**."

prophets	hoped	Jerusalem	Emmaus
weeping	great	bread	Bethany
promises	known	foolish	wondering
hearts	Nazareth	talking	peace

Thinking about God's Word

1. Why did the two disciples not fall down and worship Jesus when He began walking with them? **(Because "their eyes were kept from recognizing Him," they treated Jesus just as they would any other man who happened to join them for their travels.)**

2. Why might Jesus have asked questions of which He already knew the answer? **(He might have desired to hear, straight from the disciples, a description of what was being said about Him throughout Jerusalem.)**

3. According to these disciples, why was all hope lost that Jesus had come to redeem Israel? **(They did not think it was possible for death to be part of the Messiah's saving work.)**

4. List some pieces of information that the disciples shared "concerning Jesus of Nazareth." **(He was a prophet mighty in deed and word before God, the chief priests condemned Him to death, three days had passed since His crucifixion, some women saw a vision of angels at His tomb. Other answers may apply.)**

5. What was Jesus' reaction to the disciples' profession of doubt about Jesus being the Redeemer? **(He explained that they would have understood Jesus' divinity if they had believed all that the prophets had spoken concerning the Messiah; such writings included His suffering.)**

6. How long did Jesus stay with these two disciples? **(He sat down to eat with them, broke and blessed the bread, and vanished from their midst as soon as their eyes were opened to recognize Him.)**

Applying God's Word

1. Scripture has often been described as *Christocentric*, meaning that Jesus Christ is the central importance of what was written. How could you use this story to teach that Jesus is not simply found in the New Testament? **(A good starting point is that "beginning with Moses and all the Prophets, Jesus interpreted to [the disciples] in all the Scriptures the things concerning Himself." This shows that leaders of God's people in the Old Testament were not just raised up to guide the Israelites in the way of the Lord, but that they also pointed to Christ the Messiah's coming work.)**

2. The disciples recognized Jesus after He had broken bread, blessed it, and gave it to them. Of what sacrament is this reminiscent? **(The Lord's Supper)**

   How is the disciples' recognition of the Lord similar to what happens when God's people receive this sacrament in a worthy manner? **(Those who come to Communion properly prepared will do so by having faith in God's Word that His true body and blood are present with the bread and wine to grant to us the forgiveness of our sin. Like the disciples, our eyes are opened to see Jesus physically before us.)**

3. What immediate action did the disciples take when they realized who had just been teaching them? **(They returned to Jerusalem to tell the other disciples that "the Lord has risen indeed!")**

   Why is it important to include the resurrection when we confess our faith to others? **(We must make sure that Christ's saving work—His death and His resurrection—are kept the prominent part of our confession. As Paul writes in 1 Corinthians 15:17, our "faith is futile" without the resurrection.)**

104

Jesus Appears to Thomas (John 20)

Reviewing God's Word

Answer each question with a word or phrase from below. Not all words will be used.

1. On the evening of what day did Jesus appear to His disciples? **Sunday**
2. Whom did the disciples fear enough to stay behind locked doors? **Jewish enemies**
3. Which two scarred body parts did Jesus show them? **Hands and side**
4. Who was given to the disciples when Jesus breathed on them? **Holy Spirit**
5. Which disciple wanted physical proof that Jesus was alive? **Thomas**
6. After how many days did Jesus reappear to the disciples? **Eight**

Pilate	Two	God the Father
Thomas	Holy Spirit	Sunday
Eight	Peter	Friday
Hands and feet	Hands and side	Group of Jews

Thinking about God's Word

1. What specific words are used to describe how Jesus appeared to His disciples on both occasions?
("Jesus came and stood among them.")

2. With which words did Jesus greet the disciples?
("Peace be with you.")

3. How did the disciples react to seeing the same Jesus who had lived among them before His death?
(They no longer doubted or questioned the truth of the resurrection. Instead, they "were glad when they saw the Lord.")

4. What reason does Jesus give for sending out His disciples to preach?
(Just as His Father sent Him into the world, He is sending the disciples to preach the forgiveness of sins.)

5. What does Jesus say about the disciples' authority to not forgive someone of their sins?
("If you withhold forgiveness from any, it is withheld.")

6. By what words of Thomas is it clear that he instantly believed in the resurrected Lord after touching His wounds?
("My Lord and my God!")

7. How was Jesus' disappointment in Thomas revealed?
(Although Jesus loved Thomas no more or less than His other disciples, His question of "Have you believed because you have seen Me?" indicates that Jesus hoped Thomas would trust the testimony of the other disciples.)

Applying God's Word

1. Is it possible that a pastor's proclamation of forgiveness actually forgives repentant sinners in the congregation? Use Jesus' words to explain.
(Yes. Jesus told the disciples, "If you forgive the sins of any, they are forgiven them." He gave this authority to His Church [the disciples formed the first body of believers]. God alone can forgive, but His people speak this forgiveness.)

2. In this story, Jesus speaks about the faith that His children will have in coming generations, including yours. Which words are these?
("Blessed are those who have not seen and yet believed.")

3. How is it that a person can come to faith in Jesus as Savior if he or she has never seen the physical presence of the Lord?
(God's Spirit gives the gift of faith through God's Word.)

105

Jesus and Peter (John 21)

Reviewing God's Word

Circle Yes or No for each statement.

Statement		
1. The disciple whom Jesus loved said, "I am going fishing."	YES	(NO)
2. That night, the disciples did not catch any fish.	(YES)	NO
3. As day was breaking, Peter saw the Lord and asked Him to come to them.	YES	(NO)
4. Jesus built a charcoal fire and prepared breakfast for the disciples.	(YES)	NO
5. Their net was not torn, despite the large number of fish they had caught.	(YES)	NO
6. This was the first time Jesus had appeared since His resurrection.	YES	(NO)
7. Jesus asked Peter to stop doubting and believe.	YES	(NO)

Thinking about God's Word

1. At the beginning of Jesus' ministry, He called these disciples to follow Him. List some similarities between that event and this appearance of Jesus. Hint: see page 166 of *120 Bible Stories.*
(On both occasions, Jesus was present when the men were fishing. As they met no success in catching fish, Jesus told them where to throw in their nets and performed a miracle in that their nets became full. Jesus and Peter have the main dialogue in both stories.)

2. By what name did Jesus address the disciples at sea?
(He called them "Children."

3. How did Peter react when he realized that the Lord was standing on the shore?
("He put on his outer garment . . . and threw himself into the sea" to swim to Jesus.)

4. In what way did Jesus provide for the needs of the disciples after they arrived on shore?
(He built a charcoal fire and fed His disciples a breakfast of bread and fish.)

5. Using your own words, rephrase Jesus' question to Peter, "Simon, son of John, do you love Me more than these?"
(Peter, do you love Me more than My other disciples love Me?)

6. Why is it significant that Jesus asked Peter about his love for Him three times?
(Peter had consecutively denied knowing Jesus and being one of His disciples three times in a row on the night of Jesus' arrest.)

7. After Jesus inquired about Peter's love a third time, "Peter was grieved." What was probably the reason for this emotion?
(Peter had already twice confessed His love for the Lord. Because Jesus continued to repeat the question, Peter may have felt that Jesus did not believe he was sincere or wondered why He was asking a question of which He already knew the answer.)

Applying God's Word

1. Even after Jesus' resurrection, He continued to care for His disciples with acts of service. What are two examples in this story?
(Jesus helped them to catch fish the morning after an unsuccessful night of fishing, and after they got to shore, He served them breakfast.)
How does Jesus serve us today?
(Specific examples may vary. Possibilities include imparting to us new life in our Baptism, giving His body and blood in the Lord's Supper, interceding for us before the Father.)

2. Jesus gave Peter a similar instruction after every time that he confesses his love: he is to care for Jesus' sheep. Who then was Peter to tend? Hint: see page 200 of *120 Bible Stories.*
(Jesus' sheep; those who believe in Him.)

   How was he to care for them?
   (Peter was to be His servant by preaching the Good News to all he came in contact with and providing for the spiritual needs of those who came to faith in Christ.)

   Who has nurtured your spiritual growth?
   (Answers will vary.)

3. What do you know about the source of the love that Peter confesses, according to 1 John 4:10: "In this is love, not that we have loved God but that He loved us and sent His Son to be the propitiation for our sins"?
(Peter is only able to love Jesus because God first loved him by sending His Son to die for his sin.)

106

Jesus Ascends to Heaven

(Matthew 28; Acts 1)

Reviewing God's Word

Draw a line through the sentences that are not true. Write a corrected sentence on the blank.

1. ~~Jesus lived on earth 40 years after His resurrection.~~
Jesus lived on earth 40 days after His resurrection.

2. ~~Jesus told the disciples to leave Jerusalem and start preaching immediately.~~
Jesus told the disciples to stay in Jerusalem and wait for the promise of the Father.

3. Before He ascended into heaven, Jesus promised to be with His disciples to the end of the age.

4. ~~A legion of angels appeared, singing praises to God.~~
Two angels stood by the disciples and said that Jesus will return to earth on a cloud.

5. The disciples and some others returned to the upper room and devoted themselves to prayer.

6. ~~A man named Matthias came to the upper room and asked to be a witness.~~
The eleven disciples prayed, cast lots, and the lot for the twelfth disciple fell on Matthias.

Thinking about God's Word

1. During the time that Jesus was on earth after His resurrection, what was He speaking about?
(The kingdom of God)

2. Before Jesus' ascension, He told His disciples that they would receive a source of power in order to be His witnesses. From where would this power come?
(The Holy Spirit, who will come upon each of them)

3. In His message to the disciples, what words of Jesus told of His divine nature?
("All authority in heaven and on earth has been given to Me.")

4. List the three commands that Jesus gave to the disciples while He was still on the mountain with them.
(They are to [1] "make disciples of all nations," [2] "baptizing them in the name of the Father and of the Son and of the Holy Spirit," [3] "teaching them to observe all that" Jesus had commanded them.)

5. In what parts of the world were the disciples to be witnesses about the Good News of Christ?
(Everywhere! Jesus said, "In Jerusalem and in all Judea and Samaria, and to the end of the earth.")

6. According to Peter, what qualifications did the new disciple need to possess?
(Like the other disciples, he must have followed Jesus' ministry and witnessed His death and resurrection.)

Applying God's Word

1. All three persons of the Holy Trinity are mentioned multiple times in this story. List as many as you can find and tell what is said about each person.
(The disciples are to baptize people in the name of the triune God—Father, Son, and Holy Spirit. Jesus said the men were to wait in Jerusalem for God the Father's promise. God the Father has fixed times and seasons for His plans to take place. God the Spirit will come upon the disciples. They will then be equipped to be witnesses for God the Son.)

2. Jesus' instructions to His disciples—to make disciples, baptize, and teach—is referred to as the Great Commission. This was the task ahead of them, but only after they had received the Holy Spirit. When did God give His Spirit to you?
(Answers may vary but are likely to include, "at the time of my Baptism.")

How can we fulfill the same commission given to the disciples?
(Now that we have received the Spirit and are growing in our understanding of God's Word, we have been equipped by Him to confess the work of Jesus among our family, friends, and even people we do not know.)

3. Which words of Jesus provide a reminder that we do not need to figure out when He will come again?
(After the disciples ask about the restoration of Israel, Jesus said, "It is not for you to know times or seasons that the Father has fixed by His own authority.")

What are we to do while we wait for Him?
(We are to tell others about the person and work of Jesus Christ. And like the disciples and women in this story, it is good to devote ourselves to prayer.)

107

Pentecost

(Acts 2)

Reviewing God's Word

Underline the word or phrase that makes each sentence true.

1. On the day of Pentecost, the disciples were (away—apart—together—renounced).
2. (The Holy Spirit—The Son—The Father—The prophets) came upon the disciples.
3. The disciples began to speak (loudly—mournfully—different languages—in whispers).
4. Some Jews who had gathered to witness this sight thought the men were filled with (wine—wonder—good works—nonsense).
5. In response to the Jews' curiosity and doubt, (John—Luke—Peter—the disciples) gave a sermon about the truth of Christ.
6. To those in the crowd who were "cut to the heart," Peter said, "(Give up—Repent—Weep—Learn) and be baptized."
7. (Peter—The Holy Spirit—The disciples—Jews) opened the hearts of the people so that they believed in Christ and were forgiven.
8. About (30,000—300,000—3,000—300) people became Christians that day.

Thinking about God's Word

1. What signs indicated that the Holy Spirit entered the room in which the disciples were gathered?
   (A sound came from heaven "like a mighty rushing wind," and "tongues as of fire" came to rest on each of the disciples.)

2. By what miracle did the disciples show that the Holy Spirit had come upon them?
   (They began to speak in other tongues [languages] as the Spirit guided them.)

   Which words tell that the Holy Spirit told them what to say?
   ("As the Spirit gave them utterance")

3. Other than the disciples, who witnessed the events of Pentecost?
   (Devout Jews had traveled to Jerusalem "from every nation under heaven" and gathered to see what was happening.)

4. Which words of the Jews who gathered give an idea of what the disciples were saying while speaking other languages?
   ("How is it that we hear them telling in our own tongues the mighty works of God?")

5. Why might some of the Jews have attributed the work of the Holy Spirit to the disciples being filled with wine (drunk)?
   (They didn't believe God had blessed Jesus' followers with an outpouring of the Spirit's power.)

6. Tell how Peter began the work of "catching men" that Jesus had foretold in Luke 5:9–10.
   (He preached a powerful sermon that told about Jesus' earthly ministry and His crucifixion and exaltation.)

7. Why could Peter be so sure about everything that He preached about Christ?
   (In his sermon, Peter told the crowd that he and the disciples were witnesses of the things of which he spoke. And he, too, had received the Spirit that day.)

8. How did many in the crowd respond to Peter's sermon? Why did they react this way?
   (They wanted to know what to do to relieve the sorrow they now felt. Many were "cut to the heart" because Peter's Spirit-filled words had caused them to realize their sinfulness.)

Applying God's Word

1. How was the Holy's Spirit outpouring at Pentecost the fulfillment of what Jesus told His disciples at the time of His ascension? See page 236 of *120 Bible Stories*.
   (Jesus instructed His disciples to wait in Jerusalem until the Father's promise had been given to them; that is, the Holy Spirit.)

   Having received the Spirit, what were they prepared to do?
   (Preach the Gospel with understanding and power in order that "all nations" [Matthew 28:19] might come to faith in Jesus.)

2. According to Peter's words to the repentant Jews, what did you receive at the time of your Baptism in addition to the Holy Spirit?
   (The forgiveness of sins)

3. Are we included among the recipients of God's promise in Christ Jesus? Explain.
   (Yes, believers living today are included in the phrase "all who are far off.")

108

Peter and John Heal a Lame Man (Acts 3)

Reviewing God's Word

Fill in the blanks, using the words below. Some words will not be used.

1. Peter and **John** were going up to the temple at the hour of prayer.
2. Peter said to the man, "What I do have I give to you. In the name of Jesus Christ of Nazareth, rise up and **walk**!"
3. Peter preached, "The God of our Fathers, glorified His **servant** Jesus."
4. "I know that you acted in **ignorance**, as did also your rulers."
5. "Turn again, that your **sins** may be blotted out."
6. "You are the sons of the prophets and of the covenant that **God** made."
7. "God, having raised up His servant, sent **Jesus** to you first, to **bless** you."

Luke	bless	ignorance	sins
servant	John	rejoice	Jesus
anoint	walk	messenger	God

Thinking about God's Word

1. Why was the lame man at the gate of the temple?
(He was laid there each day so he could ask for alms, or financial help, from those entering the temple.)

2. What did the man expect Peter and John would give him?
(Money)

Which of Peter's first words to the man might have been initially disappointing to him?
(Peter began by saying, "I have no silver and gold.")

3. How did the man show his thankfulness for the healing he received?
(He went into the temple courts with Peter and John, "walking and leaping and praising God.")

4. According to Peter, how was this man healed?
(By faith in the name of Jesus Christ)

Why was it important for Peter to emphasize this fact to the astounded crowd?
(He did not want onlookers to mistakenly think that his or John's "power or piety" was responsible for the healing of the man.)

5. In what part of Peter's message to the people did he emphasize that Jesus was written about in the Old Testament?
("But what God foretold by the mouth of all the prophets, that His Christ would suffer, He fulfilled.")

6. What phrase does Peter use to describe the sinfulness of all the people in his presence?
("Your wickedness")

Applying God's Word

1. The lame man could not stand, due to a physical disability. Psalm 130:3 tells about an inability of all people: "If you, O Lord, should mark iniquities, O Lord, who could stand?" According to this verse, what cripples mankind? Is there a cure?
(Our sin makes us unworthy and unable to stand before God the Father. The cure is Christ's forgiveness applied to us: "But with You there is forgiveness, that You may be feared" [Psalm 130:4].)

2. Peter said to the Jews, "You killed the Author of life, whom God raised from the dead." Should the blame for the death of Jesus be placed completely on that group of Jews? Explain. **(No. All sinful people of all time are the ultimate reason for Jesus' crucifixion. Those who literally nailed Him to the cross were acting in sinfulness but were also being instrumental in carrying out God's plan of salvation.)**

3. What words of God's Law did Peter preach?
(Peter told the people that they had delivered over the Son of God to suffer and die.)

What were Peter's words of Gospel?
(Peter invited the people to "turn again, that your sins may be blotted out, that times of refreshing may come from the presence of the Lord, that He may send the Christ appointed for you.")

Where can you go to hear God's Law and Gospel preached?
(Specific answers may vary, but the primary place is your church.)

109

God's Servant Stephen
(Acts 6–7)

Reviewing God's Word

For the following statements, circle T for true and F for false.

1. The disciples considered giving up preaching in order to care for the neglected widows.	T	(F)
2. Stephen was among the men chosen to care for the widows.	(T)	F
3. Before he was killed, Stephen was able to see a glimpse of the glory of God in heaven.	(T)	F
4. Stephen kept silent while he was being stoned.	T	(F)
5. A young man named Saul tried to save Stephen from the hands of the mob.	T	(F)

Thinking about God's Word

1. At the beginning of this story, how do the disciples' actions communicate their determination to continue sharing God's Word with the nations?
(Instead of promising to take on another job [caring for some widows], which might limit the time they could spend spreading the Gospel, the disciples wisely decided to appoint that task to other capable Christian men.)

2. What did the disciples do for the appointed men before they sent them out?
("They prayed and laid their hands on them" as a blessing.)

3. Which words tell why Stephen could do great wonders?
(He was a man "full of grace and power.")

4. Who stirred up the people against Stephen?
(Members of the synagogue of the Freedmen and other Jews)

5. What accusations were brought against Stephen in front of the council?
("This man say[s] that Jesus of Nazareth will destroy this place and will change the customs that Moses delivered to us.")

6. Read Stephen's reply to the accusations against him. How had the fathers of the Jews been stiff-necked?
(They resisted the Holy Spirit.)

Who was the Righteous One who had been betrayed and murdered?
(Jesus)

7. Why is it clear that the assembly had hardened their hearts to God's Spirit?
(Unlike other occasions when God's Word brought forth repentance and then granted forgiveness, this time those in the assembly refused to listen and decided to silence Stephen by killing him.)

8. Whom did Stephen see when he looked into heaven?
(Jesus, the Son of Man, standing at the right hand of God)

Applying God's Word

1. Jesus' twelve disciples were like the first pastors of the Church. According to their example, what is our pastor's duty above all else?
(First and foremost, pastors should be concerned with "preaching the Word of God.")

2. Name three specific examples of how events during the end of Stephen's life (trial and stoning) mirror similar occurrences at the end of Jesus' life on earth. **(At the trials of both Jesus and Stephen, false witnesses were utilized to lead the men toward condemnation. While Stephen was being stoned, he asked the Lord to receive his spirit, similar to Jesus' "Father, into Your hands I commit My spirit." Both Stephen and Jesus asked the Father to forgive those who were killing them.)**

3. In 1 John 3:13, Scripture says, "Do not be surprised, brothers, that the world hates you." What does this mean for the life of Stephen?
(Stephen was determined to preach God's Word even when he was met with fierce opposition. Rather than cowering at his trial, he spoke the Word boldly—even up to the point of his death.)

for you? **(We, too, should expect that some people will have hard hearts when we confess our faith. But we have the same Spirit to empower and assist us.)**

110

Philip and the Ethiopian

(Acts 8)

Reviewing God's Word

Fill in the blanks, using the words below. Some words will not be used.

1. Who guided Philip to find the Ethiopian? **angel**
2. What was the Ethiopian doing in Jerusalem? **worshiping**
3. From which prophet was the man reading? **Isaiah**
4. What animal was mentioned in the passage the Ethiopian was reading from in Isaiah? **sheep (lamb)**
5. Which person of the Trinity did Philip tell the Ethiopian about? **Jesus**
6. What did the Ethiopian ask for when he saw water? **Baptism**
7. Who removed Philip from the Ethiopian's presence? **Holy Spirit**

worshiping	dove	ignorance	Isaiah
Jeremiah	Holy Spirit	drink	Jesus
help	Baptism	trading	angel
searching	walk	God	sheep

Thinking about God's Word

1. Where did the angel tell Philip to go?
("South to the road that goes down from Jerusalem to Gaza")

2. After arriving in the desert, how did Philip know whom he should speak to?
(The Holy Spirit directed him to catch up to the chariot in which the Ethiopian rode.)

3. What description of the man indicates his wealth and importance?
(He was a court official for the queen of Ethiopia. Specifically, he was in charge of the queen's treasure.)

4. Why did Philip ask the man if he understood what he was reading?
(Philip was looking for an opportunity to witness about the truth of Jesus Christ.)

5. Why was the Ethiopian confused by Isaiah's writings?
(He was unsure if the prophet was speaking "about himself or about someone else.")

6. What evidence is there that the man's heart was open to the Spirit at work in Philip's preaching of the Gospel?
(When the chariot came to some water, the man wanted to be baptized immediately. He had heard the Good News and received it as truth.)

7. What was the Ethiopian's attitude as he continued to travel after being baptized?
(He was rejoicing.)

Applying God's Word

1. Explain how the prophecy the Ethiopian read was fulfilled in Jesus.
(Jesus humbly and without protest went to the cross to suffer and die for our sins—as a sheep that is led to the slaughter.)

2. What about this account reminds us that salvation by grace through faith in Jesus is not only for the Israelites but also for all people?
(The Ethiopian was of a race other than that of the chosen people of God. Even so, the Holy Spirit created in the man faith in Jesus as he listened to the Gospel as preached by Philip.)

3. How was Philip's time with the Ethiopian a fulfillment of the three parts of Jesus' Great Commission? See page 236 of *120 Bible Stories*.
(In an effort to interpret the words of the prophet Isaiah, Philip told the Ethiopian God's Law and then taught "the Good News about Jesus." When they came to some water, Philip baptized the man for the forgiveness of his sins. The man received the Holy Spirit that day, and he rejoiced that he had been made a disciple through God's work in Philip.)

111

The Conversion of Saul

(Acts 9)

Reviewing God's Word

Underline the word or phrase that answers each question.

1. Where did Saul wish to go to persecute Christians?
   (Samaria—Tarsus—Jerusalem—<u>Damascus</u>)

2. Who spoke to Saul when he fell to the ground?
   (The men with him—<u>Jesus</u>—Ananias—God the Father)

3. What happened to Saul when he got up from the ground?
   (<u>He was blind</u>—He was alone—He began to limp—He asked for Baptism)

4. What was the name of the disciple who lived at Damascus?
   (Peter—<u>Ananias</u>—Tarsus—John)

5. What did Saul do as he waited for his sight to be restored?
   (Cried—<u>Prayed</u>—Prophesied—Preached repentance)

6. When the disciple spoke to Saul, what did he call him?
   (Child—Poor sinner—Paul—<u>Brother Saul</u>)

7. Which disciple brought Saul before the others as a witness of the truth of his conversion?
   (<u>Barnabas</u>—Peter—Paul—Ananias)

Thinking about God's Word

1. How did Saul plan to persecute the Christians in the city of Damascus?
   (After sending letters to the synagogues in Damascus, Saul hoped to learn the names of the Christians in that area. He had decided to bind these individuals and bring them to Jerusalem.)

2. What is meant by the phrase "the Way"?
   (This describes followers of Jesus Christ.)

3. What happened to Saul on the way to Damascus?
   (A light from heaven flashed around him, and he fell to the ground and heard a voice.)

   Whose voice was it that spoke to Saul? What did the voice say?
   (Jesus spoke and said, "Saul, Saul, why are you persecuting Me?")

4. After hearing the voice, in what ways did Saul have great weakness compared to his previous days of persecuting?
   (For three days, Saul could not see, and during that time, he did not eat or drink.)

5. Why did Ananias appear afraid to visit Saul?
   (Ananias told the Lord that he knew about how Saul had persecuted His Son's disciples. He probably wondered if his own life would be in danger.)

6. With which words did Ananias assure Saul that his sins were forgiven?
   ("Brother Saul, the Lord Jesus . . . has sent me so that you may regain your sight and be filled with the Holy Spirit.")

7. In what three ways did Saul respond to Ananias's words?
   (He rose, was baptized, and ate to strengthen his body.)

8. After his conversion, what did Saul testify about Jesus?
   (Jesus was the Christ.)

Applying God's Word

1. We read in 1 Corinthians 2:14, "The natural person does not accept the things of the Spirit of God, for they are folly to him, and he is not able to understand them because they are spiritually discerned." How does this verse help explain why Saul was persecuting the Church?
   (Without the gift of faith in Christ created by the Holy Spirit, Saul was not able to see his sin or understand that salvation is found in Jesus alone.)

2. This story points to a time when Saul received the Holy Spirit. When did this occur?
   (Ananias told Saul that the Lord had sent him so that Saul could be restored to "sight and be filled with the Holy Spirit." After Saul was blessed and healed by Ananias, he was baptized and received the Holy Spirit.)

   When did God create faith in you?
   (Answers may vary between these two: at the time of Baptism or upon hearing the Gospel and the Spirit worked faith within.)

3. According to Jesus, who was being persecuted when Saul harmed some of the first Christians?
   (It is Jesus Himself who is being persecuted when His disciples are hurt or threatened.)

   If we ever find ourselves being persecuted for our faith, what is a good way to respond? to not respond?
   (God would have us peacefully and boldly continue to share the Good News. Romans 12:19 says, "Beloved, never avenge yourselves, but leave it to the wrath of God." Ultimately, God will punish our persecutors.)

112

Peter and Cornelius
(Acts 10)

Reviewing God's Word

Draw a line through the sentences that are not true.

1. ~~Cornelius was a Jew by birth, but he did not believe in God.~~

2. A vision of an angel with a message prompted Cornelius to send for Peter.

3. ~~While Peter was on the housetop, he had a vision of Cornelius waiting for him.~~

4. Cornelius gathered many people together to hear God's Word as preached by Peter.

5. Peter did not want Cornelius to worship him.

6. ~~As Peter spoke to the household, the Holy Spirit fell on Cornelius, not on the others in the room.~~

7. ~~The Jewish believers who were with Peter disputed the Gentiles' faith.~~

Thinking about God's Word

1. What was Cornelius' occupation?
(He was a centurion in the Italian Cohort.)

2. What description of Cornelius indicates that he would listen to the angel's message that came to him in a vision?
("He was a devout man who feared God with all his household.")

3. Retell Peter's vision from God.
(He saw "something like a great sheet descending. . . . In it were all kinds of animals and reptiles and birds of the air.")

In what way did God explain the vision?
("What God made clean, do not call common.")

4. How did Peter know three men would be looking for him?
(The Holy Spirit told him.)

5. Why was Peter bothered by the fact that Cornelius fell at his feet to worship him?
(Peter understood that he was no greater than Cornelius, either spiritually or in any other way. He said, "Stand up. I, too, am a man.")

6. How did Cornelius communicate that he and his household would be receptive to the message of God that Peter shared?
(He said to him, "We are all here in the presence of God to hear all that you have been commanded by the Lord.")

7. Why would it have been important for Peter to share with the group "that God shows no partiality"?
(Peter was different from those gathered based on heritage — he was a Jew, but the rest in the room were Gentiles. He wanted them to understand that Jesus did not come for the Jews only.)

8. What did Peter command before he left?
(That all the new believers "be baptized in the name of Jesus Christ.")

Applying God's Word

1. According to the ceremonial law of the Old Testament, the animals that Peter saw in his vision were not to be eaten by the Jews. When God speaks, He tells Peter that this law is no longer in place. How did God use this vision to prepare Peter for visiting Cornelius?
(Cornelius was not Jewish—those called God's chosen people—but Peter learned through the vision that God's kingdom established by Christ did not belong only to Jews but to all people. He explained his new understanding when he said, "God has shown me that I should not call any person common or unclean.")

2. Peter told Cornelius that he came to his house "without objection." Without the vision from God, why would he likely have resisted witnessing to Cornelius' household?
(Peter said that it is "unlawful . . . for a Jew to associate with or to visit anyone of another nation." He was speaking of God's old covenant commands for His people's purity.)

Why might we object to sharing the Gospel with others who are unlike us?
(We could worry that we wouldn't be able to relate to them or that they might reject us. God would have us fulfill Jesus' command to bring the Gospel to all nations. God will give us the words to speak.)

3. Why were the believers who were with Peter surprised that the Holy Spirit was poured on the Gentiles?
(According to the new covenant that Jesus brought about through His saving work, forgiveness of sins is received through Christ's name only, regardless of nationality. This was still a new understanding for those accompanying Peter.)

113

Peter's Escape from Prison (Acts 12)

Reviewing God's Word

Fill in the blanks, using the words or phrases below. Some words will not be used.

King **Herod** arrested some who belonged to the Church. He put Peter in **prison**. **Peter** would go on trial after the **Passover**. One night, an **angel** appeared in Peter's cell. The **chains** fell off Peter's **hands**, and he was led through the city **gate**. Peter went to the **house** where many fellow believers were gathered. A **servant girl** told the people that Peter was free.

Saul	chains	Herod	house
gate	Peter	Spirit	servant girl
neck	resurrection	angel	centurion
temple	prison	hands	Pharaoh
apostle	Passover	court	streets

Thinking about God's Word

1. Who was the first of Jesus' disciples to be killed for his faith? **(James the brother of John)**

   How did he die?
   (King Herod killed him with the sword.)

2. Why did King Herod arrest Peter shortly after James' death?
   (Because "he saw that it [James' death] pleased the Jews," meaning he knew that a group of Jews would support the persecution of another prominent disciple.)

3. Why might Herod have decided to put four squads of soldiers in charge of guarding Peter?
   (He knew that Peter was a significant leader in the Church and might have feared that someone would try to rescue him or that Peter would escape.)

4. What were members of a church doing while Peter was in prison?
   (They were earnestly praying for him.)

5. As Peter followed the angel, did he realize that he was escaping from prison? Explain. **(No. He thought he was simply seeing a vision from God.)**

6. Who answered the door at the house where the church was gathered?
   (A servant girl name Rhoda)

7. Why was the door not opened to Peter immediately?
   (Rhoda was so excited to hear Peter's voice that she ran to tell the others instead of letting Peter in.)

Applying God's Word

1. What does this account reveal to us about the role of angels?
   (Angels serve and protect the people of God.)

   Does God send angels to earth today?
   (Yes, even if we cannot see them, God has promised to give us His protection through these heavenly beings. "For He will command His angels concerning you to guard you in all your ways" [Psalm 91:11].)

2. Peter knew the Lord's hand had delivered him "from all that the Jewish people were expecting," meaning his death. When Jesus had been arrested, He had been condemned to die. Why did God free Peter but not His Son?
   (God did not free His Son because doing so would have gone against His plan of salvation for the world. He freed Peter because He was not done using him to proclaim the Gospel.)

3. At the conclusion of the account, Peter tells how the Lord rescued him. How might we learn from Peter's eagerness to share about his freedom?
   (Each of us can tell others about how God in Christ has rescued us from sin and death. We do not need to be silent about this great news.)

114

Paul's First Missionary Journey

(Acts 13–14)

Reviewing God's Word

Circle Yes or No for each statementstatement.

Statement		
1. The Holy Spirit appointed work for Barnabas and Saul, and the two men set out immediately.	YES	(NO)
2. When Barnabas and Saul arrived at a city, they went to the synagogue.	(YES)	NO
3. The rulers of the synagogue in Antioch asked the men if they had any encouragement to share.	(YES)	NO
4. Paul's preaching did not include the fact that Jesus had died and rose to forgive the people of their sins.	YES	(NO)
5. The people at the synagogue begged for Paul to preach again.	(YES)	NO
6. Paul and Barnabas turned to preach to the Gentiles when the Good News of Jesus was rejected by the Jews.	(YES)	NO

Thinking about God's Word

1. In what way did the disciples prepare to send Barnabas and Saul out on their journey?
   (They fasted, prayed, and then laid their hands on them for a blessing.)

2. The Antioch synagogue rulers read from the Law and the Prophets. Why didn't they read the New Testament?
   (It had not yet been written down as an inspiration from the Spirit. At that time, when the Gospel was shared, it was done so verbally.)

3. What was another name for Saul?
   (Paul)

4. To whom was Paul speaking when he addressed the crowd as "men of Israel"?
   (This indicates that he was preaching to Jews.)

5. When Paul began to preach, he did not mention the name of Jesus immediately. Whom or what did he talk about before Christ?
   (As Peter spoke to the Jewish crowd, he gave a summary of their heritage by referencing their forefathers, captivity, judges, kings, and inheritance.)

6. Paul used the word "promised" twice in his sermon. What promise was he talking about?
   (God the Father's promise to send a Messiah into the world to redeem His fallen people; this promise extends as far back as the Garden of Eden.)

7. Why was Paul's message great news for those who still lived by the Law of Moses?
   (Paul told the crowd that "by [Jesus] everyone who believes is freed from everything from which you could not be freed by the Law of Moses.")

8. What reason did Paul and Barnabas give for turning to the Gentiles to preach?
   (They had spoken to some Jews, but this group had responded by disregarding their message.)

Applying God's Word

1. When the angel Gabriel appeared to Jesus' mother, Mary, he said that "the Lord God will give to Him [Jesus] the throne of His father David" (page 150 of *120 Bible Stories*). Paul also highlights that Jesus is David's offspring. How does knowing Jesus' heritage help us understand God's plan of salvation?
   (In studying Jesus' line of ancestors, we see that God was at work every step of the way throughout the history of His people. He made good come out of the sinful situations they created so that our Savior was born the way it had been prophesied.)

2. Some Jews were not happy that large crowds gathered to hear this new word from God that Paul and Barnabas shared. Similarly, many Jews opposed Jesus' unfamiliar teachings. What might this tell us about how the message of the Gospel will be received by those to whom we witness?
   (Some find the Gospel offensive and refuse to accept it. Like these Jews, they may ignore the news that eternal life comes through Christ alone.)

3. On their first missionary journey, Paul and Barnabas spoke about Christ to both Jews and Gentiles. Consider how the Gospel was received by both groups. What can we learn from their witnessing experience?
   (We cannot determine who will rejoice over the Gospel and who will reject it. Paul and Barnabas preached first to the Jews and then ended up focusing on the Gentiles. If we are witnessing to hard-hearted people, God may open doors for others to receive His Word.)

115

Paul and Timothy

(Acts 16; the Books of 1 and 2 Timothy)

Reviewing God's Word

Underline the word that makes each sentence true.

1. Paul was traveling and preaching with (Barnabas—John—Silas—Peter) when he decided to have Timothy accompany them.
2. Timothy's father was a (Jew—Italian—Roman—Greek).
3. Paul called Timothy his "true (servant—child—brother—father) in the faith."
4. Paul wrote to Timothy that Jesus displays "His perfect (patience—resistance—hope—guidance) as an example of those who were to believe in Him for eternal life."
5. "For God gave us a spirit not of (forgiveness—restlessness—fear—confusion) but of power and love and (peace—mystery—self-control—hatred)."
6. "I have finished the race, I have kept the (faith—promise—Law—joy)."

Thinking about God's Word

1. Why did Paul want Timothy to accompany him and Silas on their missionary journey?
(Timothy was "well spoken of by the brothers." They evidently knew of his strong faith.)

2. Which words indicate that the Holy Spirit was at work in the early Church, opening hearts to receive the Good News?
(The result of Paul, Silas, and Timothy's mission work was strengthened faith for the new believers and an increasing number of people who came to believe in the Gospel.)

3. Whom did Jesus come into the world to save?
(Sinners)

Which people are these?
(All people)

4. Why did Paul call himself "the foremost" of sinners? See page 248 of *120 Bible Stories*. **(Before he was called by Jesus to be His disciple, he was a prominent persecutor of Christians in the early days of the Church.)**

5. What words did Paul use to describe the Christian faith as a battle?
(He tells Timothy he must "fight the good fight of the faith.")

6. In what ways did Paul encourage Timothy to not abandon his confession of the faith and the preaching of the Word?
(He reminded him to "guard the deposit" entrusted to him, meaning the Gospel. Also, he is told to remain true to what he had "learned and . . . firmly believed.")

7. How did Paul reference that Timothy's faith had been given to him as a child?
(He recorded that Timothy had "been acquainted with the sacred writings" since his childhood. Someone had taught him about the faith.)

8. With what phrase (in the last paragraph) did Paul describe eternal life in heaven?
("The crown of righteousness")

Applying God's Word

1. In Paul's letters to Timothy, he speaks of his position in the Church. How does he describe his authority as an apostle?
(Paul emphasizes that he was made a disciple by the "command" [will] of God and of Jesus. The authority he has to preach the Word is not his own.)

In what way do these words also apply to our pastors?
(Faithful pastors are not to say whatever they want to say—they are called to teach God's Law and proclaim His Gospel in a manner that is true to what is written in Scripture. When they preach, the Word of God they speak is used by God the Holy Spirit to create, strengthen, and sustain faith.)

2. Paul told Timothy to "fight the good fight of the faith." In what way is being a Christian like being at war?
(Although the Holy Spirit strengthens us to our new life in Christ, we are still battling forces of sin and the devil—simultaneously saints and sinners.)

3. Paul said that all the faithful in Christ will receive "the crown of righteousness" on "that Day." What day is that? With what attitude may Christians anticipate this day?
(Paul spoke of Judgment Day—the day when Christ will return to judge the world. Because God will judge us according to Christ's righteousness, we don't need to fear this day. We can rejoice that eternal life is already ours.)

116

Paul Tells Lydia about Christ; Paul Writes to the Philippians (Acts 16; Philippians 1; 4)

Reviewing God's Word

For the following statements, circle T for true and F for false.

1. One night, Jesus appeared at Paul's side and urged him to go to Macedonia.	T	(F)
2. Paul sailed to Troas, a leading city of the district of Macedonia.	T	(F)
3. Some women were gathered near the riverside where Paul went to pray.	(T)	F
4. After Lydia was baptized, she volunteered to sew clothes for Paul's journey.	T	(F)
5. He who began a good work in you will bring it to completion.	(T)	F
6. Let your problems be known to everyone.	T	(F)
7. Do not be anxious about some things.	T	(F)
8. God's peace will guard your hearts and your minds in Christ Jesus.	(T)	F

Thinking about God's Word

1. Luke wrote the Book of Acts. How is his presence with Paul recorded in this account?
(Wherever the word "we" is used, it shows that Luke was accompanying Paul on his missionary journey.)

2. Even before he left for Macedonia, Paul knew the purpose for which he had been sent. What was this purpose?
(He understood that he had been called to preach the Gospel in that area.)

3. How did Paul and Luke plan to honor the Sabbath day?
(They sought out a place where they could spend time in prayer.)

Why did their plans partially change once they arrived at the riverside?
(Instead of spending the whole time in prayer, they shared the Good News with some women who were gathered at that same spot.)

4. What was Lydia's occupation?
(She sold purple goods.)

5. Why was Lydia able to come to faith in Jesus?
("The Lord opened her heart to pay attention to what Paul said.")

6. In what words did Paul tell the Philippians that he had not forgotten about them despite his physical separation from them?
("I thank my God in all my remembrance of you, always in every prayer of mine for you all making my prayer with joy.")

7. When is "the day of Jesus Christ"?
(Judgment Day)

8. According to Paul, what type of comfort are Christians given after they take their concerns to God in prayer?
(The peace of God, which surpasses all understanding)

Applying God's Word

1. When Paul and Luke went to the riverside to pray, they were not likely expecting to witness to a group of women that day. But God had other plans. What can we learn from this?
(Our time is in God's hands, and our daily plans will not always happen as we would like. God says, "My thoughts are not your thoughts, neither are your ways My ways" [Isaiah 55:8]. God will direct our lives according to His good plan.)

2. Paul told Timothy to "rejoice in the Lord always." How is it possible for us to rejoice even when bad situations happen in our lives?
(Our real reason for rejoicing is not dependent on our life circumstances. It is found in the fact that we are Christ's redeemed people and our salvation is secure in Him. Not even pending death—a loved one's or our own—can end our joy in this truth.)

3. Paul says that instead of being anxious, we should let our "requests be made known to God" in prayer. What specific worries might you pray about rather than allowing them to trouble your heart and mind?
(Answers will vary.)

117

Paul and Silas in Prison
(Acts 16)

Reviewing God's Word

Draw a line through the sentences that are not true.

1. ~~Paul hired a slave girl to tell others about him and Silas, but he soon became annoyed with her.~~

2. After being accused of speaking about unlawful customs, Paul and Silas were beat with rods.

3. ~~Paul and Silas sat in the inner prison, silently praying that they would be released.~~

4. A great earthquake loosed the bonds of all the prisoners.

5. The jailer nearly killed himself because he thought the prisoners had escaped.

6. ~~As soon as they were free, Paul and Silas ran to tell the good news to other believers.~~

7. Paul and Silas shared the Gospel with the jailer and the members of his household.

Thinking about God's Word

1. What was the slave girl saying about Paul and Silas as she followed them?
   ("These men are servants of the Most High God, who proclaim to you the way of salvation.")

   Why did she speak this repeatedly?
   (She was possessed by a "spirit," which was not of God but the devil.)

2. Why were the girl's owners angry with Paul and Silas?
   (Paul cast out the demon. It was through this girl's demon possession that she was able to earn money for her owners by fortune-telling.)

3. List some ways in which Paul and Silas were verbally and physically afflicted because of their confession of Christ.
   (False accusations were brought against them as men said that Romans [Gentiles] could not accept the "customs" of which they spoke. Their garments were torn, they were beaten with rods, and their feet were put in painful stocks in the prison.)

4. How did Paul and Silas spend their time in prison?
   (They prayed and sang hymns to God.)

5. Which words of Paul did God use to save the jailer's physical life?
   ("Do not harm yourself, for we are all here.")

   his soul?
   ("Believe in the Lord Jesus, and you will be saved.")

6. In what way did the jailer provide for Paul and Silas's physical needs after they told him and his family about salvation in Jesus?
   (He washed their wounds from the beatings, brought them into his house, and gave them food to eat.)

7. The jailer and his family was not the only group that Paul and Silas witnessed to during their night in prison. Who else may have come to faith at that time?
   (The other prisoners who were listening to Paul and Silas praising God before experiencing the earthquake that God used to free His servants.)

Applying God's Word

1. How does the unjust treatment of Paul and Silas reflect that of Jesus, beginning from when He was arrested and brought before the high priest?
   (When Jesus was brought before the religious leaders, false statements were made about His teaching, but He didn't object. Likewise, Paul and Silas could have argued that they were commanded to preach the Gospel to all nations, but they kept silent. Jesus, Paul, and Silas were all stripped of their garments and physically wounded.)

2. Fellow prisoners with Paul and Silas may have come to saving faith that night. What can this part of the story tell about how the Holy Spirit works through our actions to guide others to the truth about Christ?
   (Directly speaking about Jesus to someone is the clearest way to confess our faith, but we can also know that the Spirit is at work in the hearts of people who observe such things as how we live and the words we choose.)

3. The jailer asked, "What must I do to be saved?" In what way does this question point to a common belief that humans hold regarding their salvation?
   (It makes much more sense to us that we would have to do something to earn our salvation than the fact that "it is the gift of God" [Ephesians 2:8].)

118

Paul's Letters (The Books of Romans; Ephesians; 1 Thessalonians)

Reviewing God's Word

Fill in the blanks, using the words below. Some words will not be used.

1. "For I am not **ashamed** of the Gospel."
2. "The righteous shall live by **faith**."
3. "God . . . even when we were **dead** in our trespasses, made us alive together with **Christ**."
4. "For we are His **workmanship**, created in Christ Jesus for good **works**."
5. "When you received the Word of God, which you heard from us, you **accepted** it not as the word of men."
6. "May the Lord establish your hearts **blameless** in holiness before our God and Father."

lives	pride	accepted
faith	workmanship	dead
works	understanding	partial
rejected	Christ	truth
Moses	blameless	ashamed

Thinking about God's Word

1. Describe Paul's attitude toward preaching the Gospel to the Romans. **(Paul said he was "not ashamed of the Gospel," and was therefore "eager" to preach it to those in Rome.)**

2. Why did Paul see a need to tell the Romans that salvation belonged "also to the Greek"?
(Greeks were Gentiles, people who are not Jewish. It was still difficult for both Jews and Gentiles to wrap their mind around the fact that Christ's sacrifice brought salvation to all.)

3. What did Paul say the Romans would experience because they have been justified by faith?
("Peace with God through our Lord Jesus Christ")

4. In his Letter to the Ephesians, what phrase did Paul use to describe the meaning of "saint"?
(Those who "are faithful in Christ Jesus.")

5. Why did Paul make a point of telling the Ephesians that their salvation was not their "own doing"?
(Soon after that statement, he said that salvation comes to us in this way "so that no one may boast." Humans like to brag about things they do, but salvation, as with all other blessings that come to us and flow out of us, is from God.)

6. Which of Paul's words in his Letter to the Ephesians tell that God knows every detail of our future and plans it to happen in an exact way?
("For we are His workmanship, created in Christ Jesus for good works, which God prepared beforehand, that we should walk in them.")

7. For what reason was Paul thankful for the Thessalonians?
(He knew that they carried out good works as enabled by God in faith, their work was done in love, and their hope remained placed in Christ.)

8. According to Paul's First Letter to the Thessalonians, what would be a mistake when receiving the Word of God?
(Those who hear the Word and believe are never to trust in it as being the words of the men who wrote it. There is no power in man's words.)

Applying God's Word

1. When Paul greeted the Ephesians, he called them saints because they "are faithful in Christ Jesus." Are we, sinners who fall short of God's Law, saints as well? Explain. **(Yes, we are numbered among God's saints not because we earned the title or always live in an upright manner. We are saints in God's kingdom because the Spirit has called us to faith in Christ Jesus. "So then you are no longer strangers and aliens, but you are fellow citizens with the saints and members of the household of God [Ephesians 2:19].**

2. Some people say that in order for Jesus to save you, you must make a decision to follow Him. If "we were dead in our trespasses" when God gave us new life, is it really possible that we could decide we need a Savior? Explain.
(No, it's not possible for our salvation to depend on our actions. Since we were spiritually dead in our sin, only God could open our hearts to receive and believe in His Son.)

3. Is the Bible only a collection of stories and ideas that men wrote down about God? Share your answer using Paul's argument. **(No. After hearing and receiving the Scripture, God's Spirit desires us to trust in it for "what it really is"; that is, the Word of God. In another letter, Paul said that "all Scripture is breathed out by God" [2 Timothy 3:16].)**

119

Paul Sails to Rome

(Acts 27–28)

Reviewing God's Word

Underline the word that makes each sentence true.

1. Paul was sailing to (Rome—Antioch—Malta—Philippi).
2. Julius allowed Paul to receive the care of (warmth—medicine—friends—God) while on the journey.
3. A (cry—storm—famine—fight) came up while the group was at sea.
4. The sailors began to throw (Paul—Paul's friends—cargo—themselves) overboard.
5. Paul said, "I urge you to take heart, for there will be no loss of (morale—food—sight—life) among you."
6. On the island of Malta, the native people showed the shipwrecked group unusual (hostility—kindness—wealth—curiosity).
7. When Paul finally arrived in Rome, the (women—Roman officials—brothers—high priest) came to meet him and his friends.

Thinking about God's Word

1. Why was Paul sailing to Rome?
   (After he was arrested in the temple, he asked to be tried before Caesar, whose palace was in Rome.)

2. Who was Julius?
   (Julius was a Roman centurion who had been appointed to take Paul to Rome for his trial.)

3. Paul had spent much time at sea when he made the observation that their journey would be dangerous. But, to whom did Julius listen instead of Paul?
   (He "paid more attention to the pilot and to the owner of the ship.")

4. Which words indicate that the storm did not last for only a matter of hours?
   ("Neither sun nor stars appeared for many days")

5. What encouragement did Paul offer the hungry men?
   (He told them that he had been visited by an angel who said he should not be afraid. The angel said that God would save him and those who were with him on board. Paul expressed his trust that God would provide for them.)

6. What did the soldiers plan to do when the ship hit land? Why?
   (Kill the prisoners so they could not escape)

7. How did Julius take action to save Paul and those with him?
   (He ordered the men who could swim to jump overboard and head for land. To those who could not swim, he gave wooden planks from the ship so they could float.)

Applying God's Word

1. Paul told the sailors that God would save them. To what message of greater salvation had Paul dedicated his life?
   (Paul was called by Jesus to become His apostle. After that, he spent his life sharing with both Jews and Gentiles the Good News of salvation by grace through faith in Jesus.)

2. Once Paul arrived in Rome and was met by the brothers, his first response was to thank God. What might we learn from Paul's example?
   (God would have us thank and praise Him for all He has done and continues to do for us.)

3. Tell how this account from Paul's journey is a metaphor of the Christian life. **(Jesus promises to remain with us during our earthly life. The Spirit sustains and encourages us in all the storms of life, and God finally calls us to live with Him in heaven. We are not guaranteed to avoid all bodily harm, but our comfort is in the eternal life already ours through Christ.)**

120

John's Vision of Heaven (Revelation 21–22)

Reviewing God's Word

Circle Yes or No for each statement.

Statement		
1. The dwelling place of God is not with man. Instead, He will dwell above them.	YES	(NO)
2. In this new Jerusalem, death shall be no more.	(YES)	NO
3. The gates of the city will bear inscriptions of the sermons of Jesus and Paul.	YES	(NO)
4. A temple made of gold will be shining in the center of the city.	YES	(NO)
5. Rather than a sun or moon, the city is lit by the glory of God.	(YES)	NO
6. The tree of life was on either side of the flowing river.	(YES)	NO
7. Both the Spirit and the Bridegroom say, "Come."	YES	(NO)

Thinking about God's Word

1. What is the name of the holy city?
(The new Jerusalem)

How will this city be prepared?
("As a bride adorned for her husband")

2. The loud voice that John heard told him what would not be a part of life in this city. Name some of these things.
(Death, mourning, crying, pain)

3. In what two ways does John state that the water of life will not cost anything to God's people?
(He recalled that the One sitting on the throne said, "To the thirsty I will give from the spring of the water of life without payment," and He Himself proclaimed, "Let the one who desires take the water of life without price.")

4. What will be on the twelve foundations of the city's wall?
(The twelve names of the twelve apostles of the Lamb)

5. Who is "the Lamb"? Hint: see John the Baptist's words on page 166 of *120 Bible Stories*.
(Jesus Christ)

6. Why is there no need for a temple in this coming holy city?
(The temple, or place of worship, was what God gave to His people so He could meet them while they were living on the old, fallen earth. In God's immediate presence, such a building isn't necessary.)

7. By the city's light, or the glory of God, "will the nations walk." What is meant by "the nations"?
(This refers to all of God's redeemed people who were given faith in Christ during their life on earth.)

8. What did Jesus reveal to John regarding the time when He would be returning?
(He did not give an exact date. He said nothing more than "I am coming soon.")

Applying God's Word

1. Revelation describes the new Jerusalem as the Bride of Christ. A husband is to love and provide for his wife, as well as protect her and make sacrifices for her. With these things in mind, how is Christ a perfect Husband to the Church?
("Christ loved the church and gave Himself up for her" [Ephesians 5:25] by dying on a cross. In this way, He sacrificed Himself in order to provide forgiveness and new life for sinners. Jesus' perfect love opened the way for our salvation and protects us from eternal separation from God.)

2. Jesus said He will freely give "the water of life" to anyone who is thirsty. What life-giving water does God give to us right now? How does this water prepare us for the holy city?
(God gives us the water of the Sacrament of Holy Baptism. When we are baptized, we are forgiven of our sins and given the gift of faith. The Holy Spirit, who comes to dwell in us, will strengthen us to keep us in that faith until God calls us to heaven or Christ returns.)

3. Genesis 2:9 says that "the tree of life was in the midst of the garden" when God created the world. The tree of life will also be in the new Jerusalem. What happened in the Garden of Eden that will not be part of the new Jerusalem? (See page 10 of *120 Bible Stories*.) Why is this a reason to rejoice?
(In the Garden, Adam and Eve doubted God's commands and committed the first sin. Since then, sin has corrupted God's beautiful creation and His people too. Because of Christ Jesus, sin will not enter His people's dwelling place in the holy city. Thanks be to God!)

9780758641700.